Fro W9-CGL-316

P O R T A B L E
Puerto Rico

2nd Edition

by Darwin Porter & Danforth Prince

WILEY
Wiley Publishing, Inc.

Published by:

WILEY PUBLISHING, INC.

909 Third Ave.
New York, NY 10022

ISBN 0-7645-2439-9
ISSN 1532-995X

Editor: Lisa Torrance Duffy
Production Editor: Bethany André
Photo Editor: Richard Fox
Cartographer: John Decamillis
Production by Wiley Indianapolis Composition Services

For information on our other products and services or to obtain technical support, please contact our Customer Care Department within the U.S. at 800-762-2974, outside the U.S. at 317-572-3993 or fax 317-572-4002.

Wiley also publishes its books in a variety of electronic formats. Some content that appears in print may not be available in electronic formats.

Manufactured in the United States of America

5 4 3 2 1

& Other Exciting News from Frommer's!

In our continuing effort to publish the savviest, most up-to-date, and most appealing travel guides available, we've added some great new features.

Frommer's guides now include a new **star-rating system.** Every hotel, restaurant, and attraction is rated from 0 to 3 stars to help you set priorities and organize your time.

We've also added **seven brand-new features** that point you to the great deals, in-the-know advice, and unique experiences that separate travelers from tourists. Throughout the guide, look for:

(Finds	Special finds—those places only insiders know about
(Fun Fact	Fun facts—details that make travelers more informed and their trips more fun
(Kids	Best bets for kids—advice for the whole family
(Moments	Special moments—those experiences that memories are made of
(Overrated	Places or experiences not worth your time or money
(Tips	Insider tips—some great ways to save time and money
(Value	Great values—where to get the bes

Contents

List of Maps

About the Authors

A native of North Carolina, **Darwin Porter** was a bureau chief for the *Miami Herald* when he was 21 and later worked in TV advertising. This veteran travel writer is the author of numerous best-selling Frommer's guides, including *Frommer's Caribbean,* the most candid and up-to-date guide to island vacations on the market. He is assisted by **Danforth Prince,** formerly of the Paris bureau of the *New York Times.* Both writers have traveled widely in the Caribbean for years and happily share their secrets and discoveries with you.

An Invitation to the Reader

In researching this book, we discovered many wonderful places—hotels, restaurants, shops, and more. We're sure you'll find others. Please tell us about them, so we can share the information with your fellow travelers in upcoming editions. If you were disappointed with a recommendation, we'd love to know that, too. Please write to:

Frommer's Portable Puerto Rico, 2nd Edition
Wiley Publishing, Inc. • 909 Third Ave. • New York, NY 10022

An Additional Note

Please be advised that travel information is subject to change at any time— and this is especially true of prices. We therefore suggest that you write or call ahead for confirmation when making your travel plans. The authors, editors, and publisher cannot be held responsible for the experiences of readers while traveling. Your safety is important to us, however, so we encourage you to stay alert and be aware of your surroundings. Keep a close eye on cameras, purses, and wallets, all favorite targets of thieves and pickpockets.

What the Symbols Mean

The following abbreviations are used for credit cards:

AE	American Express	DISC	Discover	V	Visa
DC	Diners Club	MC	MasterCard		

FROMMERS.COM

Now that you have the guidebook to a great trip, visit our website at **www.frommers.com** for travel information on nearly 2,500 destinations. With features updated regularly, we give you instant access to the most current trip-planning information available. At Frommers.com, you'll also find the best prices on airfares, accommodations, and car rentals—and you can even book travel online through our travel booking partners. At Frommers.com, you'll also find the following:

- Online updates to our most popular guidebooks
- Vacation sweepstakes and contest giveaways
- Newsletter highlighting the hottest travel trends
- Online travel message boards with featured travel discussions

The Best of Puerto Rico

Whatever you want to do on a tropical vacation or business trip—play on the beach with the kids (or gamble away their college funds), enjoy a romantic honeymoon, or have a little fun after a grueling negotiating session—you'll find it in Puerto Rico. But you don't want to waste precious hours after you get here searching for the best deals and the best experiences. We've done that work for you. During our years of traveling through the islands that form the Commonwealth of Puerto Rico, we've tested the beaches, toured the sights, reviewed countless restaurants, inspected hotels, and sampled the best outdoor activities. We've even learned where to get away from it all when it's time to escape the crowds.

Here's what we consider to be the best that Puerto Rico has to offer.

1 The Best Beaches

White sandy beaches put Puerto Rico and its offshore islands on tourist maps in the first place. Many other Caribbean destinations have only jagged coral outcroppings or black volcanic-sand beaches that get very hot in the noonday sun.

- **Best for Singles (Straight & Gay):** Sandwiched between the Condado and Isla Verde beaches along San Juan's beachfront, **Ocean Park Beach** attracts more adults and less of the family trade. Only Isla Verde beach to the east matches Ocean Park for its broad beach and good swimming. The people-watching here is nothing compared to the well-stuffed bikinis (both male and female) found on South Miami Beach or Rio de Janeiro. However, for the Caribbean, Ocean Park is as good as it gets. Because many gay boarding houses lie in Ocean Park, a lot of the beach here is frequented by gay young men, mainly from New York. However, straight people looking to meet someone while wearing swimwear will find plenty of lookers (and perhaps takers). See "Diving, Fishing, Tennis & Other Outdoor Pursuits" in chapter 6.

- **Best Beach for Families:** Winning without contest, **Luquillo Beach,** 30 miles (48km) east of San Juan, attracts both local families, mainly from San Juan, and visitors from Condado and Isla Verde beaches in San Juan. Beach buffs heading for Luquillo know they will get better sands and clearer waters there than in San Juan. The vast sandy beach opens onto a crescent-shaped bay edged by a coconut grove. Coral reefs protect the crystal-clear lagoon from the often rough Atlantic waters that can buffet the northern coast, making Luquillo a good place for young children to swim. Much-photographed because of its white sands, Luquillo also has tent sites and other facilities, including picnic areas with changing rooms, lockers, and showers. See "Luquillo Beach" in chapter 7.
- **Best for Swimming:** Whereas on much of the northwest coast of Puerto Rico, rough Atlantic waters often deter bathers but attract surfers, the south coast waters are calmer. On the south coast, **Playa de Ponce,** outside Ponce, Puerto Rico's second-largest city, consists of a long strip of beautiful white sand that opens onto the tranquil waters of the Caribbean. Less crowded than Luquillo, Playa de Ponce is an ideal place to swim year-round in clearer, less polluted waters than those along the more heavily populated northern coastline. See "Ponce" in chapter 8.
- **Best for Snorkeling:** Puerto Rico offers top-notch snorkeling even though freshwater run-offs from tropical outbursts feeding into the sea can momentarily cloud the ocean's waters. In most places, when conditions are right, visibility extends from 50 to 75 feet. The best snorkeling on the main island is found near the town of **Fajardo,** to the east of San Juan and along the tranquil eastern coast. (See chapter 10.) Remote **Mona Island** off the west coast of Puerto Rico offers the best snorkeling. The reefs here, the most pristine in Puerto Rico, are home to a wide variety of rainbow-hued fish, turtles, octopuses, moray eels, rays, puffers, and clownfish: the single largest concentration of reef fish life in Puerto Rico. You must bring your snorkeling equipment to the island, however, as there are no rentals available once you are here. See "Mona Island: The Galápagos of Puerto Rico" in chapter 8.
- **Best for Windsurfing:** Rincón's winter surf, especially at **Playa Higüero,** puts Malibu to shame. Today surfers from all over the world are attracted to Rincón, which they have dubbed "Little Malibu." From Borinquén Point south to Rincón, nearly all the beaches along the western coast are ideal

for surfing from November to April. As the windsurfing capital of the Caribbean, the Rincón area was put on the map when it was the site of the 1968 world surfing championships. Some of the 16-foot breakers here equal those on the north shore of Oahu. See "Rincón" in chapter 9.

2 The Best Golf & Tennis

- **Westin Rio Mar Golf Course** (Palmer): A 45-minute drive from San Juan on the northeast coast, the 6,145-yard Rio Mar Golf Course is shorter than those at both Palmas del Mar and Dorado East. One avid golfer recommended it to "those whose games and egos have been bruised by the other two courses." Wind here can seriously influence the outcome of your game. The greens fees are a lot lower than those of its two major competitors. See "Diving, Fishing, Tennis & Other Outdoor Pursuits" in chapter 6.

- **Hyatt Resorts at Dorado** (Hyatt Dorado Beach Resort & Country Club; Hyatt Regency Cerromar Beach Hotel): With 72 holes, Dorado has the highest concentration of golf on the island. Two courses—east and west—belong to the Hyatt Regency Cerromar and the Hyatt Dorado Beach resorts. Dorado East is our favorite. Designed by Robert Trent Jones, Sr., it was the site of the Senior PGA Tournament of Champions throughout the 1990s.

  True tennis buffs head here, too. The Dorado courts are the best on the island, and both hotels sponsor tennis weeks and offer special tennis packages. The Hyatt Regency Cerromar has 14 Laykold courts alone, two of them lit for night play. The Hyatt Dorado Beach Resort & Country Club weighs in with seven Laykold courts, two of them lighted. See "Dorado" in chapter 7.

- **Wyndham El Conquistador Resort & Country Club** (Las Croabas): This sprawling resort east of San Juan is one of the island's finest tennis retreats, with seven Har-Tru courts and a pro on hand to offer guidance and advice. If you don't have a partner, the hotel will find one for you. Only guests of the hotel are allowed to play here. See the section on tennis under "Las Croabas" in chapter 10.

- **Palmas del Mar Golf Club** (Humacao): Lying on the southeast coast on the grounds of a former coconut plantation, the Palmas del Mar resort boasts the second-leading course in

Puerto Rico—a par-72, 6,803-yard layout designed by Gary Player. Crack golfers consider holes 11 through 15 the toughest five successive holes in the Caribbean. See "Palmas del Mar" in chapter 10.

- **Tennis Center at Palmas del Mar** (Humacao): On the eastern coastline, this resort complex on the grounds of a former coconut plantation has 20 courts, 5 of which are Har-Tru and 15 are Tenne-flex (a harder surface). Seven of the courts are lighted. The resort offers tennis packages, and an on-site pro conducts private lessons. See "Palmas del Mar" in chapter 10.

3 The Best Natural Wonders

- **Río Camuy Caves:** Some 2½ hours west of San Juan, visitors board a tram to descend into this forest-filled sinkhole at the mouth of the Clara Cave. They walk the footpaths of a 170-foot-high cave to a deeper sinkhole. Once they're inside, a 45-minute tour helps everyone, including kids, learn to differentiate stalactites from stalagmites. At the Pueblos sinkhole, a platform overlooks the Camuy River, passing through a network of cave tunnels. See "Arecibo & Camuy" in chapter 7.

- **El Yunque:** Forty-five minutes by road east of San Juan in the Luquillo Mountains, and protected by the U.S. Forest Service, El Yunque is Puerto Rico's greatest natural attraction. Some 100 billion gallons of rain fall annually on this home to four forest types containing 240 species of tropical trees. Families can walk one of the dozens of trails that wind past waterfalls, dwarf vegetation, and miniature flowers, while the island's colorful parrots fly overhead. You can hear the sound of Puerto Rico's mascot, the coquí, a small frog. See "El Yunque" in chapter 7.

- **Las Cabezas de San Juan Nature Reserve:** This 316-acre nature reserve about 45 minutes from San Juan encompasses seven different ecological systems, including forestland, mangroves, lagoons, beaches, cliffs, and offshore coral reefs. Five days a week (Wed–Sun), the park staff conducts tours in Spanish and English, the latter at 2pm only. Each tour lasts 2½ hours and is conducted with electric trolleys that traverse most of the park. Tours end with a climb to the top of the still-working 19th-century lighthouse for views over Puerto Rico's eastern coast and nearby Caribbean islands. Call to reserve space before going, as bookings are based on stringent restrictions as to the number of persons who can tour the park without damage to its landscape or ecology. The cost is a relative bargain, $5 for adults, $2 for children under 13, and $2.50 for seniors. See "To the Lighthouse: Exploring Las Cabezas de San Juan Nature Reserve" in chapter 10.

4 The Best Family Resorts

Puerto Rico has a bounty of attractions, natural wonders, and resorts that welcome families who choose to play together. Here are some of the best.

- **Condado Plaza Hotel & Casino** (San Juan): This resort offers Camp Taíno, a regular program of activities and special events for children ages 5 to 12. The cost of $25 per child includes lunch. The main pool has a kids' water slide that starts in a Spanish castle turret, plus a toddler pool. For teenagers, the hotel has a video game room, tennis courts, and various organized activities. For the whole family, the resort offers two pools and opens onto a public beach. It also has the best collection of restaurants of any hotel on the Condado. See p. 70.

- **Wyndham El San Juan Hotel & Casino** (San Juan): The grandest hotel in Puerto Rico lies on Isla Verde, the less-famous strip of beach connected to the Condado. Its Kids Klub features trained counselors and group activities for the 5-to-13-year-old set. A daily fee of $28 buys lunch and an array of activities. The hotel opens onto a good beachfront and has some of the best restaurants in San Juan. See p. 80.

- **Hyatt Resorts at Dorado** (Hyatt Dorado Beach Resort & Country Club; Hyatt Regency Cerromar Beach Hotel): Sitting 18 miles (29km) west of San Juan, the Hyatt Regency Cerromar Beach Resort & Casino and the Hyatt Dorado Beach Resort & Country Club share a Camp Coquí program available for guests ages 3 to 12. Certified counselors direct programs of educational, environmental, and cultural activities. In the evening, movies, talent shows, and video games occupy the agenda. All this costs $40 a day per kid. Parents find one of the largest beaches and resort complexes in the Caribbean, including the world's longest freshwater river pool. See p. 139.

- **Wyndham El Conquistador Resort & Country Club** (Las Croabas): Located 31 miles (50km) east of San Juan, this resort offers Camp Coquí on Palomino Island for children 3 to 12 years of age. The hotel's free water taxi takes kids to the island for a half or full day of watersports, and nature hikes. This resort has some of the best facilities and restaurants in eastern Puerto Rico. See p. 188.

- **Doral Palmas del Mar Resort** (Humacao): The major rival in the east to El Conquistador, this sprawling resort has an Adventure Club for children ages 3 to 13. Supervised activities include arts, crafts, and sports, plus horseback riding for those old enough. For nonguests, the cost is $30 per half day or $35 per day, including lunch; guests are free. The resort is one of the most extensive in the Caribbean, with beaches, restaurants, and lots of watersports. See p. 192.

5 The Best Big Resort Hotels

- **Wyndham El San Juan Hotel & Casino** (San Juan): An opulent circular lobby sets the haute style at the Caribbean's most elegant resort. From its location along Isla Verde Beach, it houses some of the capital's finest restaurants and is the city's major entertainment venue. Guest rooms are tropically designed and maintained in state-of-the-art condition. See p. 80.

- **Ritz-Carlton San Juan Hotel, Spa & Casino** (San Juan): At last Puerto Rico has a Ritz-Carlton, and this truly deluxe, oceanfront property is one of the island's most spectacular resorts. Guests are pampered in a setting of elegance and beautifully furnished guest rooms. Hotel dining is second only to that at El San Juan, and a European-style spa features 11 treatments "for body and beauty." See p. 77.

- **Hyatt Dorado Beach Resort & Country Club** (Dorado): Lying on the former stamping grounds of the Rockefellers, these low-rise buildings blend into the lush surroundings of a grapefruit-and-coconut plantation. Spacious rooms open onto a long stretch of secluded beach, and grounds include an 18-hole championship golf course designed by Robert Trent Jones, Sr. Tennis, windsurfing, swimming, and dozens of watersports are available, as is the most elegant dining in Dorado. See p. 139.

- **Westin Rio Mar Beach Resort, Country Club & Ocean Villas** (Rio Grande): This $180 million 481-acre resort, 19 miles (31km) east of the San Juan airport, is one of the three largest hotels in Puerto Rico. Despite its size, personal service and style are hallmarks of the property. Twelve restaurants and lounges boast an array of cuisines. Along with its proximity to two golf courses, entertainment, such as an extensive program of live music, is a key ingredient in the hotel's success. See p. 145.

- **Wyndham El Conquistador Resort & Country Club** (Las Croabas): The finest resort in Puerto Rico, this is a world-class destination—a sybaritic haven for golfers, honeymooners, families, and anyone else. Three intimate "villages" combine with one grand hotel, draped along 300-foot bluffs overlooking both the Atlantic and the Caribbean at Puerto Rico's northeastern tip. The 500 landscaped acres include tennis courts, an 18-hole Arthur Hills–designed championship golf course, and a marina filled with yachts and charter boats. See p. 188.

- **Doral Palmas del Mar Resort** (Humacao): Although not as impressive as El Conquistador, this sprawling complex evokes a Mediterranean village, opening onto over 3 miles (5km) of beach on the east coast of Puerto Rico. Palm trees grow everywhere. The complex boasts the largest tennis center in the Caribbean and an 18-hole Gary Player championship golf course. Additional amenities include a horseback-riding center for beach rides, watersports galore, an outstanding scuba-diving program, and deep-sea fishing charters. There's even a casino and nine restaurants. See p. 192.

6 The Best Attractions

- **The Historic District of Old San Juan:** There's nothing like it in the Caribbean. Partially enclosed by old walls dating from the 17th century, Old San Juan was designated a U.S. National Historic Zone in 1950. Some 400 beautifully restored buildings fill this district, which is chockablock with tree-shaded squares, monuments, and open-air cafes, as well as shops, restaurants, and bars. If you're interested in history, there is no better stroll in the West Indies. See "Seeing the Sights" in chapter 6.

- **Castillo de San Felipe del Morro** (Old San Juan): In Old San Juan and nicknamed El Morro, this fort was originally built in 1540. It guards the bay from a rocky promontory on the northwestern tip of the old city. Rich in history and legend, the site covers enough territory to accommodate a nine-hole golf course. See p. 108.

- **The Historic District of Ponce:** Second only to Old San Juan in terms of historic significance, the central district of Ponce is a blend of Ponce Créole and Art Deco building styles, dating mainly from the 1890s to the 1930s. One street, Calle Isabel, offers an array of Ponceño architectural styles, which often incorporate neoclassic details. The city underwent a massive restoration preceding the celebration of its 300th anniversary in 1996. See "Ponce" in chapter 8.

- **Museo de Arte de Ponce** (Ponce): This museum has the finest collection of European and Latin American art in the Caribbean. The building was designed by Edward Durell Stone, who also designed the Museum of Modern Art in New York City. Contemporary works by Puerto Ricans are displayed, as well as works by an array of old masters, including Renaissance and baroque pieces from Italy. See p. 152.

- **Tropical Agriculture Research Station:** These tropical gardens contain one of the largest collections of tropical species intended for practical use. These include cacao, fruit trees, spices, timbers, and ornamentals. Adjacent to the Mayagüez campus of the University of Puerto Rico, the site attracts botanists from around the world. See "Mayagüez" in chapter 8.

7 The Best Restaurants

- **Parrot Club** (San Juan): This San Juan establishment is one of the finest and most innovative restaurants on the island. Its chef serves a Nuevo Latino cuisine that is a happy medley of Puerto Rican delights, drawing upon the Spanish, African, and even Taíno influences of the island. Menu items are based on updated interpretations of old-fashioned regional dishes—everything from criolla-styled flank steak to a pan-seared tuna served with a sauce of dark rum and essence of oranges. See p. 86.

- **La Belle Epoque** (San Juan): Jeremie Cruz is being celebrated as the finest chef of the Caribbean. From his elegant Condado setting, he serves a combined fusion and French cuisine that is about as close to perfection as it gets on the Condado. The cuisine is exquisitely prepared, and the selections of vintage wines are dazzling. See p. 94.

- **Ramiro's** (San Juan): Chef Jesús Ramiro has some of the most innovative cookery along the Condado beachfront strip, along with the city's best wine list. Ramiro has made his culinary reputation with such dishes as quail stuffed with lamb in a port sauce and lamb loin in a tamarind coriander sauce, both equally delectable. His dessert menu is two pages long, including the town's best soufflés. His death-by-chocolate mousse on a green grape leaf is equaled only by his caramelized fresh mango napoleon. See p. 95.

- **Ajili Mójili** (San Juan): On the Condado beachfront, Ajili Mójili provides the most refined interpretation of classic Puerto Rican cookery on the island. Locals find it evocative of the food they enjoyed at their mother's table, one example being *mofongos*—green plantains stuffed with veal, chicken, shrimp, or pork. The chefs take that cliché dish *arroz con pollo* (stewed chicken with saffron rice) and raise it to celestial levels. The restaurant takes its name from the lemon-garlic sweet chile salsa that's traditionally served here with fish or meat. See p. 94.

- **Mark's at the Meliá** (Ponce): Mark French has elevated Puerto Rican dishes to a new high at this endearing restaurant that also serves an impeccable international cuisine. He took over what was a backwater and turned the place into an enclave of refined dining with such imaginative and good-tasting dishes as tamarind barbecued lamb with yucca mojo. See p. 158.

- **The Landing** (Barrios Puntas/Playa Antonio): One of the best dining spots along the western coast of Puerto Rico, this restaurant has a setting like a stylish private home. Its international cuisine draws hundreds of patrons nightly who enjoy jerk chicken and lobster kebabs, among other dishes, while taking in a view of the legendary Rincón surf. See p. 175.

2

Planning Your Trip to Puerto Rico

This chapter discusses the where, when, and how of your trip to Puerto Rico—everything required to plan your trip and get it on the road. Here we've concentrated on what you need to do *before* you go.

1 The Regions in Brief

Although the many geological divisions of Puerto Rico might not be immediately apparent to the ordinary visitor, its people take great pride in the island's diversity. The most important geological and political divisions are detailed below.

SAN JUAN

The largest and best-preserved complex of Spanish colonial architecture in the Caribbean, Old San Juan (founded in 1521) is the oldest capital city under the U.S. flag. Once a linchpin of Spanish dominance in the Caribbean, it has three major fortresses, miles of solidly built stone ramparts, a charming collection of antique buildings, and a modern business center. The city's economy is the most stable and solid in all of Latin America.

San Juan is the site of the official home and office of the governor of Puerto Rico (La Fortaleza), the 16th-century residence of Ponce de León's family, and several of the oldest places of Christian worship in the Western Hemisphere. Its bars, restaurants, shops, and nightclubs attract an animated group of fans. In recent years the old city has become surrounded by densely populated modern buildings, including an ultramodern airport, which makes San Juan one of the most dynamic cities in the West Indies.

THE NORTHWEST: ARECIBO, RIO CAMUY, RINCON & MORE

A fertile area with many rivers bringing valuable water for irrigation from the high mountains of the Cordillera, the northwest also offers

Puerto Rico

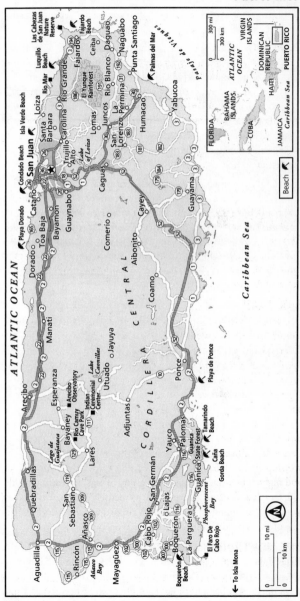

abundant opportunities for sightseeing. The region's districts include the following:

ARECIBO   Located on the northern coastline a 2-hour drive west of San Juan, Arecibo was originally founded in 1556. Although little remains of its original architecture, the town is well known to physicists and astronomers around the world because of the radar/radio-telescope that fills a concave depression between six of the region's hills. Equal in size to 13 football fields and operated jointly by the National Science Foundation and Cornell University, it studies the shape and formation of the galaxies by deciphering radio waves from space.

RINCON   Named after the 16th-century landowner Don Gonzalo Rincón, who donated its site to the poor of his district, the tiny town of Rincón is famous throughout Puerto Rico for its world-class surfing and beautiful beaches. The lighthouse that warns ships and boats away from dangerous offshore reefs is one of the most powerful on Puerto Rico.

RIO CAMUY CAVE PARK   Located near Arecibo, this park's greatest attraction is underground, where a network of rivers and caves provides some of the most enjoyable spelunking in the world. At its heart lies one of the largest known underground rivers. Above-ground, the park covers 300 acres.

DORADO & THE NORTH COAST

Playa Dorado, directly east of San Juan at Dorado, is actually a term for a total of six white-sand beaches along the northern coast, reached by a series of winding roads. Dorado is the island's oldest resort town, the center of golf, casinos, and two major Hyatt resorts (p. 139). At the Hyatt resorts at Dorado, you'll find 72 holes of golf, the greatest concentration in the Caribbean—all designed by Robert Trent Jones, Sr. The complex is quite family-friendly, with its Camp Coquí, which offers programs for children ages 3 to 15. There is also a water playground at the Hyatt Regency Cerromar Beach Hotel, with a 1,776-foot-long fantasy pool—the world's longest freshwater swimming pool.

Another resort of increasing importance is also found along the north coast: Wyndham El Conquistador Resort & Country Club at Palomino Island, a private island paradise with sandy beaches and recreational facilities. This resort lies near Las Croabas, a fishing village on the northeasternmost tip of Puerto Rico's north coast.

Challenging both the Hyatt resorts and El Conquistador is the Westin Rio Mar Beach Resort, Country Club & Ocean Villas, which lies 19 miles (31km) to the east of the San Juan international airport.

THE NORTHEAST: EL YUNQUE, A NATURE RESERVE & FAJARDO

The capital city of San Juan (see above) dominates Puerto Rico's northeast. Despite the region's congestion, there are still many remote areas, including some of the island's most important nature reserves. Among the region's most popular towns, parks, and attractions are the following:

EL YUNQUE   The rain forest in the Luquillo Mountains, 25 miles (40km) east of San Juan, El Yunque is a favorite escape from the capital. Teeming with plant and animal life, it is a sprawling tropical forest (actually a national forest) whose ecosystems are strictly protected. Some 100 billion gallons of rainwater fall here each year, allowing about 250 species of trees and flowers to flourish.

FAJARDO   Small and sleepy, this town was originally established as a supply depot for the many pirates who plied the nearby waters. Today, a host of private yachts bob at anchor in its harbor, and the many offshore cays provide visitors with secluded beaches. From Fajardo, ferryboats make choppy but frequent runs to the offshore islands of Vieques and Culebra.

LAS CABEZAS DE SAN JUAN NATURE RESERVE   About an hour's drive from San Juan, this is one of the island's newest ecological refuges. It was established in 1991 on 316 acres of forest, mangrove swamp, offshore cays, coral reefs, and freshwater lagoons—a representative sampling of virtually every ecosystem on Puerto Rico. There is a visitor center, a 19th-century lighthouse (El Faro) that still works, and ample opportunity to forget the pressures of urban life.

THE SOUTHWEST: PONCE, MAYAGÜEZ & MORE

One of Puerto Rico's most beautiful regions, the southwest is rich in local lore, civic pride, and natural wonders.

BOQUERON   Famous for the beauty of its beach and the abundant birds and wildlife in the nearby Boquerón Forest Reserve, this sleepy village is now ripe for large-scale tourism-related development. During the early 19th century, the island's most-feared pirate, Roberto Cofresi, terrorized the Puerto Rican coastline from a secret lair in a cave nearby.

CABO ROJO   Established in 1772, Cabo Rojo reached the peak of its prosperity during the 19th century, when immigrants from around the Mediterranean, fleeing revolutions in their own countries, arrived to establish sugar-cane plantations. Today, cattle graze peacefully on land originally devoted almost exclusively to sugar cane, and the area's many varieties of exotic birds draw bird-watchers from throughout North America. Even the offshore waters are fertile; it's estimated that nearly half of all the fish consumed on Puerto Rico are caught in waters near Cabo Rojo.

MAYAGÜEZ   The third-largest city on Puerto Rico, Mayagüez is named after the *majagua,* the Amerindian word for a tree that grows abundantly in the area. Because of an earthquake that destroyed almost everything in town in 1917, few old buildings remain. The town is known as the commercial and industrial capital of Puerto Rico's western sector. Its botanical garden is among the finest on the island.

PONCE   Puerto Rico's second-largest city, Ponce has always prided itself on its independence from the Spanish-derived laws and taxes that governed San Juan and the rest of the island. Long-ago home of some of the island's shrewdest traders, merchants, and smugglers, it is enjoying a renaissance as citizens and visitors rediscover its unique cultural and architectural charms. Located on Puerto Rico's southern coast, about 90 minutes by car from the capital, Ponce contains a handful of superb museums, one of the most charming main squares in the Caribbean, an ancient cathedral, dozens of authentically restored colonial-era buildings, and a number of outlying mansions and villas that, at the time of their construction, were among the most opulent on the island.

THE SOUTHEAST: PALMAS DEL MAR & MORE

The southeastern quadrant of Puerto Rico has some of the most heavily developed, as well as some of the least developed, sections of the island.

COAMO   Although today Coamo is a bedroom community for San Juan, originally it was the site of two different Taíno communities. Founded in 1579, it now has a main square draped with bougainvillea and one of the best-known Catholic churches on Puerto Rico. Even more famous, however, are the mineral springs whose therapeutic warm waters helped President Franklin D. Roosevelt during his recovery from polio. (Some historians claim that these springs inspired the legend of the Fountain of Youth, which in turn set Ponce de León off on his vain search of Florida.)

PALMAS DEL MAR   This sprawling vacation and residential resort community is located near Humacao. A splendid golf course covers some of the grounds. Palmas del Mar is at the center of what has been called the "New American Riviera"—3 miles (5km) of white-sand beaches on the eastern coast of the island. Palmas del Mar is the largest resort in Puerto Rico, lying to the south of Humacao on 2,800 acres of a former coconut plantation—now devoted to luxury living and the sporting life.

The Equestrian Center at Palmas is the finest riding headquarters in Puerto Rico, with trails cutting through an old plantation and jungle along the beach. The resort is ideal for families and has a supervised summer activities program for children ages 5 to 12.

2 Visitor Information

For information before you leave home, visit **www.prtourism.com** or contact one of the following **Puerto Rico Tourism Company** offices: 666 Fifth Ave., New York, NY 10103 (© **800/223-6530** or 212/586-6262); 3575 W. Cahuenga Blvd., Suite 405, Los Angeles, CA 90068 (© **800/874-1230** or 213/874-5991); or 901 Ponce de León Blvd., Suite 604, Coral Gables, FL 33134 (© **800/815-7391** or 305/445-9112).

In Canada contact the company at 230 Richmond St. W., Suite 902, Toronto, ON MSV 1V6 (© **416/368-2680**).

If you have Internet access, visit **CityNet** (www.citynet.com), which has links, organized by location and then by subject, to sites with information about many destinations. To find Puerto Rico, click on the "Caribbean" heading; when a map of the region appears, click on the island. Here you will find a number of links pertaining to Puerto Rico.

One of the best Caribbean websites is **Caribbean-On-Line** (www.webcom.com/earleltd), a series of virtual guidebooks full of information on hotels, restaurants, and shopping, along with sights and detailed maps of the islands. The site also includes links to travel agents and cruise lines that are up on the Web.

Other helpful websites include **Municipality of Ponce** (www.ponceweb.org), **Municipality of Rincón** (www.Rincon.org), and **Puerto Rico Travel Maps** (www.travelmaps.com).

You might also want to contact the U.S. State Department for background bulletins, which supply up-to-date information on crime, health concerns, import restrictions, and other travel matters. Write the **Superintendent of Documents, U.S. Government Printing Office,** Washington, DC 20402 (✆ **202/512-1800**).

A good travel agent can be a source of information. Make sure your agent is a member of the American Society of Travel Agents (ASTA). If you get poor service from an ASTA agent, you can write to the **ASTA Consumer Affairs Department,** 1101 King St., Alexandria, VA 22314 (✆ **703/739-8739;** www.astanet.com).

3 Entry Requirements & Customs

ENTRY REQUIREMENTS

DOCUMENTS   Because Puerto Rico is a Commonwealth, **U.S. citizens** coming from mainland destinations do not need any documents to enter Puerto Rico. It is the same as crossing from Georgia into Florida. They do not need to carry proof of citizenship or to produce documents. However, because of new airport security measures, it is necessary to produce a government-issued photo ID (federal, state, or local) to board a plane; this is most often a driver's license.

Be sure to carry plenty of documentation. You might need to show a government-issued photo ID (federal, state, or local) at various airport checkpoints. Be sure that your ID is *up-to-date:* an expired driver's license or passport, for example, might keep you from boarding a plane.

For **Canadians,** proof of citizenship is required to land in Puerto Rico. This could be in the form of a province-issued birth certificate or a Canadian identification card. A valid passport is preferred but not required. In addition, some form of photo ID, usually a driver's license, is also required.

Visitors from **other countries** need a valid passport to land in Puerto Rico. For those from countries requiring a visa to enter the U.S., the same visa is necessary to enter Puerto Rico, unless these nationals are coming directly from the U.S. mainland and have already cleared U.S. Immigration and Customs there.

CUSTOMS

U.S. citizens do not need to clear Puerto Rican Customs upon arrival by plane or ship from the U.S. mainland. All non-U.S. citizens must clear Customs and are permitted to bring in items intended for their personal use, including tobacco, cameras, film, and a limited supply of liquor (usually 40 oz.).

WHAT YOU CAN TAKE HOME

U.S. CUSTOMS   On departure, U.S.-bound travelers must have their luggage inspected by the U.S. Agriculture Department because laws prohibit bringing fruits and plants to the U.S. mainland. Fruits and vegetables are not allowed, but otherwise, you can bring back as many purchased goods as you want without paying duty.

For more information, contact the **U.S. Customs Service,** 1300 Pennsylvania Ave. NW, Washington, DC 20229 (© **877/287-8867;** www.customs.gov [click on "Traveler Information" and then "Know Before You Go Brochure"]) and request the free pamphlet *Know Before You Go.*

CANADIAN CUSTOMS   For a clear summary of Canadian rules, write for the booklet *I Declare,* issued by the **Canada Customs and Revenue Agency** (© **800/461-9999** in Canada or 204/983-3500; www.ccra-adrc.gc.ca). Canada allows its citizens a C$750 exemption, and you're allowed to bring back duty-free one carton of cigarettes, one can of tobacco, 40 imperial ounces of liquor, and 50 cigars. In addition, you're allowed to mail gifts to Canada valued at less than C$60 per day, provided they're unsolicited and don't contain alcohol or tobacco (write on the package "Unsolicited gift, under $60 value"). All valuables should be declared on the Y-38 form before departure from Canada, including serial numbers of valuables already owned, such as expensive foreign cameras. *Note:* The $750 exemption can only be used once per year and only after an absence of 7 days.

U.K. CUSTOMS   U.K. citizens returning from a non-EU country have a customs allowance of: 200 cigarettes; 50 cigars; 250 grams of smoking tobacco; 2 liters of still table wine; 1 liter of spirits or strong liqueurs (over 22% volume); 2 liters of fortified wine, sparkling wine or other liqueurs; 60cc (ml) perfume; 250cc (ml) of toilet water; and £145 worth of all other goods, including gifts and souvenirs. People under 17 cannot have the tobacco or alcohol allowance. For more information, contact HM Customs & Excise at © **0845/010-9000** (from outside the U.K., 020/8929-0152), or consult their website at www.hmce.gov.uk.

AUSTRALIA CUSTOMS   The duty-free allowance in Australia is A$400 or, for those under 18, A$200. Citizens can bring in 250 cigarettes or 250 grams of loose tobacco, and 1,125 milliliters of alcohol. If you're returning with valuables you already own, such as foreign-made cameras, you should file form B263. A helpful brochure available from Australian consulates or Customs offices is *Know Before You Go*. For more information, call the **Australian Customs Service** at ✆ **1300/363-263,** or log on to www.customs. gov.au.

NEW ZEALAND CUSTOMS   The duty-free allowance for New Zealand is NZ$700. Citizens over 17 can bring in 200 cigarettes, 50 cigars, or 250 grams of tobacco (or a mixture of all three if their combined weight doesn't exceed 250g); plus 4.5 liters of wine and beer, or 1.125 liters of liquor. New Zealand currency does not carry import or export restrictions. Fill out a certificate of export, listing the valuables you are taking out of the country; that way, you can bring them back without paying duty. Most questions are answered in a free pamphlet available at New Zealand consulates and Customs offices: *New Zealand Customs Guide for Travellers, Notice no. 4.* For more information, contact **New Zealand Customs,** The Customhouse, 17–21 Whitmore St., Box 2218, Wellington (✆ **04/473-6099** or 0800/428-786; www.customs.govt.nz).

4 Money

CURRENCY   The U.S. dollar is the coin of the realm. Keep in mind that once you leave Ponce or San Juan, you might have difficulty finding a place to exchange foreign money (unless you're staying at a large resort), so it's wise to handle your exchange needs before you head off into rural parts of Puerto Rico.

ATMS   ATMs are linked to a network that most likely includes your bank at home. **Cirrus** (✆ **800/424-7787;** www.mastercard. com) and **Plus** (✆ **800/843-7587;** www.visa.com) are the two most popular networks in the U.S.; call or check online for ATM locations at your destination. Be sure you know your four-digit PIN before you leave home and be sure to find out your daily withdrawal limit before you depart. You can also get cash advances on your credit card at an ATM. Keep in mind that credit-card companies try to protect themselves from theft by limiting the funds someone can withdraw away from home; it's therefore best to call your credit-card company before you leave and let them know where you're going and how much you plan to spend. You'll get the best exchange rate if you withdraw money from an ATM, but keep in mind that many banks impose a fee every time a card is used at an ATM in a different city or bank. On top of this, the bank from which you withdraw cash may charge its own fee.

What Things Cost in Puerto Rico	US $	British £
Taxi from airport to Condado	12.00	8.00
Average taxi fare within San Juan	6.00	4.00
Typical bus fare within San Juan	.25–.50	.16–.33
Local telephone call	.10	.07
Double room at the Caribe Hilton (very expensive)	250.00	167.00
Double room at El Canario by the Lagoon (moderate)	145.00	97.00
Double room at At Wind Chimes Inn (inexpensive)	80.00	54.00
Lunch for one at Amadeus (moderate)	16.00	11.00
Lunch for one at La Bombonera (inexpensive)	8.00	5.25
Dinner for one at Ramiro's (expensive)	46.00	31.00
Dinner for one at El Patio de Sam (moderate)	26.00	18.00
Dinner for one at Tony Roma's (inexpensive)	16.00	10.50
Bottle of beer in a bar	3.00	2.00
Glass of wine in a restaurant	3.75	2.50
Roll of ASA 100 color film, 36 exposures	8.50	5.50
Movie ticket	5.00–6.50	3.25–4.25
Theater ticket	15.00–65.00	10–44.00

CURRENCY EXCHANGE   The currency exchange facilities at any large international bank within Puerto Rico's larger cities can exchange non-U.S. currencies for dollars. You can also exchange money at the Luis Muñoz Marín International Airport. Also, you'll find foreign-exchange facilities in large hotels and at the many banks in Old San Juan or Avenida Ashford in Condado. In Ponce, look for foreign-exchange facilities at large resorts and at banks such as **Banco Popular,** Plaza Las Delicias (© **787/843-8000**).

5 When to Go

CLIMATE

Puerto Rico has one of the most unvarying climates in the world. Temperatures year-round range from 75°F to 85°F (24°C–29°C). The island is wettest and hottest in August, averaging 81°F (27°C) and 7 inches of rain. San Juan and the northern coast seem to be cooler and wetter than Ponce and the southern coast. The coldest weather is in the high altitudes of the Cordillera, the site of Puerto Rico's lowest recorded temperature—39°F (4°C).

THE HURRICANE SEASON

The hurricane season, the curse of Puerto Rican weather, lasts—officially, at least—from June 1 to November 30. But there's no cause for panic. In general, satellite forecasts give adequate warnings so that precautions can be taken.

If you're heading to Puerto Rico during the hurricane season, you can call your local branch of the **National Weather Service** (listed in your phone directory under the U.S. Department of Commerce) for a weather forecast.

It'll cost 95¢ per query, but you can get information about the climate conditions in any city you plan to visit by calling ℂ **800/WEATHER.** When you're prompted, enter your Visa or MasterCard account number and then punch in the name of any of 1,000 cities worldwide whose weather is monitored by the **Weather Channel** (www.weather.com).

Average Temperatures on Puerto Rico

	Jan	Feb	Mar	Apr	May	June	July	Aug	Sept	Oct	Nov	Dec
Temp. (°F)	75	75	76	78	79	81	81	81	81	81	79	77
Temp. (°C)	25	24	24	24	26	26	27	27	27	27	27	26

THE "SEASON"

In Puerto Rico, hotels charge their highest prices during the peak winter period from mid-December to mid-April, when visitors fleeing from cold northern climates flock to the islands. Winter is the driest season along the coasts but can be wet in mountainous areas.

If you plan to travel in the winter, make reservations 2 to 3 months in advance. At certain hotels it's almost impossible to book accommodations for Christmas and the month of February.

SAVING MONEY IN THE OFF-SEASON

Puerto Rico is a year-round destination. The island's "off-season" runs from late spring to late fall, when temperatures in the mid-80s (about 29°C) prevail throughout most of the region. Trade winds ensure comfortable days and nights, even in accommodations without air-conditioning. Although the noonday sun may raise the temperature to around 90°F (32°C), cool breezes usually make the morning, late afternoon, and evening more comfortable here than in many parts of the U.S. mainland.

Dollar for dollar, you'll spend less money by renting a summer house or fully equipped unit in Puerto Rico than you would on Cape Cod, Fire Island, Laguna Beach, or the coast of Maine.

The off-season in Puerto Rico—roughly from mid-April to mid-December (rate schedules vary from hotel to hotel)—amounts to a summer sale. In most cases, hotel rates are slashed from 20% to a startling 60%. It's a bonanza for cost-conscious travelers, especially families who like to go on vacations together. In the chapters ahead, we'll spell out in dollars the specific amounts hotels charge during the off-season.

HOLIDAYS

Puerto Rico has many public holidays when stores, offices, and schools are closed: New Year's Day, January 6 (Three Kings Day), Washington's Birthday, Good Friday, Memorial Day, July 4, Labor Day, Thanksgiving, Veterans Day, and Christmas, plus such local holidays as Constitution Day (July 25) and Discovery Day (Nov 19). Remember, U.S. federal holidays are holidays in Puerto Rico, too.

PUERTO RICO CALENDAR OF EVENTS

January

Three Kings Day, islandwide. On this traditional gift-giving day in Puerto Rico, there are festivals with lively music, dancing, parades, puppet shows, caroling troubadours, and traditional feasts. January 6.

February

Carnival Ponceño, Ponce. The island's Carnival celebrations feature float parades, dancing, and street parties. One of the most vibrant festivities is held in Ponce, known for its masqueraders wearing brightly painted horned masks. Live music includes the folk rhythms of the plena, which originated in Africa. Festivities include the crowning of a carnival queen and the closing "burial of the sardine." For more information, call © **787/284-4141.** February 6 to February 12, 2003.

March

Emancipation Day, islandwide. Commemoration of the emancipation of Puerto Rico's slaves in 1873, held at various venues. March 22.

April

Good Friday and Easter, islandwide. Celebrated with colorful ceremonies and processions. April 18 through 20, 2003.

June

Casals Festival, Performing Arts Center in San Juan. *Sanjuaneros* and visitors alike eagerly look forward to the annual Casals Festival, the Caribbean's most celebrated cultural event. The bill at San Juan's Performing Arts Center includes a glittering array of international guest conductors, orchestras, and soloists. They come to honor the memory of Pablo Casals, the renowned cellist who was born in Spain to a Puerto Rican mother. When Casals died in Puerto Rico in 1973 at the age of 97, the Casals Festival was 16 years old and attracting the same class of performers who appeared at the Pablo Casals Festival in France, founded by Casals after World War II. When he moved to Puerto Rico in 1957 with his wife, Marta Casals Istomin (former artistic director of the John F. Kennedy Center for the Performing Arts), he founded not only this festival but also the Puerto Rico Symphony Orchestra to foster musical development on the island.

Ticket prices for the Casals Festival range from $20 to $40. A 50% discount is offered to students, people over 60, and persons with disabilities. Tickets are available through the **Performing Arts Center** in San Juan (© **787/721-7727**). Information is also available from the **Puerto Rico Tourism Company,** 666 Fifth Ave., New York, NY 10103 (© **800/223-6530** or 212/586-6262). The festivities take place June 2 through 17, 2003.

San Juan Bautista Day, islandwide. Puerto Rico's capital and other cities celebrate the island's patron saint with weeklong festivities. At midnight, Sanjuaneros and others walk backward into the sea (or nearest body of water) three times to renew good luck for the coming year. June 24.

July

Loíza Carnival. An annual folk and religious ceremony honoring Loíza's patron saint, John (Santiago) the Apostle. Colorful processions take place, with costumes, masks, and bomba dancers (the bomba has a lively Afro-Caribbean dance rhythm). This jubilant celebration reflects the African and Spanish heritage of the region. For more information, call ☎ **787/876-3570.** July 24 through August 3, 2003.

October

La Raza Day (Columbus Day), islandwide. Commemoration of Columbus's landing in the New World. October 12.

National Plantain Festival, Corozal. This annual festivity involves crafts, paintings, agricultural products, exhibition, and sale of plantain dishes; *neuva trova* music and folk ballet are performed. For more information, call ☎ **787/859-1259.** End of October through the beginning of November.

November

Puerto Rico Discovery Day, islandwide. This day commemorates the "discovery" by Columbus in 1493 of the already inhabited island of Puerto Rico. Columbus is thought to have come ashore at the northwestern municipality of Aguadilla, although the exact location is unknown. November 19.

Festival of Puerto Rican Music, San Juan. Annual classical and folk music festival. One of its highlights is a *cuatro*-playing contest. (A *cuatro* is a guitar-like instrument with 10 strings.) For more information, call ☎ **787/721-5274.** Mid-November.

December

Old San Juan's White Christmas Festival, Old San Juan. Special musical and artistic presentations take place in stores, with window displays. December 1 through January 12.

Bacardi Artisans' Fair, San Juan. The best and largest artisans' fair on the island features more than 100 artisans who turn out to exhibit and sell their wares. The fair includes shows for adults and children, a Puerto Rican troubadour contest, rides, and typical food and drink—all sold by nonprofit organizations. Held on the grounds of the world's largest rum-manufacturing plant in Cataño, an industrial suburb set on a peninsula jutting into San Juan Bay. For more information, call ☎ **787/788-1500.** First two Sundays in December.

YEAR-ROUND FESTIVALS

In addition to the individual events described above, Puerto Rico has two year-long series of special events.

Many of Puerto Rico's most popular events are during the **Patron Saint Festivals** (*fiestas patronales*) in honor of the patron saint of each municipality. The festivities, held in each town's central plaza, include religious and costumed processions, games, local food, music, and dance.

At **Festival La Casita,** prominent Puerto Rican musicians, dance troupes, and orchestras perform; puppet shows are staged; and painters and sculptors display their works. It happens every Saturday at Puerto Rico Tourism's "La Casita" Tourism Information Center, Plaza Darsenas, across from Pier 1, Old San Juan.

For more information about all these events, contact the **Puerto Rico Tourism Company,** 666 Fifth Ave., New York, NY 10103 (© **800/223-6530** or 212/586-6262).

6 Staying Healthy

Puerto Rico poses no major health problem for most travelers. If you have a chronic condition, however, you should check with your doctor before visiting the islands. For conditions such as epilepsy, diabetes, or heart problems, wear a **MedicAlert Identification Tag** (© **800/825-3785;** www.medicalert.org), which will immediately alert doctors to your condition and give them access to your records through MedicAlert's 24-hour hot line.

If you worry about getting sick away from home, consider purchasing **medical travel insurance** and carry your ID card in your purse or wallet. In most cases, your existing health plan will provide the coverage you need.

Finding a good doctor in Puerto Rico is easy, and most speak English. See "Fast Facts: Puerto Rico," later in this chapter, for the locations of hospitals. If you get sick, consider asking your hotel concierge to recommend a local doctor—even his or her own. You can also try the emergency room at a local hospital; many have walk-in clinics for emergency cases that are not life threatening. You might not get immediate attention, but you won't pay the high price of an emergency-room visit (usually a minimum of $300 just for signing your name).

You can also contact the **International Association for Medical Assistance to Travellers** (IAMAT; © **716/754-4883** or 416/652-0137; www.sentex.net/~iamat) for tips on travel and health concerns in Puerto Rico and lists of local, English-speaking doctors.

Pack **prescription medications** in your carry-on luggage, and carry prescription medications in their original containers. Also bring along copies of your prescriptions in case you lose your medication or run out. Carry the generic name of prescription medicines, in case a local pharmacist is unfamiliar with the brand name.

And don't forget **sunglasses** and an extra pair of **contact lenses** or **prescription glasses.**

It's best to stick to **bottled mineral water** here. Although tap water is said to be safe to drink, many visitors experience diarrhea, even if they follow the usual precautions. The illness usually passes quickly without medication if you eat simply prepared food and drink only mineral water until you recover. If symptoms persist, consult a doctor.

The **sun** can be brutal, especially if you haven't been exposed to it in some time. Experts advise that you limit your time on the beach the first day. If you do overexpose yourself, stay out of the sun until you recover. If your exposure is followed by fever or chills, a headache, or a feeling of nausea or dizziness, see a doctor.

Sandflies (or "no-see-ums") are one of the biggest insect menaces in Puerto Rico. They appear mainly in the early evening, and even if you can't see these tiny bugs, you sure can "feel-um," as any native Puerto Rican will attest. Screens can't keep them out, so you'll need to use your favorite insect repellent.

Although **mosquitoes** are a nuisance, they do not carry malaria in Puerto Rico.

Hookworm and other **intestinal parasites** are relatively common in the Caribbean, though you are less likely to be affected in Puerto Rico than on other islands. Hookworm can be contracted by just walking barefoot on an infected beach. *Schistosomiasis* (also called *bilharzia*), caused by a parasitic fluke, can be contracted by submerging your feet in rivers and lakes infested with a certain species of snail.

7 Tips for Travelers with Special Needs

TRAVELERS WITH DISABILITIES

Most disabilities shouldn't stop anyone from traveling. There are more options and resources out there today than ever before.

The Americans with Disabilities Act is enforced as strictly in Puerto Rico as it is on the U.S. mainland—in fact, a telling example of the act's enforcement can be found in Ponce, where the sight-seeing trolleys are equipped with ramps and extra balustrades to accommodate travelers with disabilities. Unfortunately, hotels rarely give much publicity to the facilities they offer persons with disabilities, so it's always wise to contact the hotel directly, in advance, if you need special facilities. Tourist offices usually have little data about such matters.

The U.S. National Park Service offers a **Golden Access Passport** that gives free lifetime entrance to all properties administered by the National Park Service—including those in Puerto Rico—for persons who are blind or permanently disabled, regardless of age. You may pick up a Golden Access Passport at any NPS entrance fee area by showing proof of medically determined disability and eligibility for receiving benefits under federal law. Besides free entry, the Golden Access Passport also offers a 50% discount on federal-use fees charged for such facilities as camping, swimming, parking, boat launching, and tours. For more information, go to www.nps.gov/fees_passes.htm or call ✆ **888/467-2757.**

Many travel agencies offer customized tours and itineraries for travelers with disabilities. **Flying Wheels Travel** (✆ **507/451-5005;** www.flyingwheelstravel.com) offers escorted tours and cruises that emphasize sports and private tours in minivans with lifts.

Organizations that offer assistance to disabled travelers include the **Moss Rehab Hospital** (www.mossresourcenet.org), which provides a library of accessible-travel resources online, and the **Society for Accessible Travel and Hospitality** (✆ **212/447-7284;** www.sath.org; annual membership fees: $45 adults, $30 seniors and students), which offers a wealth of travel resources for all types of disabilities and informed recommendations on destinations and services.

GAY & LESBIAN TRAVELERS

Puerto Rico is the most gay-friendly destination in the Caribbean, with lots of accommodations, restaurants, clubs, and bars that actively cater to a gay clientele. A free monthly newsletter, *Puerto Rico Breeze,* lists items of interest to the island's gay community. It's distributed at the Atlantic Beach Hotel (p. 73) and many of the gay-friendly clubs mentioned in this book.

The International Gay & Lesbian Travel Association (IGLTA) (✆ **800/448-8550** or 954/776-2626; www.iglta.org) is the trade association for the gay and lesbian travel industry, and offers an online directory of gay- and lesbian-friendly travel businesses; go to their website and click on "Members."

Many agencies offer tours and travel itineraries specifically for gay and lesbian travelers. **Above and Beyond Tours** (✆ **800/397-2681;** www.abovebeyondtours.com) is the exclusive gay and lesbian tour operator for United Airlines. **Now, Voyager** (✆ **800/255-6951;** www.nowvoyager.com) is a well-known San Francisco–based gay-owned and operated travel service.

SENIOR TRAVEL

Mention the fact that you're a senior when you first make your travel reservations. All major airlines and many Puerto Rican hotels offer discounts for seniors.

Though much of the island's sporting and nightlife activity is geared toward youthful travelers, Puerto Rico also has much to offer the senior. The best source of information for seniors is the Puerto Rico Tourism Company (see "Visitor Information," earlier in this chapter), or, if you're staying in a large resort hotel, the activities director or the concierge.

Members of **AARP** (formerly known as the American Association of Retired Persons), 601 E St. NW, Washington, DC 20049 (© **800/ 424-3410** or 202/434-2277; www.aarp.org), get discounts on hotels, airfares, and car rentals. AARP offers members a wide range of benefits, including *AARP: The Magazine* and a monthly newsletter. Anyone over 50 can join.

The **U.S. National Park Service** offers a **Golden Age Passport** that gives seniors 62 years or older lifetime entrance to all properties administered by the National Park Service—national parks, monuments, historic sites, recreation areas, and national wildlife refuges—for a one-time processing fee of $10, which must be purchased in person at any NPS facility that charges an entrance fee. Besides free entry, a Golden Age Passport also offers a 50% discount on federal-use fees charged for such facilities as camping, swimming, parking, boat launching, and tours. For more information, go to www.nps.gov/fees_passes.htm or call © **888/467-2757.**

Elderhostel (© **877/426-8056;** www.elderhostel.org) arranges study programs for those ages 55 and over (and a spouse or companion of any age) in the U.S. and in more than 80 countries around the world. Most courses last 5 to 7 days in the U.S. (2–4 weeks abroad), and many include airfare, accommodations in university dormitories or modest inns, meals, and tuition.

FAMILY TRAVEL

The family vacation is a rite of passage for many households, one that in a split second can devolve into a *National Lampoon* farce. But as any veteran family vacationer will assure you, a family trip can be among the most pleasurable and rewarding times of your life.

Puerto Rico is a terrific family destination. The smallest toddlers can spend blissful hours on sandy beaches and in the shallow seawater or pools specifically constructed for them. There's no end to the fascinating pursuits available for older children, ranging from boat rides to shell collecting to horseback riding and hiking. Perhaps your children are old enough to learn to snorkel and explore the wonderland of underwater Puerto Rico. Skills such as swimming and windsurfing are taught here, and there are a variety of activities unique to the islands. Most resort hotels will advise you on what there is in the way of fun for the young, and many have play directors and supervised activities for various age groups.

Refer to chapter 4 for some recommendations of family-friendly accommodations, and to chapter 5 for our pick of family-friend restaurants. In chapter 6, look for the section "Especially for Kids" for special activities.

Families will be especially interested in some of the activities outlined in chapter 7, including Arecibo Observatory and Río Camuy cave park. A trip to the El Yunque rain forest and an afternoon at Luquillo Beach are other family favorite highlights. Chapter 7 also contains recommendations of two Hyatt properties at Dorado that are among the most family-friendly accommodations in Puerto Rico.

You can find good family-oriented vacation advice on the Internet from sites like the **Family Travel Network** (www.familytravel network.com) and **Family Travel Files** (www.thefamilytravelfiles. com), which offers an online magazine and a directory of off-the-beaten-path tours and tour operators for families.

8 Getting There: Flying to Puerto Rico

Puerto Rico is by far the most accessible of the Caribbean islands, with frequent airline service. It's also the major airline hub of the Caribbean Basin.

THE AIRLINES

With San Juan as its hub for the entire Caribbean, **American Airlines** (© 800/433-7300; www.aa.com) offers nonstop daily flights to San Juan from Baltimore, Boston, Chicago, Dallas–Fort Worth, Hartford, Miami, Newark, New York (JFK), Orlando, Philadelphia, Tampa, Fort Lauderdale, and Washington (Dulles), plus flights to San Juan from both Montréal and Toronto with changes in Chicago or Miami. There are also at least two daily flights from Los Angeles to San Juan that touch down in Dallas or Miami.

American, because of its wholly owned subsidiary, **American Eagle,** is also the undisputed leader among the short-haul local commuter flights of the Caribbean. It usually flies in propeller planes carrying between 34 and 64 passengers. Collectively, American Eagle, along with its larger associate, American Airlines, offers service to 37 destinations on 31 islands of the Caribbean and The Bahamas, more than any other carrier.

Delta (℗ **800/221-1212;** www.delta-air.com) has four daily nonstop flights from Atlanta Monday through Friday, six nonstop on Saturday, and four nonstop on Sunday. Flights into Atlanta from around the world are frequent, with excellent connections from points throughout Delta's network in the South and Southwest. There is also one daily nonstop flight from Cincinnati.

United Airlines (℗ **800/241-6522;** www.ual.com) offers daily nonstop flights from Chicago to San Juan. **Northwest** (℗ **800/ 225-2525;** www.nwa.com) has one daily nonstop flight to San Juan from Detroit, as well as at least one (and sometimes more) connecting flights to San Juan from Detroit. United also offers flights to San Juan, some of them nonstop, from both Memphis and Minneapolis, with a schedule that varies according to the season and the day of the week.

US Airways (℗ **800/428-4322;** www.usairways.com) has daily direct flights between Charlotte, N.C., and San Juan. The airline also offers three daily nonstop flights to San Juan from Philadelphia, and one daily nonstop flight to San Juan from Pittsburgh.

British travelers can take a **British Airways** (℗ **0845/773-3377** in the U.K., 800/247-9297 in the U.S.) weekly flight direct from London to San Juan on Sunday. **Lufthansa** (℗ **01/803-803-803** in Germany, 800/645-3880 in the U.S.) passengers can fly on Saturday (one weekly flight) from Frankfurt to San Juan via Condor (a subsidiary operating the flight). And **Iberia** (℗ **1/902-400-500** in Spain, 800/772-4642 in the U.S.; www.iberia.com) has two weekly flights from Madrid to San Juan, leaving on Thursday and Saturday.

FLYING FOR LESS: TIPS FOR GETTING THE BEST AIRFARE

Passengers within the same airplane cabin are rarely paying the same fare. Business travelers who need to purchase tickets at the last minute, change their itinerary at a moment's notice, or get home for the weekend pay the premium rate. Passengers who can book their ticket long in advance, who can stay over Saturday night, or who are willing to travel on a Tuesday, Wednesday, or Thursday after 7pm, will pay a fraction of the full fare. On many flights, even the shortest hops, the full fare is close to $1,000 or more, while a 7- or 14-day advance purchase ticket may cost less than half that amount. Here are a few other easy ways to save.

Airlines periodically lower prices on their most popular routes. Check the travel section of your Sunday newspaper for advertised discounts or call the airlines directly and ask if any **promotional rates** or special fares are available. You'll almost never see a sale during the peak winter season in Puerto Rico, or during the Thanksgiving or Christmas seasons. If your schedule is flexible, say so, and ask if you can secure a cheaper fare by staying an extra day, by flying midweek, or by flying at less-trafficked hours. If you already hold a ticket when a sale breaks, it may even pay to exchange your ticket, which usually incurs a $100 to $150 charge. *Note:* The lowest-priced fares are often nonrefundable, require advance purchase of 1 to 3 weeks and a certain length of stay, and carry penalties for changing dates of travel.

Find out about great **last-minute deals** available through free weekly e-mail services provided directly by the airlines. Most of these are announced on Tuesday or Wednesday and must be purchased online. Sign up for weekly e-mail alerts at airline websites or check mega-sites that compile comprehensive lists of last-minute specials, such as **Smarter Living** (smarterliving.com). For last-minute trips, **site59.com** in the U.S. and **lastminute.com** in Europe often have better deals than the major-label sites.

Join a travel club such as **Moment's Notice** (© 718/234-6295; www.moments-notice.com) or **Sears Discount Travel Club** (© 800/433-9383, or 800/255-1487 to join; www.travelersadvantage.com), which supply unsold tickets at discounted prices. You pay an annual membership fee to get the club's hot-line number. Of course, you're limited to what's available, so you have to be flexible.

9 Escorted Tours, Package Deals & Special-Interest Vacations

Before you start your search for the lowest airfare, you might want to consider booking your flight as part of a travel package such as an escorted tour or a package tour. What you lose in adventure, you'll gain in time and money saved when you book accommodations, and maybe even food and entertainment, along with your flight.

PACKAGE TOURS FOR INDEPENDENT TRAVELERS

Package tours are not the same thing as escorted tours. With a package tour, you travel independently but pay a group rate. Packages usually include airfare, a choice of hotels, and car rentals, and packagers often offer several options at different prices. In many cases, a package that includes airfare, hotel, and transportation to and from the airport will cost you less than just the hotel alone would have, had you booked it yourself. That's because packages are sold in bulk to tour operators—who resell them to the public at a cost that drastically undercuts standard rates.

RECOMMENDED U.S. PACKAGE TOUR OPERATORS

One good source of package deals is the airlines themselves. Most major airlines offer air/land packages, including **American Airlines Vacations** (© **800/321-2121;** http://aav1.aavacations.com), **Delta Vacations** (© **800/221-6666;** www.deltavacations.com), **US Airways Vacations** (© **800/455-0123** or 800/422-3861; www.usairways vacations.com), **Continental Airlines Vacations** (© **800/301-3800;** www.coolvacations.com), and **United Vacations** (© **888/854-3899;** www.unitedvacations.com).

Online Vacation Mall (© **800/839-9851;** www.onlinevacation mall.com) allows you to search for and book packages offered by a number of tour operators and airlines. The **United States Tour Operators Association's** website (www.ustoa.com) has a search engine that allows you to look for operators that offer packages to a specific destination. Travel packages are also listed in the travel section of your local Sunday newspaper. **Liberty Travel** (© **888/271-1584;** www.libertytravel.com), one of the biggest packagers in the Northeast, often runs full-page ads in Sunday papers. Or check ads in the national travel magazines such as *Arthur Frommer's Budget Travel Magazine, Travel & Leisure, National Geographic Traveler*, and *Condé Nast Traveler.*

To save time comparing the price and value of all the package tours out there, consider calling **TourScan Inc.,** P.O. Box 2367, Darien, CT 06820 (© **800/962-2080** or 203/655-8091; fax 203/655-6689; www.tourscan.com). Every season the company gathers and computerizes the contents of about 200 brochures containing 10,000 different vacations in the Caribbean, The Bahamas, and Bermuda. TourScan selects the best value at each hotel and condo. Two catalogs are printed each year. Each lists a broad-based choice of hotels on most of the islands of the Caribbean, in all price ranges. Write to TourScan for their catalogs, costing $4 each, the price of which is credited to any TourScan vacation.

Other options for general independent packages include:

Horizon Tours, 1634 Eye St. NW, Suite 301, Washington, DC 20006 (© **877/TRIPSAI** or 202/393-8390; fax 202/393-1547;

www.horizontours.com), specializes in all-inclusive upscale resorts in Puerto Rico.

AAA Tours, 1759 Pinero Ave., Summit Hills, San Juan (*©* 787/ 793-3678), offers some good packages ranging from 2 days to 2 weeks.

ESCORTED TOURS

An escorted tour is a structured group tour with a group leader. The price usually includes everything from airfare to hotel, meals, tours, admission costs, and local transportation.

RECOMMENDED ESCORTED TOUR OPERATORS

Puerto Rico Tours, Condo Inter-Suite, Suite 5M on Isla Verde in San Juan (*©* **787/306-1540;** fax 787/791-5479), offers specially conducted private sightseeing tours of Puerto Rico, including trips to the rain forest, Luquillo Beach, the caves of Camuy, and other attractions, such as a restored Taíno Indian village.

Backstage Partners (*©* **787/791-0099;** fax 787/791-2760) offers customized tours that take in a wide range of island attractions, including ecotours, deep-sea fishing, scuba diving and snorkeling, safaris, and golf packages.

Other leading escorted tour operators include **Crown Imperial Travel**, Loiza Street Station in San Juan (*©* **787/791-7075**), known for such major destinations as Ponce, El Yunque, and the Camuy Caverns; **Northwestern Land Tour** (*©* **787/447-7804**), which helps you take in all the major sights of the island from Ponce to El Yunque; and **Sunshine Tours** (*©* **787/791-4500**; www.puerto-rico-sunshinetours. com), which covers much the same ground as the others.

SPECIAL-INTEREST TOURS

If you'd like to explore Puerto Rico as part of a horseback riding tour package, consult **PRwest Vacation Services** (*©* **888/779-3788**). A dozen well-trained Paso Fino horses are available to accommodate both the advanced and novice rider. In northwest Puerto Rico, you can explore cavernous cliffs and tropical forests—all on horseback. Tours last 7 days and 6 nights.

Several other tour operators cater to special tastes, including **Castillo Tours & Travel Service**, 2413C Laurel St., Punta Las Marias, San Juan (*©* **787/791-6995;** www.castillotours.com), which is known for some of the best deep-sea fishing tours. **Encantada Tours,** 654 Muñoz Rivera Ave., Suite 908, IBM Plaza, San Juan (*©* **888/711-2901;** www.encantadatours.com), offers gastronomical tours of the island.

Hillbilly Tours, Route 181, km 13.4, San Juan (℃ **787/760-5618**), specializes in nature-based and countryside tours in the rain forest.

AdvenTours, Luquillo (℃ **787/530-8311;** aventura@coqui.net), features customized private tours that include such activities as bird-watching, hiking, camping, visits to coffee plantations, and kayaking. **Aventuras Tierra Adentro,** 268 Piñero Avenue, San Juan (℃ **787/766-0470;** www.aventurastierraadentro.com), specializes in rock climbing, body rafting, caving, and canyoning.

Eco Xcursion Aquatica, Route 191, km 1.7, Rio Grande, Fajardo (℃ **787/888-2887**), offers some of the best rain-forest hikes and mountain bike tours for both individuals and groups.

10 Getting Around

BY PLANE

American Eagle (℃ **800/433-7300** or 787/749-1747; www.aa.com) flies from Luis Muñoz Marín International Airport to Mayagüez, which can be your gateway to western Puerto Rico. Round-trip fares are $99 to $242.

BY RENTAL CAR

There is good news and bad news about driving in Puerto Rico. First, the good news. Puerto Rico offers some of the most scenic drives in all the Caribbean. Driving around and discovering its little hidden beaches, coastal towns, mountain villages, vast forests, and national parks is reason enough to visit the island. In fact, if you want to explore the island in any depth, driving a private car is about the only way, as public transportation is woefully inadequate.

Of course, if you want to stay only in San Juan, having a car is not necessary. You can get around San Juan on foot or by bus, taxi, and in some cases, hotel minivan.

Now the bad news. Renting a car and driving in Puerto Rico, depending on the routes you take, can lead to a number of frustrating experiences, as our readers relate to us year after year. These readers point out that local drivers are often dangerous, as evidenced by the number of fenders with bashed-in sides. The older coastal highways provide the most scenic routes but are often congested. Some of the roads, especially in the mountainous interior, are just too narrow for automobiles. If you do rent a car, proceed with caution along these poorly paved and maintained roads, which most often follow circuitous routes. Cliffslides or landslides are not uncommon.

Some local agencies may tempt you with special reduced prices. But if you're planning to tour the island by car, you won't find any local branches that will help you if you experience trouble. And some of the agencies widely advertising low-cost deals won't take credit cards and want cash in advance. Also, watch out for "hidden" extra costs, which sometimes proliferate among the smaller and not very well known firms, and difficulties connected with resolving insurance claims.

If you do rent a vehicle, it's best to stick with the old reliables: **Avis** (© **800/331-1212** or 787/253-5926; www.avis.com), **Budget** (© **800/527-0700** or 787/791-3685; https://rent.drivebudget.com), or **Hertz** (© **800/654-3131** or 787/791-0840; www.hertz.com). Each of these companies offers minivan transport to its office and car depot. Be alert to the minimum-age requirements for car rentals in Puerto Rico. Both Avis and Hertz require that renters be 25 or older; at Budget, renters must be 21 or older, but those between the ages of 21 and 24 pay a $5 daily surcharge to the agreed-upon rental fee. None of these companies rents Jeeps, SUVs, or convertibles.

Added security comes from an antitheft double-locking mechanism that has been installed in most of the rental cars available in Puerto Rico. Car theft is common in Puerto Rico, so extra precautions are always needed.

Distances are often posted in kilometers rather than miles (1km = .62 mile), but speed limits are displayed in miles per hour.

INSURANCE   Each company offers an optional collision damage waiver priced at around $14 to $20 a day. Purchasing the waiver eliminates most or all of the financial responsibility you would face in case of an accident. With it, you can simply go home, leaving the rental company to sort it all out. Without it, you would be liable for up to the full value of the car in case it was damaged. Paying for the rental with certain credit or charge cards sometimes eliminates the need to buy this extra insurance. Also, your own automobile insurance policy might cover some or all of the damages. You should check with both your own insurer and your credit-card issuers before leaving home.

GASOLINE   There is usually an abundant supply of gasoline in Puerto Rico, especially on the outskirts of San Juan, where you'll see all the familiar signs, such as Mobil. Gasoline stations are also plentiful along the main arteries traversing the island. However, if you're going to remote areas of the island, especially on Sunday, it's advisable to start out with a full tank. *Note:* In Puerto Rico, gasoline is

Highway Signs

Road signs using international symbols are commonplace in the San Juan metropolitan area and other urban centers, but they are written in Spanish. The following translations will help you figure out what they mean:

Spanish	English
Autopista	Expressway
Balneario	Public beach
Calle sin salida	Dead end
Carretera cerrada	Road closed to traffic
Carretera dividida	Divided highway
Carretera estrecha	Narrow road
Cruce	Crossroad
Cruce de peatones	Pedestrian crossing
Cuesta	Hill
Desprendimiento	Landslide
Desvío	Detour
Estación de peaje	Toll station
Manténgase a la derecha	Keep right
No entre	Do not enter
No estacione	Do not park
Parada de guaguas	Bus stop
Peligro	Danger
Puente estrecho	Narrow bridge
Velocidad máxima	Speed limit
Zona escolar	School zone

sold by the liter, not by the gallon. The cost of gasoline is often somewhat cheaper than in the United States. A liter usually sells for 26¢, which comes to about $1.25 per gallon.

DRIVING RULES   Driving rules can be a source of some confusion. Speed limits are often not posted on the island, but when they are, they're given in miles per hour. For example, the limit on the San Juan–Ponce *autopista* (expressway) is 70 mph. Speed limits elsewhere, notably in heavily populated residential areas, are much lower. Because you're not likely to know what the actual speed limit is in some of these areas, it's best to confine your speed to no more than 30 mph. The highway department places *lomas* (speed bumps) at strategic points to deter speeders. Sometimes these are called "sleeping policemen."

Like U.S. and Canadian motorists, *Puerto Ricans drive on the right-hand side of the road.*

ROAD MAPS   One of the best and most detailed road maps of Puerto Rico is published by **International Travel Maps** and distributed in the United States by Rand McNally. It's available in some bookstores and is a good investment at $8.95. The *Gousha Puerto Rico Road Map,* which sells for $8.95 in the United States and Canada, has a good street map of San Juan but lacks detailed information about minor highways on the island and is very similar to the map of Puerto Rico distributed free at tourist offices.

BREAKDOWNS AND ASSISTANCE   All the major towns and cities have garages that will come to your assistance and tow your vehicle for repairs if necessary. There's no national emergency number to call in the event of a mechanical breakdown. If you have a rental car, call the rental company first. Usually, someone there will bring motor assistance to you. If your car requires extensive repairs because of a mechanical failure, a new one will be sent to replace it.

BY PUBLIC TRANSPORTATION

Cars and minibuses known as *públicos* provide low-cost transportation around the island. Their license plates have the letters "P" or "PD" following the numbers. They serve all the main towns of Puerto Rico; passengers are let off and picked up along the way, both at designated stops and when someone flags them down. Rates are set by the Public Service Commission. *Públicos* usually operate during daylight hours, departing from the main plaza (central square) of a town.

Information about público routes between San Juan and Mayagüez is available at **Lineas Sultana,** Calle Esteban González 898, Urbanización Santa Rita, Río Piedras (*©* 787/765-9377). Information about público routes between San Juan and Ponce is available from **Choferes Unidos de Ponce,** Terminal de Carros Públicos, Calle Vive in Ponce (*©* 787/764-0540).

Fares vary according to whether the público will make a detour to pick up or drop off a passenger at a specific locale. (If you want to deviate from the predetermined routes, you'll pay more than if you wait for a público beside the main highway.) Fares from San Juan to Mayagüez range from $16 to $30; from San Juan to Ponce, from $15 to $25. Be warned that although prices of públicos are low, the routes are slow, with frequent stops, often erratic routing, and lots of inconvenience.

Beach Warning

Don't go walking along the beaches at night, even as tempting as it may be to do with your lover. Even if you find the secluded, hidden beach of your dreams, proceed with caution. On unguarded beaches, you will have no way to protect yourself or your valuables should you be approached by a robber or mugger, which happens frequently.

11 The Active Vacation Planner

Puerto Rico offers a wide variety of sports, including golf, tennis, horseback riding, and all kinds of watersports—from scuba diving to deep-sea fishing.

Many resorts offer a large choice of sports activities, and various all-inclusive sports-vacation packages are available from hotels and airlines serving Puerto Rico.

Dorado Beach, Cerromar Beach, and Palmas del Mar are the chief centers for golf, tennis, and beach life. San Juan's hotels on the Condado–Isla Verde coast also generally offer a complete array of watersports.

BEACHES

With 272 miles (438km) of Atlantic and Caribbean coastline, Puerto Rico obviously has plenty of beaches—more than 250 of them. No two beaches are alike. Some are long, straight, and very popular, with active and lively waves. Others have calmer waters, are more intimate, and are off the beaten path.

Puerto Rico's public beaches are called *balnearios;* they charge for parking and for use of facilities such as lockers and showers. Some of Puerto Rico's balnearios are practically deserted. They are closed on Monday, except if Monday is a holiday; in that case, they are open then but closed on Tuesday. In winter, public beach hours are from 9am to 5pm; in summer, from 9am to 6pm. For more information about the island's many beaches, call the **Department of Sports and Recreation** at © 787/728-5668.

BOATING & SAILING

The waters off Puerto Rico provide excellent boating in all seasons. Winds average 10 to 15 knots virtually year-round. Marinas provide facilities and services on par with any others in the Caribbean, and many have powerboats or sailboats for rent, crewed or bareboat charter.

Major marinas include the **San Juan Bay Marina,** Fernandez Juncos Avenue (© **787/721-8062**); **Marina Puerto Chico,** at Puerto Chico (© **787/863-0834**); **Marina de Palmas Shipyard** at Palmas del Mar in Humacao (© **787/850-2065**); and **Marina de Salinas** (© **787/752-8484**) in Salinas. The Caribbean's largest and most modern marina, **Puerto del Rey,** RD 3, km 51.4 (© **787/860-1000**), is located on the island's east coast, in Fajardo.

DEEP-SEA FISHING

The offshore fishing here is top-notch! Allison tuna, white and blue marlin, sailfish, wahoo, dolphin, mackerel, and tarpon are some of the fish that can be caught in Puerto Rican waters, where some 30 world records have been broken.

Charter arrangements can be made through most major hotels and resorts. In San Juan, **Benitez Fishing Charters** sets the standard by which to judge other captains (see "Diving, Fishing, Tennis & Other Outdoor Pursuits" in chapter 6). In Palmas del Mar, which has some of the best year-round fishing in the Caribbean, you'll find **Capt. Bill Burleson** (see "Palmas del Mar" in chapter 10).

GOLF

Home to 13 golf courses, including 8 championship links, Puerto Rico is justifiably known as the "Scotland of the Caribbean." In fact, the 72 holes at the Hyatt resorts at Dorado offer the greatest concentration of golf in the Caribbean.

The courses at the **Hyatt Dorado Beach Resort & Country Club** and the **Hyatt Regency Cerromar Beach Resort** are among the 25 best courses created by Robert Trent Jones, Sr. Jack Nicklaus rates the challenging 13th hole at the Hyatt Dorado as one of the top 10 in the world. See "Dorado," in chapter 7 for more details.

On the southeast coast, crack golfers consider holes 11 through 15 at the **Golf Club at Palmas del Mar** to be the toughest five successive holes in the Caribbean. At **Wyndham El Conquistador Resort & Country Club,** the spectacular $250 million resort at Las Croabas east of San Juan, the course's 200-foot changes in elevation provide panoramic vistas. With the exception of the El Conquistador Resort and Country Club, these courses are open to the public. See chapter 10 for more details on the major golf clubs east of San Juan.

HIKING

The mountainous interior of Puerto Rico provides ample opportunities for hill climbing and nature treks. These are especially appealing because panoramas open at the least-expected moments, often revealing spectacular views of the distant sea.

The most popular, most beautiful, and most spectacular trekking spot is **El Yunque,** the sprawling "jungle" maintained by the U.S. Forest Service and the only rain forest on U.S. soil.

El Yunque is part of the **Caribbean National Forest,** which lies a 45-minute drive east of San Juan. More than 250 species of trees and some 200 types of ferns have been identified here. Some 60 species of birds inhabit El Yunque, including the increasingly rare Puerto Rican parrot. Such rare birds as the elfin woods warbler, the green mango hummingbird, and the Puerto Rican lizard-cuckoo live here.

Park rangers have clearly marked the trails that are ideal for walking. See "El Yunque" in chapter 7 for more details.

A lesser forest, but one that is still intriguing to visit, is the **Maricao State Forest,** near the coffee town of Maricao. This forest is in western Puerto Rico, east of the town of Mayagüez. For more details, see "Mayagüez" in chapter 8.

Ponce is the best center for exploring some of the greatest forest reserves in the Caribbean Basin, notably the **Guánica State Forest,** ideal for hiking and bird-watching. For details, see "Ponce" in chapter 8.

Equally suitable for hiking are the protected lands (especially the **Río Camuy Cave Park**) whose topography is characterized as "karst"—that is, limestone riddled with caves, underground rivers, and natural crevasses and fissures. Although these regions pose additional risks and technical problems for trekkers, some people prefer the opportunities they provide for exploring the territory both above and below its surface. See "Arecibo & Camuy" in chapter 7 for details about the Río Camuy Caves.

For more information about any of the national forest reserves of Puerto Rico, call the **Department of Sports & Recreation** at © **787/728-5668.**

SCUBA DIVING & SNORKELING

SCUBA DIVING The continental shelf, which surrounds Puerto Rico on three sides, is responsible for an abundance of coral reefs, caves, sea walls, and trenches for scuba diving and snorkeling.

Open-water reefs off the southeastern coast near **Humacao** are visited by migrating whales and manatees. Many caves are located near Isabela on the west coast. The **Great Trench,** off the island's south coast, is ideal for experienced open-water divers. Caves and the sea wall at **La Parguera** are also favorites. **Mona Island** offers unspoiled reefs at depths averaging 80 feet; seals are one of the attractions. Uninhabited islands, such as **Icacos,** off the northeastern coast near Fajardo, are also popular with both snorkelers and divers.

These sites are now within reach because many of Puerto Rico's dive operators and resorts offer packages that include daily or twice-daily dives, scuba equipment, instruction, and excursions to Puerto Rico's popular attractions.

In San Juan, **Caribe Aquatic Adventures** offers an array of sailing, scuba, and snorkeling trips, as well as boat charters and fishing (see "Diving, Fishing, Tennis & Other Outdoor Pursuits," in chapter 6). At the Palmas del Mar Resort, **Palmas Dive Center** features daily two-tank open-water dives for certified divers, plus snorkeling trips to Monkey Island (see "Palmas del Mar," in chapter 10). Elsewhere on the island, several other companies offer scuba and snorkeling instruction. We provide details in each chapter.

SNORKELING   Because of its overpopulation, the waters around San Juan aren't the most ideal for snorkeling. In fact, the entire north shore of Puerto Rico fronts the Atlantic, where the waters are often turbulent. Windsurfers—not snorkelers—gravitate to the waves and surf in the northwest.

The best snorkeling on the main island is found near the town of **Fajardo,** to the east of San Juan and along the tranquil eastern coast (see chapter 10).

The calm, glasslike quality of the clear Caribbean along the south shore is also ideal for snorkeling. The most developed tourist mecca here is the city of Ponce. Few rivers empty their muddy waters into the sea along the south coast, resulting in gin-clear waters offshore. You can snorkel off the coast without having to go on a boat trip. One good place is at **Playa La Parguera,** where you can rent snorkeling equipment from kiosks along the beach. This beach lies east of the town of Guánica, to the east of Ponce. Here tropical fish add to the brightness of the water, which is generally turquoise. The addition of mangrove cays in the area also makes La Parguera more alluring for snorkelers. Another good spot for snorkelers is **Caja de Muertos** off the coast of Ponce. Here a lagoon coral reef boasts a large number of fish species (see "Ponce," in chapter 8).

SURFING

Puerto Rico's northwest beaches attract surfers from around the world. Called the "Hawaii of the East," Puerto Rico has hosted a number of international competitions. October through February are the best surfing months, but the sport is enjoyed in Puerto Rico from August to April. The most popular areas are from Isabela around Punta Borinquén to Rincón—at beaches such as Wilderness, Surfers, Crashboat, Los Turbos in Vega Baja, Pine Grove in Isla Verde, and La Pared in Luquillo. Surfboards are available at many watersports shops.

International competitions held in Puerto Rico have included the 1968 and 1988 World Amateur Surfing Championships, the annual Caribbean Cup Surfing Championship, and the 1989 and 1990 Budweiser Puerto Rico Surfing Challenge events.

TENNIS

Puerto Rico has approximately 100 major tennis courts. Many are at hotels and resorts; others are in public parks throughout the island. Several paradores also have courts. A number of courts are lighted for nighttime play.

In San Juan, the **Caribe Hilton** and the **Condado Plaza Hotel & Casino** have tennis courts. Also in the area are the **public courts** at the San Juan Central Municipal Park. See chapter 6.

The **Hyatt Regency Cerromar Beach Hotel** and the **Hyatt Dorado Beach Resort & Country Club** maintain a total of 21 courts between them (see "Dorado," in chapter 7). The **Tennis Center** at **Palmas del Mar** in Humacao, the largest in Puerto Rico, features 20 courts (see "Palmas del Mar," in chapter 10).

WINDSURFING

Windsurfing is a popular watersport in Puerto Rico; the sheltered waters of the **Condado Lagoon** in San Juan are a favorite spot. Other sites include **Ocean Park, Enseñada, Boquerón,** and **Honda Beach.** Puerto Rico hosted its first major windsurfing tournament, the Ray-Ban Windsurfing World Cup, in 1989.

Many companies that offer snorkeling and scuba diving also provide windsurfing equipment and instruction, and dozens of hotels have facilities on their own premises.

One of the best places to arrange for windsurfing in San Juan is **Caribe Aquatic Adventures** (see "Diving, Fishing, Tennis & Other Outdoor Pursuits," in chapter 6). Windsurfing is excellent at the beachfront of the Hyatt Dorado Beach Resort & Country Club, where **Penfield Island Adventures** offers lessons and rentals (see "Dorado," in chapter 7).

12 Tips on Choosing Your Accommodations

HOTELS & RESORTS

There is no rigid classification of Puerto Rican hotels. The word "deluxe" is often used—or misused—when "first class" might be a more appropriate term. Self-described first-class hotels often aren't that nice. We've presented fairly detailed descriptions of the hotels in this book, so you'll get an idea of what to expect once you're there.

Even in the real deluxe and first-class properties, however, don't expect top-rate service and efficiency. The slow tropical pace is what folks mean when they talk about "island time." Also, things often don't work as well in the tropics as they do in some of the fancy resorts of California or Europe. You might even experience power failures.

Ask detailed questions when booking a room. Don't just ask to be booked into a certain hotel, but specify your likes and dislikes. There are several logistics of getting the right room in a hotel. Entertainment in Puerto Rico is often alfresco, so light sleepers obviously won't want a room directly over a steel band. In general, back rooms cost less than oceanfront rooms, and lower rooms cost less than upper-floor units. Therefore, if budget is a major consideration for you, opt for the cheaper rooms. You won't have a great view, but you'll pay less. Just make sure that it isn't next to the all-night drummers.

Transfers from the airport or the cruise dock are included in some hotel bookings, most often in a package plan but usually not in ordinary bookings. This is true of first-class and deluxe resorts but rarely of medium-priced or budget accommodations. Always ascertain whether transfers (which can be expensive) are included.

When using the facilities at a resort, make sure that you know exactly what is free and what costs money. For example, swimming in the pool is nearly always free, but you might be charged for use of a tennis court. Nearly all watersports cost extra, unless you're booked on some special plan such as a scuba package. Some resorts seem to charge every time you breathe and might end up costing more than a deluxe hotel that includes most everything in the price.

Some hotels are right on the beach. Others involve transfers to the beach by taxi or bus, so factor in transportation costs, which can mount quickly if you stay 5 days to a week. If you want to go to the beach every day, it might be wise to book a hotel on the Condado and not stay in romantic Old San Juan, from which you'll spend a lot of time and money transferring back and forth between your hotel and the beach.

Most hotels in Puerto Rico are on the windward side of the island, with lots of waves, undertow, and surf. If a glasslike smooth sea is imperative for your stay, you can book on the leeward (eastern shore) or Caribbean (southeast coast) sides, which are better for snorkeling. The major centers in these areas are the resort complex of Palmas del Mar and the "second city" of Ponce.

MAP VS. AP, OR DO YOU WANT TO GO CP OR EP?

All resorts offer a **European Plan** (EP) rate, which means you pay only for the price of a room. That leaves you free to dine around at night at various other resorts or restaurants without restriction. Another plan preferred by many is the **Continental Plan** (CP), which means you get your room and a continental breakfast of juice, coffee, bread, jam, and so on, included in a set price. This plan is preferred by many because most guests don't like to "dine around" at breakfast time.

Another major option is the **Modified American Plan** (MAP), which includes breakfast and one main meal of the day, either lunch or dinner. The final choice is the **American Plan** (AP), which includes breakfast, lunch, and dinner.

At certain resorts you will save money by booking either the MAP or AP because discounts are granted. If you dine a la carte for lunch and dinner at various restaurants, your final dining bill will no doubt be much higher than if you stayed on the MAP or AP.

These plans might save you money, but if as part of your holiday you like to eat in various places, you might be disappointed. You face the same dining room every night, unless the resort you're staying at has many different restaurants on the dining plan. Often they don't. Many resorts have a lot of specialty restaurants, serving, say, Japanese cuisine, but these more expensive restaurants are not included in MAP or AP; rather, they charge a la carte prices.

One option is to ask if your hotel has a dine-around plan. You might still keep costs in check, but you can avoid a culinary rut by taking your meals in some other restaurants if your hotel has such a plan. Such plans are rare in Puerto Rico, which does not specialize in all-inclusive resorts the way that Jamaica and some other islands do.

Before booking a room, check with a good travel agent or investigate on your own what you are likely to save by booking in on a dining plan. Under certain circumstances in winter, you might not have a choice if MAP is dictated as a requirement for staying there. It pays to investigate, of course.

PUERTO RICAN GUESTHOUSES

A unique type of accommodation is the guesthouse, where Puerto Ricans themselves usually stay when they travel. Ranging in size from 7 to 25 rooms, they offer a familial atmosphere. Many are on or near the beach, some have pools or sun decks, and a number serve meals.

In Puerto Rico, however, the term "guesthouse" has many meanings. Some guesthouses are like simple motels built around pools. Others have small individual cottages with their own kitchenettes, constructed around a main building in which you'll often find a bar and a restaurant serving local food. Some are surprisingly comfortable, often with private baths and swimming pools. You may or may not have air-conditioning. The rooms are sometimes cooled by ceiling fans or by the trade winds blowing through open windows at night.

For value, the guesthouse can't be topped. If you stay at a guesthouse, you can journey over to a big beach resort and use its seaside facilities for only a small fee. Although bereft of frills, the guesthouses we've recommended are clean and safe for families or single women. However, the cheapest ones are not places where you'd want to spend a lot of time because of their modest furnishings.

For further information on guesthouses, contact the **Puerto Rico Tourism Company,** 575 Fifth Ave., New York, NY 10017 (© **800/ 223-6530** or 212/586-6262).

PARADORES

In an effort to lure travelers beyond the hotels and casinos of San Juan's historic district to the tranquil natural beauty of the island's countryside, the Puerto Rico Tourism Company offers *paradores puertorriqueños* (**charming country inns**) which are comfortable bases for exploring the island's varied attractions. Vacationers seeking a peaceful idyll can also choose from several privately owned and operated guesthouses.

Using Spain's *parador* system as a model, the Puerto Rico Tourism Company established the paradores in 1973 to encourage tourism across the island. Each of the paradores is situated in a historic place or site of unusual scenic beauty and must meet high standards of service and cleanliness. (See the map "Paradores & Country Inns of Puerto Rico" on p. 45.)

Some of the paradores are located in the mountains and others by the sea. Most have pools, and all offer excellent Puerto Rican cuisine. Many are within easy driving distance of San Juan.

Paradores & Country Inns of Puerto Rico

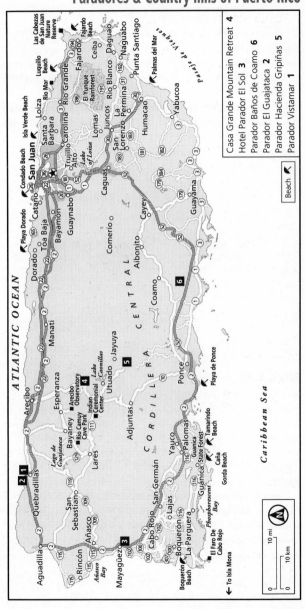

Casa Grande Mountain Retreat **4**
Hotel Parador El Sol **3**
Parador Baños de Coamo **6**
Parador El Guajataca **2**
Parador Hacienda Gripiñas **5**
Parador Vistamar **1**

Beach ⟩

Our favorite paradores are all in western Puerto Rico. (See "Paradores of Western Puerto Rico" in chapter 9.) **Parador Posada Portlamar** in La Parguera gives you a taste of the good life in a simple fishing village. For a plantation ambience and an evocation of the Puerto Rico of colonial times, there is the **Parador Hacienda Gripiñas** at Jayuya, some 30 miles (48km) southwest of San Juan; it was a former coffee plantation. **Parador Vistamar,** at Quebradillas, one of the largest paradores in Puerto Rico, enjoys a mountain location with beautiful gardens of tropical flowers.

VILLAS & VACATION HOMES

You can often secure good deals in Puerto Rico by renting privately owned villas and vacation homes.

Almost every villa has a staff, or at least a maid who comes in a few days a week. Villas also provide the essentials of home life, including bed linen and cooking paraphernalia. Condos usually come with a reception desk and are often comparable to life in a suite at a big resort hotel. Nearly every condo complex has a swimming pool, and some have more than one.

Private apartments are rented either with or without maid service. This is more of a no-frills option than the villas and condos. An apartment might not be in a building with a swimming pool, and it might not have a front desk to help you. Among the major categories of vacation homes, cottages offer the most freewheeling way to live. Most cottages are fairly simple, many opening in an ideal fashion onto a beach, whereas others may be clustered around a communal pool. Many contain no more than a simple bedroom together with a small kitchen and bath. For the peak winter season, reservations should be made at least 5 or 6 months in advance.

Dozens of agents throughout the United States and Canada offer these types of rentals (see "Rental Agencies," below, for some recommendations). You can also write to local tourist-information offices, which can advise you on vacation-home rentals.

Travel experts agree that savings, especially for a family of three to six people, or two or three couples, can range from 50% to 60% over what a hotel would cost. If there are only two in your party, these savings probably don't apply.

RENTAL AGENCIES

Agencies specializing in renting properties in Puerto Rico include:

- **Villas of Distinction,** P.O. Box 55, Armonk, NY 10504 (© **800/289-0900** or 914/273-3331; fax 914/273-3387;

www.villasofdistinction.com), is one of the best rental agencies offering "complete vacations," including airfare, rental car, and domestic help. Some private villas have two to five bedrooms, and almost every villa has a swimming pool.

- **Caribbean Connection Plus Ltd.,** P.O. Box 261, Trumbull, CT 06611 (© **800/634-4907** or 203/261-8603; fax 203/261-8295; www.islandhoppingexperts.com), offers many apartments, cottages, and villas in the Caribbean. Caribbean Connection specializes in island hopping with JetAir, and it offers especially attractive deals for U.S. West Coast travelers. This is one of the few reservations services whose staff has actually been on the islands, so members can talk to people who know from experience and not from a computer screen.

- **VHR, Worldwide,** 235 Kensington Ave., Norwood, NJ 07648 (© **800/633-3284** or 201/767-9393; fax 201/767-5510; www.vhrww.com), offers the most comprehensive portfolio of luxury villas, condominiums, resort suites, and apartments for rent in the Caribbean, including complete packages for airfare and car rentals. The company's more than 4,000 homes and suite resorts are handpicked by the staff, and accommodations are generally less expensive than comparable hotel rooms.

- **Hideaways International,** 767 Islington St., Portsmouth, NH 03801 (© **800/843-4433** or 603/430-4433; fax 603/430-4444; www.hideaways.com), provides a 144-page guide with illustrations of its accommodations in the Caribbean so that you can get an idea of what you're renting. Most of its villas, which can accommodate up to three couples or a large family of about 10, come with maid service. You can also ask this travel club about discounts on plane fares and car rentals.

 FAST FACTS: Puerto Rico

American Express See "Fast Facts: San Juan" in chapter 3.

Area Code The telephone area code for Puerto Rico is **787.** For calls on the island, the area code is not used.

ATM Networks See "Money," earlier in this chapter.

Banks All major U.S. banks have branches on Puerto Rico; their hours are from 8am to 2:30pm Monday through Friday and from 9:45am to noon on Saturday.

Business Hours Regular business hours are Monday through Friday from 8am to 5pm. Shopping hours vary considerably. Regular shopping hours are Monday through Thursday and Saturday from 9am to 6pm. On Friday, stores have a long day: 9am to 9pm. Many stores also open on Sunday from 11am to 5pm.

Car Rentals See "Getting Around," earlier in this chapter.

Climate See "When to Go," earlier in this chapter.

Currency See "Money," earlier in this chapter.

Customs See "Entry Requirements & Customs," earlier in this chapter.

Driving Rules See "Getting Around," earlier in this chapter.

Drugs A branch of the Federal Narcotics Strike Force is permanently stationed on Puerto Rico, where illegal drugs and narcotics are a problem. Convictions for possession of marijuana can bring severe penalties, ranging from 2 to 10 years in prison for a first offense. Possession of hard drugs, such as cocaine or heroin, can lead to 15 years or more in prison.

Drugstores It's a good idea to carry enough prescription medications with you to last the duration of your stay. If you're going into the hinterlands, take along the medicines you'll need. If you need any additional medications, you'll find many drugstores in San Juan and other leading cities. One of the most centrally located pharmacies in Old San Juan is the **Puerto Rican Drug Co.,** Calle San Francisco 157 (*©* **787/725-2202**); it's open daily from 7:30am to 9:30pm.

Electricity The electricity is 110 volts AC, as it is in the continental United States and Canada.

Embassies & Consulates Because Puerto Rico is part of the United States, there is no U.S. embassy or consulate. Instead, there are branches of all the principal U.S. federal agencies. Canada has no embassy or consulate either. There are no special provisions or agencies catering to British travel needs in Puerto Rico, nor are there agencies serving citizens of Australia or New Zealand.

Emergencies In an emergency, dial *©* **911.** Or call the local police (*©* **787/343-2020**), fire department (*©* **787/343-2330**), ambulance (*©* **787/343-2550**), or medical assistance (*©* **787/754-3535**).

Health Care Medical-care facilities, including excellent hospitals and clinics, in Puerto Rico are on par with those in the

United States. Hotels can arrange for a doctor in case of an emergency. Most major U.S. health insurance plans are recognized here, but it's advisable to check with your carrier or insurance agent before your trip, because medical attention is very expensive.

Holidays See "When to Go," earlier in this chapter.

Hospitals In a medical emergency, call ⓒ **911. Ashford Presbyterian Community Hospital,** Av. Ashford 1451, San Juan (ⓒ **787/721-2160**), maintains 24-hour emergency service. Service is also provided at **Clinica Las Americas,** 400 Franklin Delano Roosevelt Ave., Hato Rey (ⓒ **787/765-1919**), and at **Río Piedras Medical Center,** Av. Americo Miranda, Río Piedras (ⓒ **787/777-3535**).

Information See "Visitor Information," earlier in this chapter.

Internet Access Public access to the Internet is available at some large-scale resorts; the staff often provides access from their own computers. Another place to try is **Cybemet Café,** Av. Ashford Condado 1126 (ⓒ **787/724-4033**), which is open Monday through Thursday from 9am to 10pm, Friday and Saturday from 9am to midnight, and Sunday from 10am to 9pm. It charges $3 for 15 minutes, $5 for 30 minutes, $7 for 45 minutes, and $9 for 1 hour.

Language English is understood at the big resorts and in most of San Juan. Out in the island, Spanish is still *numero uno*.

Liquor Laws You must be 21 years of age to purchase liquor in stores or buy drinks in hotels, bars, and restaurants.

Maps See "Getting Around," earlier in this chapter.

Marriage Requirements There are no residency requirements for getting married in Puerto Rico. You need parental consent if either of you is under 18. Blood tests are required, although a test conducted in your home country within 10 days of the ceremony will suffice. A doctor must sign the license after an examination of the bride and groom. For complete details, contact the **Commonwealth of Puerto Rico Health Department,** Demographic Register, Franklin Delano Roosevelt Ave., Hato Rey (P.O. Box 11854), San Juan, PR 00910 (ⓒ **787/ 281-8868**).

Newspapers & Magazines The San Juan Star, a daily English-language newspaper, has been called the "*International Herald Tribune* of the Caribbean." It concentrates extensively on news from the United States. You can also pick up copies of *USA Today* at most news kiosks. If you read Spanish, you might enjoy *El Nuevo Día,* the most popular local tabloid. Few significant magazines are published on Puerto Rico, but *Time* and *Newsweek* are available at most newsstands.

Passports See "Visitor Information," earlier in this chapter.

Pets To bring your pet in, you must produce a health certificate from a U.S. mainland veterinarian and show proof of vaccination against rabies. Very few hotels allow animals, so check in advance.

Postal Services Because the U.S. Postal Service is responsible for handling mail on Puerto Rico, the regulations and tariffs are the same as on the mainland United States. Stamps can be purchased at any post office, all of which are open Monday through Friday from 8am to 5pm. Saturday hours are from 8am to noon (closed Sun). As on the mainland, you can purchase stamps at vending machines in airports, stores, and hotels. First-class letters to addresses within Puerto Rico, the United States, and its territories cost 37¢; postcards, 23¢. Letters and postcards to Canada both cost 60¢ for the first half-ounce. Letters and postcards to other countries cost 80¢ for the first half-ounce. *Note:* These rates will rise during the life of this edition.

Safety Crime exists here as it does everywhere. Use common sense and take precautions. Muggings are commonplace on the Condado and Isla Verde beaches, so you might want to confine your moonlit beach nights to the fenced-in and guarded areas around some of the major hotels. The countryside of Puerto Rico is safer than San Juan, but caution is always in order. Avoid narrow country roads and isolated beaches, night or day.

Smoking Antismoking regulation is less stringent here than it is on the U.S. mainland. Anyone over 18 can smoke in any bar here. Smoking is permitted in restaurants, within designated sections, but not necessarily everywhere. Most hotels have smoking and nonsmoking rooms.

Taxes All hotel rooms in Puerto Rico are subject to a tax, which is not included in the rates given in this book. At casino hotels, the tax is 11%; at noncasino hotels, it's 9%. At country inns you pay a 7% tax. Most hotels also add a 10% service charge. If they don't, you're expected to tip for services rendered. When you're booking a room, it's always best to inquire about these added charges. There is no airport departure tax.

Telephone & Fax Coin-operated phones can be found throughout the island, with a particularly dense concentration in San Juan. After depositing your coins, you can dial a seven-digit number at the sound of the dial tone. If you're calling long distance within Puerto Rico, add a **1** before the numbers. When you're placing a call to the U.S. mainland or to anywhere else overseas, preface the number with **011**. An operator (or a recorded voice) will tell you how much money to deposit, although you'll probably find it more practical to use a calling card issued by such long-distance carriers as Sprint, AT&T, or MCI. Public phones that allow credit cards such as American Express, Visa, or MasterCard to be inserted or "swiped" through a magnetic slot are rare on the island. Most of these are located at the San Juan airport. Most phone booths contain printed instructions for dialing. Local calls are 10¢. Most Puerto Ricans buy phone cards valid for between 15 and 100 units. The 30-unit card costs $14; the 60-unit card, $28. The card provides an even less expensive and usually more convenient way of calling within Puerto Rico or to the U.S. mainland. They are for sale in most drugstores and gift shops on the island.

Most hotels can send a telex or fax for you and bill the costs to your room, and in some cases, they'll even send a fax for a nonguest if you agree to pay a charge. Barring that, several agencies in San Juan will send a fax anywhere you want for a fee. Many are associated with print shops/photocopy stands. **Eagle Print,** 1229 Franklin Delano Roosevelt Blvd., Puerto Nuevo, San Juan, PR 00920 (© **787/782-7830**), charges $2 per page for faxes sent to the U.S. mainland.

Time Puerto Rico is on Atlantic Standard Time, which is 1 hour later than Eastern Standard Time. Puerto Rico does not go on daylight saving time, however, so the time here is the same year-round.

Tipping Tipping is expected here, so hand over the money as you would on the U.S. mainland. That usually means 15% in restaurants, 10% in bars, and 10% to 15% for taxi drivers, hairdressers, and other services, depending on the quality of the service rendered. Tip a porter, either at the airport or at your hotel, $1 per bag. The U.S. government imposes income tax on wait staff and other service-industry workers whose income is tip-based according to the gross receipts of their employers; therefore, if you don't tip them, those workers could end up paying tax anyway.

Visitor Information See "Visitor Information," earlier in this chapter.

Water See "Staying Healthy," earlier in this chapter.

Weights & Measures There's a mixed bag of measurements in Puerto Rico. Because of its Spanish tradition, most weights (meat and poultry) and measures (gasoline and road distances) are metric. But because of the U.S. presence, speed limits appear in miles per hour and liquids such as beer are sold by the ounce.

3

Getting to Know San Juan

All but a handful of visitors arrive in San Juan, the capital city. It is the political base, economic powerhouse, and cultural center of the island, and it's home to about one-third of all Puerto Ricans.

The second-oldest city in the Americas (behind Santo Domingo in the Dominican Republic), this metropolis presents two different faces. On one hand, the charming historic district, Old San Juan, is strongly reminiscent of the Spanish Empire. On the other hand, modern expressways outside the historic district cut through urban sprawl to link towering concrete buildings and beachfront hotels resembling those of Miami Beach.

Old San Juan is a 7-square-block area that was once completely enclosed by a wall erected by the Spanish with slave labor. The most powerful fortress in the Caribbean, this fortified city repeatedly held off would-be attackers. By the 19th century, however, it had become one of the Caribbean's most charming residential and commercial districts. Today it's a setting for restaurants and shops. Most of the major resort hotels are located nearby, along the Condado beachfront and at Isla Verde (see chapter 4).

1 Orientation

ARRIVING BY PLANE & GETTING FROM THE AIRPORT INTO THE CITY

Visitors from overseas arrive at **Luis Muñoz Marín International Airport** (✆ 787/791-1014), the major transportation center of the Caribbean. The airport is on the easternmost side of the city, rather inconvenient to nearly all hotels except the resorts and small inns at Isla Verde.

The airport offers services such as a tourist-information center, restaurants, hair stylists, coin lockers for storing luggage, bookstores, banks, currency-exchange kiosks, and a bar (open daily noon–4pm) that offers Puerto Rican rums.

BY TAXI   Some of the larger hotels send vans to pick up airport passengers and transport them to various properties along the

San Juan

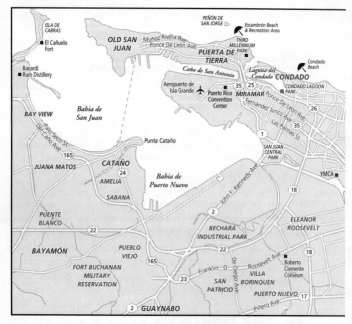

beachfront. It's wise to find out if your hotel offers this service when making a reservation. If your hotel doesn't have shuttle service between the airport and its precincts, you'll have to get there on your own steam—most likely by taxi. Dozens of taxis line up outside the airport to meet arriving flights, so you rarely have to wait. Fares can vary widely, depending on traffic conditions. Again depending on traffic, figure on about a 30-minute drive from the airport to your hotel along the Condado.

Although technically cab drivers should turn on their meters, more often than not they'll quote a flat rate before starting out. The rate system seems effective and fair, and if you're caught in impenetrable traffic, it might actually work to your advantage. The island's **Public Service Commission**, or PSC (© **787/756-1401**), establishes flat rates between the Luis Muñoz Marín International Airport and major tourist zones as listed here: From the airport to any hotel in Isla Verde, the fee is $8; to any hotel in the Condado district, the charge is $12; and to any hotel in Old San Juan, the cost is $16. Normal tipping supplements of between 10% and 15% of that fare are appreciated.

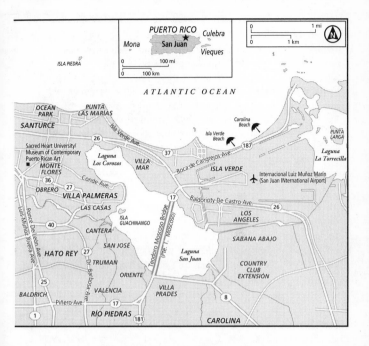

BY MINIVAN OR LIMOUSINE A wide variety of vehicles at the San Juan airport call themselves *limosinas* (their Spanish name). One outfit whose sign-up desk is in the arrivals hall of the international airport, near American Airlines, is the **Airport Limousine Service** (© 787/791-4745). It offers minivan service from the airport to various San Juan neighborhoods for prices that are lower than what a taxi would charge. When 8 to 10 passengers can be accumulated, the fare for transport, with luggage, is $35 to $55 per van to any hotel in Isla Verde, $55 to $75 per van to the Condado or Old San Juan.

For conventional limousine service, **Bracero Limousine** (© 787/253-1133) offers cars with drivers that will meet you and your entourage at the arrivals terminal for luxurious, private transportation to your hotel. Transport to virtually anywhere in San Juan ranges from $85 to $105; transport to points throughout the island varies from $150 to $275. Ideally, transport should be arranged in advance, so that a car and driver can be waiting for you near the arrivals terminal.

BY CAR All the major car-rental companies have kiosks at the airport. Although it's possible to rent a car once you arrive, your best

The Way to Go: Tren Urbano in 2003

In late 2003, San Juan will be linked to its major suburbs such as Santurce, Bayamón, and Guaynabo by a $1.25 billion urban train called *Tren Urbano*. This will be the first mass-transit project in the history of Puerto Rico. The new train system is designed to bring a fast and easy mode of transportation to the most congested areas of metropolitan San Juan. Trains will run every 4 minutes during peak hours in the morning and afternoon. For more information, call ℂ 787/765-0927.

bet is to reserve one before you leave home. See the "Getting Around" section of chapter 2 for details.

To drive into the city, head west along Route 26, which becomes Route 25 as it enters Old San Juan. If you stay on Route 25 (also called Av. Muñoz Rivera), you'll have the best view of the ocean and the monumental city walls.

Just before you reach the capital building, turn left between the Natural Resources Department and the modern House of Representatives office building. Go 2 blocks, until you reach the intersection of Paseo de Covadonga, and then take a right past the Treasury Building, and park your car in the **Covadonga Parking Garage** (ℂ 787/7222-337) on the left. The garage is open 24 hours; the first hour costs $1, the second hour 65¢, and 24 hours costs $16. A free shuttle-bus service loops the Old Town from here on two different routes.

BY BUS   Those with little luggage can take the T1 bus, which runs to the center of the city.

VISITOR INFORMATION

Tourist information is available at the **Luís Muñoz Marín Airport** (ℂ 787/791-1014). Another office is at **La Casita,** Pier 1, Old San Juan (ℂ 787/722-1709). These offices are open Sunday through Wednesday from 9am to 8pm, Thursday and Friday from 9am to 5:30pm.

CITY LAYOUT

Metropolitan San Juan includes the old walled city on San Juan Island; the city center on San Juan Island (called Puerta de Tierra), containing the capitol building; Santurce, on a larger peninsula, which is reached by causeway bridges from San Juan Island (the lagoon-front section here is called Miramar); Condado, the narrow peninsula that stretches from San Juan Island to Santurce; Hato Rey, the business center; Río Piedras, site of the University of Puerto Rico; and Bayamón, an industrial and residential quarter.

The Condado strip of beachfront hotels, restaurants, casinos, and nightclubs is separated from Miramar by a lagoon. Isla Verde, another resort area, is near the airport, which is separated from the rest of San Juan by an isthmus.

FINDING AN ADDRESS   Finding an address in San Juan isn't always easy. You'll have to contend not only with missing street signs and numbers but also with street addresses that appear sometimes in English and at other times in Spanish. The most common Spanish terms for thoroughfares are *calle* (street) and *avenida* (avenue). When it is used, the street number follows the street name; for example, the El Convento hotel is located at Calle del Cristo 100, in Old San Juan. Locating a building in Old San Juan is relatively easy. The area is only 7 square blocks, so by walking around, it's possible to locate most addresses.

STREET MAPS   *Qué Pasa?,* the monthly tourist magazine distributed free by the tourist office, contains accurate, easy-to-read maps of San Juan and the Condado that pinpoint the major attractions.

NEIGHBORHOODS IN BRIEF

OLD SAN JUAN   This is the most historic area in the West Indies. Filled with Spanish colonial architecture and under constant restoration, it lies on the western end of an islet. It's encircled by water; on the north is the Atlantic Ocean and on the south and west is the tranquil San Juan Bay. Ponte San Antonio bridge connects the Old Town with "mainland" Puerto Rico. Ramparts and old Spanish fortresses form its outer walls.

PUERTA DE TIERRA   Translated as "gateway to the land" or "gateway to the island," Puerta de Tierra lies just east of the old city walls of San Juan. It is split by Avenida Ponce de León and interconnects Old San Juan with the Puerto Rican "mainland." Founded by freed black slaves, the settlement today functions as the island's administrative center and is the site of military and government buildings, including the capital and various U.S. naval reserves.

MIRAMAR   Miramar is an upscale residential neighborhood across the bridge from Puerta de Tierra. Yachts anchor in its waters on the bay side of Ponte Isla Grande, and some of the finest homes in Puerto Rico are found here. It's also the site of Isla Grande Airport, where you can board flights to the islands of Vieques and Culebra.

CONDADO   Linked to Puerta de Tierra and Old San Juan by a bridge built in 1910, the Condado was once known as the Riviera of the Caribbean, enjoying a voguish reputation in the 1920s. This beach-bordering district is wedged between the Atlantic Ocean and several large inland bodies of water, including the lakelike Los Corozos and Lagunas Condado. Over the years the area has declined. It is now a cliché to compare it to Miami Beach. But like Miami Beach, the Condado is making major improvements, although many parts of it remain seedy and in need of restoration. The *putas* (prostitutes), pimps, and drug dealers are still here, but there are many fine deluxe hotels as well. Much of the Condado architecture today is viewed as "kitsch," the way Art Deco on Miami Beach is prized. The area is especially popular with gays, but straights also flock here, especially those attracted to the beaches during cruise-ship stopovers. Much of the Condado has been turned into time-share condos.

OCEAN PARK   Dividing the competitive beach resort areas of the Condado and Isla Verde, Ocean Park is a beachfront residential neighborhood that's sometimes plagued by flooding, especially during hurricanes. It's completely built up today with houses that are smaller and more spread out than those in the Condado district. Beaches here are slightly less crowded than those at Condado or Isla Verde. Because several gay guesthouses are located here, some of the beaches of Ocean Park are popular with gay men.

ISLA VERDE   East of the Condado, en route to the airport, Isla Verde—technically known as the "Carolina" section of San Juan—is the chief rival of the Condado. Because much of the Condado is in need of massive rejuvenation, many of the great resorts have fled east to Isla Verde, which has better, cleaner beaches. Don't come here for history or romance. Two features put Isla Verde on the tourist map: some of San Juan's best beaches and its most deluxe hotels. This district appeals to travelers who like a hotel to be a virtual theme park, with everything under one roof—entertainment, vast selections of dining, convenient shopping, pools, and an array of planned activities. Isla Verde is the Las Vegas of San Juan. The area roughly lies between Ocean Park and the San Juan airport. When visitors get tired of all this glamour and glitz, they can taxi into Old San Juan for museum hopping and shopping.

HATO REY   Situated to the south of the Martín Peña canal, this area was a marsh until landfill and concrete changed it forever. Today it is the Wall Street of the West Indies, filled with many high-rises, a large federal complex, and many business and banking offices.

2 Getting Around

BY TAXI   Except for a handful of important, high-profile tourist routes, public taxis are metered within San Juan (or should be). Normal tipping supplements of between 10% and 15% are appreciated. Passengers traveling between most other destinations within greater San Juan are charged by meter readings. The initial charge is $1, plus 10¢ for each quarter mile (.5km) and 50¢ for every suitcase, with a minimum fare of $3. These rates apply to conventional *taxis turisticos,* which are usually white-painted vehicles with official logos on their doors. Owned by a medley of individual outfitters within San Juan, they maintain standards that are higher than those of the cheaper but more erratic and inconvenient *públicos,* which are described in chapter 2. Call the **PSC** (© 787/756-1401) to request information or to report any irregularities.

Taxis are invariably lined up outside the entrance to most of the island's hotels, and if they're not, a staff member can almost always call one for you. But if you want to arrange a taxi on your own, call the **Rochdale Cab Company** (© 787/721-1900) or the **Mejor Cab Company** (© 787/723-2460).

You'll have to negotiate a fare with the driver, usually at a flat rate, for trips to far-flung destinations within Puerto Rico.

BY BUS   The **Metropolitan Bus Authority** (© 787/767-7979 for route information) operates buses in the greater San Juan area. Bus stops are marked by upright metal signs or yellow posts that say PARADA. There's one bus terminal in the dock area and another at the Plaza de Colón. A typical fare is 25¢ to 50¢.

Most of the large hotels of the Condado and Isla Verde maintain air-conditioned buses that make free shuttle runs into Old San Juan. Clients are usually deposited at the Plaza de Colón. Public buses also make the run along the Condado, stopping at clearly designated bus stops placed near the major hotels. Public buses usually deposit their clients at the Plaza Colón and the main bus terminal across the street from the Cataño ferryboat pier. This section of Old San Juan is the starting point for many of the city's metropolitan bus routes.

Here are some useful public bus routes: Bus no. 2 goes from the Plaza de Colón along the Condado, eventually reaching the

Value Great Discounts Through the LeLoLai VIP Program

For the $10 it will cost you to join San Juan's **LeLoLai VIP (Value in Puerto Rico)** program, you can enjoy the equivalent of up to $250 in travel benefits. You'll get discounts on admission to folklore shows, guided tours of historic sites and natural attractions, lodgings, meals, shopping, activities, and more. Of course, most of the experiences linked to LeLoLai are of the rather touristy type, but it can still be a good investment.

With membership, the *paradores puertorriqueños,* the island's modestly priced network of country inns, give cardholders 10% to 20% lower room rates Monday through Thursday. Discounts of 10% to 20% are offered at many restaurants, from San Juan's toniest hotels to several *mesones gastronómicos,* government-sanctioned restaurants that serve Puerto Rican fare. Shopping discounts are offered at many stores and boutiques, and, best yet, cardholders get 10% to 20% discounts at many island attractions.

The card also entitles you to free admission to some of the island's folklore shows. At press time, the pass included *Jolgorio,* presented every Wednesday at 8:30pm at the Caribe Terrace of the Caribe Hilton, although the specifics might change by the time you arrive in Puerto Rico.

For more information about this card, call ℅ **787/722-1709** or go to the El Centro Convention Center at Avenida Ashford on the Condado. Although you can call for details before you leave home, you can only sign up for this program once you reach Puerto Rico. Many hotel packages include participation in this program as part of their offerings.

commercial section of San Juan, Hato Rey; bus no. A7 passes from Old San Juan to the Condado and goes on to Avenida Isla Verde; and no. T1 heads for Avenida de Diego in the Condado district, then makes a long run to Isla Verde and the airport.

ON FOOT   This is the only way to explore Old San Juan. All the major attractions can easily be covered in a day. If you're going from

Old San Juan to Isla Verde, however, you'll need to rely on public transportation.

BY TROLLEY   When you tire of walking around Old San Juan, you can board one of the free trolleys that run through the historic area. Departure points are the Marina and La Puntilla, but you can board along the route by flagging the trolley down (wave at it and signal for it to stop) or by waiting at any of the clearly designated stopping points. Relax and enjoy the sights as the trolleys rumble through the old and narrow streets.

BY RENTAL CAR   See "Getting Around" in chapter 2 for details—including some reasons you shouldn't plan to drive in Puerto Rico.

BY FERRY   The **Agua Expreso** (✆ 787/788-1155) connects Old San Juan with the industrial and residential communities of Hato Rey and Cataño, across the bay. Ferries depart daily every 30 minutes from 6am to 9pm. The one-way fare to Hato Rey is 75¢, and the one-way fare to Cataño is 50¢. Departures are from the San Juan Terminal at the pier in Old San Juan. However, it's best to avoid rush hours because hundreds of locals who work in town use this ferry. Each ride lasts about 20 minutes.

 FAST FACTS: San Juan

Airport   See "Arriving by Plane & Getting from the Airport into the City," earlier in this chapter.

American Express   The agency is represented in San Juan by **Travel Network,** Av. Ashford 1135, Condado (✆ **787/725-0960**). The office is open Monday through Friday from 9am to 5pm, Saturday from 9 to 11:30am.

Bus Information   For information about bus routes in San Juan, call ✆ **787/729-1512.**

Camera & Film   Both **Cinefoto** (✆ **787/753-7238**) and **Foto World** (✆ **787/753-8778**), located in the Plaza Las Americas Shopping Mall in Hato Rey, offer a wide variety of photographic supplies. Cinefoto is open Monday through Saturday from 9am to 9pm. Foto World is open Monday through Saturday from 9am to 9pm, Sunday from 11am to 5pm.

Car Rentals   See "Getting Around" in chapter 2. If you want to reserve after you've arrived in Puerto Rico, call **Avis**

((© 787/791-2500), **Budget** ((© 787/791-3685), or **Hertz** ((© 787/791-0840).

Currency Exchange The unit of currency is the U.S. dollar. Most banks provide currency exchange, and you can also exchange money at the **Luis Muñoz Marín International Airport**. See "Money" in chapter 2.

Drugstores One of the most centrally located pharmacies is **Puerto Rican Drug Co.**, Calle San Francisco 157 ((© 787/725-2202), in Old San Juan. It's open daily from 7:30am to 9:30pm. **Walgreen's**, Av. Ashford 1130, Condado ((© 787/725-1510), is open 24 hours.

Emergencies In an emergency, dial (© 911. Or call the local police ((© 787/343-2020), fire department ((© 787/343-2330), ambulance ((© 787/343-2550), or medical assistance ((© 787/754-3535).

Eyeglasses Services are available at **Pearle Vision Express**, Plaza Las Americas Shopping Mall ((© 787/753-1033). Hours are Monday through Saturday from 9am to 9pm and Sunday from 11am to 5pm.

Hospitals **Ashford Presbyterian Community Hospital**, Av. Ashford 1451 ((© 787/721-2160), maintains a 24-hour emergency room.

Information See "Visitor Information," earlier in this chapter.

Internet Access Public access to the Internet is available at **Soapy's Station**, 111 Gilberto Concepción de Gracia, Old San Juan ((© 787/289-0344), in an annex of the Wyndham Old San Juan Hotel & Casino.

Maps See "City Layout," earlier in this chapter.

Police Call (© 787/343-2020 for the local police.

Post Office In San Juan, the **General Post Office** is at Av. Roosevelt 585 ((© 787/767-3604). If you don't know your address in San Juan, you can ask that your mail be sent here "c/o General Delivery." This main branch is open Monday through Friday from 6am to 9pm, Saturday from 8am to 2pm. A letter from Puerto Rico to the U.S. mainland will arrive in about 4 days. See "Fast Facts: Puerto Rico," in chapter 2, for more information.

Restrooms Restrooms are not public facilities accessible from the street. It's necessary to enter a hotel lobby, cafe, or restaurant to gain access to a toilet. Fortunately, large-scale hotels are familiar with this situation, and someone looking for a restroom usually isn't challenged during his or her pursuit.

Safety At night, exercise extreme caution when walking along the back streets of San Juan, and don't venture onto the unguarded public stretches of the Condado and Isla Verde beaches at night. All these areas are favorite targets for muggings.

Salons Most of San Juan's large resort hotels, including the Condado Plaza, the Marriott, and the Wyndham Old San Juan, maintain hair salons.

Taxis See "Getting Around," earlier in this chapter.

Telephone/Fax Many public telephones are available at **World Service Telephone (AT&T),** Pier 1, Old San Juan (© **787/ 721-2520**). To send a fax, go to **Eagle Print,** 1229 F. D. Roosevelt Blvd., Puerto Nuevo (© **787/782-7830**). For more information, see "Fast Facts: Puerto Rico" in chapter 2.

Tourist Offices See "Visitor Information," earlier in this chapter.

4

Where to Stay in San Juan

Whatever your preferences in accommodations—a beachfront resort or a place in historic Old San Juan, sumptuous luxury or an inexpensive base from which to see the sights—you can find a perfect fit in San Juan.

In addition to checking the recommendations listed here, you might want to contact a travel agent; there are package deals galore that can save you money and match you with an establishment that meets your requirements. See "Escorted Tours, Package Deals & Special-Interest Vacations" in chapter 2.

Before talking to a travel agent, you should refer to our comments about how to select a room in Puerto Rico. See "Hotels & Resorts" under "Tips on Choosing Your Accommodations" in chapter 2.

Not all hotels here have air-conditioned rooms. We've pointed them out in the recommendations below. If air-conditioning is important to you, make sure "A/C" appears after "*In room:*" at the end of the listing.

If you prefer shopping and historic sights to the beach, then Old San Juan might be your preferred nest. The high-rise resort hotels lie primarily along the Condado beach strip and the equally good sands of Isla Verde. The hotels along Condado and Isla Verde attract the cruise-ship and casino crowds. The hotels away from the beach in San Juan, in such sections as Santurce, are primarily for business clients.

All hotel rooms in Puerto Rico are subject to a **tax** that is not included in the rates given in this book. At casino hotels, the tax is 11%; at noncasino hotels, it's 9%. At country inns you pay a 7% tax. Most hotels also add a 10% service charge. If they don't, you're expected to **tip** for services rendered. When you're booking a room, it's a good idea to ask about these charges.

1 Old San Juan

Old San Juan is 1½ miles (2.5km) from the beach. You should choose a hotel here if you're more interested in shopping and attractions than you are in watersports.

EXPENSIVE

El Convento ☼☼   Puerto Rico's most famous hotel had deteriorated into a shabby version of its former self, but it came majestically back to life when it was restored and reopened in 1997, at cost of $275,000 per room. El Convento offers some of the most charming and historic hotel experiences anywhere in the Caribbean. As one observer put it, El Convento "is an exquisitely wrought David on an island of otherwise glitzy Goliaths." Built in 1651 in the heart of the old city, it was the New World's first Carmelite convent, but over the years it played many roles, from a dance hall to a flophouse to a parking lot for garbage trucks. It first opened as a hotel in 1962.

The roomy accommodations include Spanish-style furnishings, throw rugs, elaborate paneling, and handmade Andalusian terra-cotta floor tiles. Each unit contains two double or twin beds, fitted with fine linen. The small bathrooms, with tub-and-shower combinations, contain scales and second phones. For the ultimate in luxury, ask for Gloria Vanderbilt's restored suite or ask for no. 508, a corner room with dramatic views. Although the facilities here aren't as diverse as those of some resorts on the Condado or in Isla Verde, this hotel's sweeping charm and Old Town location usually compensate. A possible drawback for some is that El Convento is a 15-minute walk to the nearest beach. The lower two floors feature a collection of shops, bars, and restaurants.

Calle de Cristo 100, San Juan, PR 00901. ✆ **800/468-2779** or 787/723-9020. Fax 787/721-2877. www.elconvento.com. 58 units. Winter $265–$375 double; off-season $150–$285 double. Year-round from $400 suite. AE, DC, DISC, MC, V. Parking $10. Bus: Old Town trolley. **Amenities:** 4 restaurants; 2 bars; fitness center; Jacuzzi; massage. *In room:* A/C, TV, VCR, coffeemaker, hair dryer, iron, safe, stereo.

Wyndham Old San Juan Hotel & Casino ☼   Opened in 1997, this dignified, nine-story waterfront hotel is part of a $100 million renovation of San Juan's cruise-port facilities. The hotel has an unusual and desirable position between buildings erected by the Spanish monarchs in the 19th century and the city's busiest and most modern cruise-ship terminals. Most of the major cruise ships dock nearby, making this a worthwhile choice if you want to spend time in San Juan before boarding a ship. On days when cruise ships pull into port, the hotel's lobby and bars are likely to be jammed with passengers stretching their legs after a few days at sea.

Although the pastel building is modern, iron railings and exterior detailing convey a sense of colonial San Juan. The triangular shape of the building encircles an inner courtyard that floods light into the tasteful and comfortable bedrooms, each of which has two phone lines and a modem connection for laptop computers. Other than that, the smallish rooms lack character. Each room has a compact bathroom with a shower stall. Think of a Holiday Inn geared for business travelers. If you want Old Town character and atmosphere, head for El Convento (see above) instead. Most of the lobby level here is devoted to a 10,000-square-foot casino. The upscale dining room serves perfectly fine, if unremarkable, international cuisine, with some regional specialties.

Calle Brumbaugh 100, San Juan, PR 00902. ℭ **800/WYNDHAM** or 787/721-5100. Fax 787/721-1111. www.wyndham.com. 240 units. Winter $230–$340 double, $290–$390 suite; off-season $135–$200 double, $185–$290 suite. AE, DC, DISC, MC, V. Free self-parking; valet parking $15. Bus: A7. **Amenities:** 8 restaurants; 14 bars; nightclub; casino; 2 pools; 3 tennis courts; fitness center; 5 Jacuzzis; room service (6:30–11:30pm). *In room:* A/C, TV, dataport, minibar, coffeemaker, hair dryer, iron.

MODERATE

Gallery Inn at Galería San Juan 𝒜 *Finds*   This hotel's location and ambience are unbeatable, though the nearest beach is a 15-minute ride away. Set on a hilltop in Old Town, with a sweeping sea view, this unusual hotel contains a maze of verdant courtyards. In the 1700s it was the home of an aristocratic Spanish family. Today it's the most whimsically bohemian hotel in the Caribbean. Jan D'Esopo and Manuco Gandia created this inn out of their art studio. They cast bronze in their studio when not attending to their collection of birds, including macaws and cockatoos. The entire inn is covered with clay and bronze figures as well as other original art. We suggest booking one of the least expensive doubles; even the cheapest units are fairly roomy and attractively furnished, with good beds and small but adequate shower-only bathrooms. *Note to lovers:* The honeymoon suite has a Jacuzzi on a private balcony with a panoramic view of El Morro. From the rooftop terrace there is a 360-degree view of the historic Old Town and the port. This is the highest point in San Juan and the most idyllic place to enjoy a breeze at twilight and a glass of wine.

Calle Norzagaray 204–206, San Juan, PR 00901. ℭ **787/722-1808.** Fax 787/ 977-3929. www.thegalleryinn.com. 22 units (some with shower only). Year-round $145–$270 double, $350 suite. Rates include continental breakfast. AE, DC, MC, V. There are 6 free parking spaces, plus parking on the street. Bus: Old Town trolley. **Amenities:** Breakfast room. *In room:* A/C, hair dryer, safe.

Old San Juan Accommodations

El Convento **2**
Gallery Inn at Gallería San Juan **1**
Hotel Milano **4**
Wyndham Old San Juan Hotel & Casino **3**

Information (i) City Walls

Hotel Milano Old Town's newest hotel was created in April 1999 in a 1920s warehouse. You enter a wood-sheathed lobby at the lower, less desirable end of Calle Fortaleza before ascending to one of the clean, well-lit bedrooms. Despite its location in historic Old Town, there's not much charm about this place. The simple, modern rooms have cruise-ship–style decor and unremarkable views. The more expensive accommodations contain small refrigerators and dataports.

The building's fifth floor (the elevator goes only to the 4th floor) contains an alfresco Italian and Puerto Rican restaurant called the Panoramic, which has views of San Juan's harbor.

Calle Fortaleza 307, San Juan, PR 00901. ✆ **877/729-9050** or 787/729-9050. Fax 787/722-3379. 30 units. Winter $85–$150 double; off-season $75–$125 double. Rates include continental breakfast. AE, MC, V. Bus: Old Town trolley. **Amenities:** Restaurant; bar; babysitting. *In room:* A/C, TV, dataport in some, fridge in some, hair dryer.

2 Puerta de Tierra

Stay in Puerta de Tierra only if you have a desire to be at either the Caribe Hilton or the Normandie Hotel, because when you stay there, you're sandwiched halfway between Old San Juan and the Condado, but you're not getting the advantages of staying right in the heart of either.

Caribe Hilton 🏨🏨 Thanks to rivers of money being poured into its radical renovation, this deluxe hotel is one of the most up-to-date spa and convention hotels in San Juan. Thanks to an unusual configuration of natural barriers and legal maneuverings, the hotel has the only private beach on the island (and the only garden incorporating an antique naval installation: the semi-ruined colonial Fort San Gerónimo). Because this beachfront hotel was the first Hilton ever built outside the U.S. mainland (in 1949), the chain considers it its most historic property. The Caribe's size (17 acres of parks and gardens) and sprawling facilities often attract conventions and tour groups. Only the Condado Plaza and the Wyndham El San Juan rival it for nonstop activity.

Rooms were radically upgraded in the late 1990s; variations in price are related to the views outside and the amenities within. Each room has a larger-than-expected bathroom with a tub-and-shower combo, as well as comfortable tropical-inspired furniture. In the Caribe Terrace Bar, you can order the bartender's celebrated piña colada, which was once enjoyed by movie legends Joan Crawford and Errol Flynn. A newly restored oceanfront spa and fitness center is the only beachside spa in Puerto Rico. It features such tantalizing

Eastern San Juan Accommodations

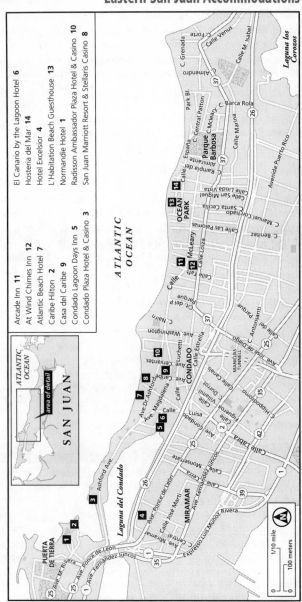

Arcade Inn **11**
At Wind Chimes Inn **12**
Atlantic Beach Hotel **7**
Caribe Hilton **2**
Casa del Caribe **9**
Condado Lagoon Days Inn **5**
Condado Plaza Hotel & Casino **3**

El Canario by the Lagoon Hotel **6**
Hostería del Mar **14**
Hotel Excelsior **4**
L'Habitation Beach Guesthouse **13**
Normandie Hotel **1**
Radisson Ambassador Plaza Hotel & Casino **10**
San Juan Marriott Resort & Stellaris Casino **8**

delights as couples massages, body wraps, hydrotherapy tub treatments, and soothing cucumber sun therapies. A 12,400-square-foot casino is adjacent to the lobby atrium area.

Calle Los Rosales, San Juan, PR 00902. ⓒ 800/HILTONS or 787/721-0303. Fax 787/725-8849. www.caribehilton.com. 644 units. Winter $310–$365 double; off-season $205–$290 double. Year-round $255–$1,000 suite. Children 16 and under stay free in parent's room (maximum 4 people per room). AE, DC, DISC, MC, V. Self-parking $10; valet parking $20. Bus: B21. **Amenities:** 6 restaurants; 3 bars; pool; 6 tennis courts; health club and spa; playground; business center (6am–1am); babysitting; laundry/dry cleaning. In room: A/C, TV, minibar, hair dryer, safe.

Normandie Hotel   It isn't as well accessorized as its nearby competitor the Hilton, but for a clientele of mostly business travelers, it doesn't really matter. One guest, however, found the Hilton bright and festive, the Normandie "dark and haunting." The hotel first opened in 1939 and remains one of the purest examples of Art Deco architecture in Puerto Rico. Originally built for a Parisian cancan dancer by her tycoon husband, the building has a curve-sided design that was inspired by the famous French ocean liner, *Le Normandie.* The gardens are not particularly extensive, and the beach is unexceptional. But several multimillion-dollar renovations, most recently in 2000 after devastation by a 1998 hurricane, have given the place a conservative, vaguely historic charm. Bedrooms are tastefully outfitted, each with a neatly tiled tub-and-shower bathroom. The lobby retains its original Art Deco zest, soaring upward into an atrium whose centerpiece is a bubbling aquarium.

Av. Muñoz-Rivera, San Juan, PR 00902. ⓒ 877/987-2929 or 787/729-2929. Fax 787/729-3083. www.normandiepr.com. 176 units. Winter $250–$350 double, $550 suite; off-season $185–$205 double, $450 suite. AE, DC, MC, V. Parking $10. Bus: B5 or B21. **Amenities:** Restaurant; bar; pool; gym; room service; babysitting; laundry/dry cleaning. *In room:* A/C, TV, coffeemaker, hair dryer, iron, safe.

3 Condado

This is where you'll find the city's best beaches. Once the Condado area was filled with the residences of the very wealthy, but all that changed with the construction of the Puerto Rico Convention Center. Private villas gave way to high-rise hotel blocks, restaurants, and nightclubs. The Condado shopping area, along Ashford and Magdalena avenues, has an extraordinary number of boutiques. There are good bus connections into Old San Juan, and taxis are plentiful.

VERY EXPENSIVE

Condado Plaza Hotel & Casino 🗲🗲 (Kids   This is one of the busiest hotels in Puerto Rico, with enough facilities, restaurants, and distractions to keep visitors occupied for weeks. It is the most prominent of San Juan's hotels, set on a popular strip of beachfront on the Condado. It's a favorite of business travelers, tour groups, and conventions, but it also attracts independent travelers, especially families, because of its wide array of amenities. The Hilton is its major rival, but we prefer this hotel's style and flair, especially after its recent $40 million overhaul.

Each unit has a private terrace and is spacious, bright, and airy, fitted with deluxe beds, either one king-size, two doubles, or two twins. The good-sized bathrooms contain tub-and-shower combos. The complex's most deluxe section, the Plaza Club, has 80 units (including 5 duplex suites), a VIP lounge reserved exclusively for the use of its guests, and private check-in/checkout service.

The hotel is owned by the same consortium that owns the somewhat more upscale Wyndham El San Juan Hotel & Casino (see below). Use of the facilities at one hotel can be charged to a room at the other. Only the Wyndham El San Juan Hotel has a more dazzling array of dining options. This place is known for its charming restaurants with culinary diversity that attract many local residents. The hotel's premier restaurant—a hot ticket on San Juan's dining scene—is Cobia, winner of several culinary awards.

Av. Ashford 999, San Juan, PR 00907. (✆) **800/468-8588** or 787/721-1000. Fax 787/721-4613. www.condadoplaza.com. 570 units. Winter $325–$475 double, $460–$1,350 suite; off-season $225–$390 double, $350–$945 suite. AE, DC, DISC, MC, V. Valet parking $10. Bus: A7. **Amenities:** 6 restaurants; 3 bars; casino; 3 pools; 2 tennis courts; health club and spa; 3 Jacuzzis; watersports; children's programs, car rental; salon; 24-hr. room service; laundry/dry cleaning. *In room:* A/C, TV, minibar, coffeemaker, hair dryer, iron, safe.

San Juan Marriott Resort & Stellaris Casino (✸)

It's the tallest building on the Condado, a 21-story landmark that Marriott spent staggering sums to renovate in a radically different format after a tragic fire gutted the premises in 1989. The current building packs in lots of postmodern style, and one of the best beaches on the Condado is right outside. Furnishings in the soaring lobby were inspired by Chippendale. If there's a flaw, it's the decor of the comfortable but bland bedrooms, with pastel colors that look washed out when compared to the rich mahoganies and jewel tones of the rooms in the rival Condado Plaza Hotel. Nonetheless, the units here boast one of the most advanced telephone networks on the island, and good security and fire-prevention systems. They're generally spacious, with good views of the water, and each has a tiled bathroom with tub-and-shower combination. We suggest having only one dinner in-house—at Ristorante Tuscany (p. 96).

Av. Ashford 1309, San Juan, PR 00907. ℭ 800/464-5005 or 787/722-7000. Fax 787/722-6800. www.marriottpr.com. 538 units. Winter $205–$340 double; off-season $180–$225 double. Year-round $610 suite. Suite rate includes breakfast. AE, DC, DISC, MC, V. Parking $10. Bus: B21. **Amenities:** 3 restaurants; 2 bars; casino; 2 pools; 2 tennis courts; health club; Jacuzzi; sauna; concierge; tour desk; car rental; salon; 24-hr. room service; babysitting; laundry/dry cleaning. *In room:* A/C, TV, dataport, minibar, coffeemaker, hair dryer, iron, safe.

EXPENSIVE

Radisson Ambassador Plaza Hotel & Casino ℛ   At the eastern edge of the Condado, a short walk from the beach, the Ambassador is now competitive with its more glamorous neighbors, after a local entrepreneur poured $40 million into its restoration in 1990. Since then, it has evolved into a competent but not particularly exciting hotel. What's missing (especially at these prices) are the resort amenities associated with the Hilton, the Condado Plaza, the Ritz-Carlton, and the Wyndham El San Juan. Nor does this hotel have the sense of whimsy and fun that's so much a part of those glitzy competitors.

Accommodations are in a pair of towers, one of which is devoted to suites. The decor is inspired variously by 18th-century Versailles, 19th-century London, imperial China, and Art Deco California. However, despite the gaudy, glitzy overlay, the hotel used to be a Howard Johnson's, a fact that's evident in the relatively small size of the standard rooms. Each unit has a balcony with outdoor furniture. The beds (twins or doubles) are fitted with fine linen, and each bathroom has generous shelf space and a tub-and-shower combination.

Av. Ashford 1369, San Juan, PR 00907. ℭ 800/333-3333 or 787/721-7300. Fax 787/723-6151. www.radisson.com. 233 units. Winter $260–$290 double, $290–$320 suite; off-season $185–$215 double, $215–$225 suite. Self-parking $8. Bus: B21 or C10. **Amenities:** 3 restaurants; 3 bars; casino; rooftop pool; gym; sauna; babysitting; laundry/dry cleaning. *In room:* A/C, TV, coffeemaker, hair dryer, iron, safe (in suites).

MODERATE

Condado Lagoon Days Inn *Kids*   This family-oriented hotel, remodeled in 1996, rises seven stories above a residential neighborhood across the street from Condado Beach. The accommodations are small and not particularly imaginative in their decor. Each room has either one or two queen beds, and each has a tub-and-shower bathroom. Some rooms have sofas that convert into beds for children. There's a small swimming pool on the premises. The bars, restaurants, and facilities of the Condado neighborhood are within walking distance.

Calle Clemenceau 6, Condado, San Juan, PR 00907. © 800/858-7407 or 787/721-0170. www.daysinn.com. 50 units. Winter $119 double, $200–$210 suite; off-season $89 double, $149–$189 suite. AE, DC, DISC, MC, V. Parking $7. Bus: 5, 9, 21, or 22. **Amenities:** Pool; babysitting; laundry/dry cleaning. *In room:* A/C, TV, hair dryer, iron, safe.

El Canario by the Lagoon Hotel   A relaxing, informal European-style hotel, El Canario is in a quiet residential neighborhood just a short block from Condado Beach. The place is a bit run-down and the staff is not too helpful, but it charges affordable rates. The hotel is very much in the Condado styling, which evokes Miami Beach in the 1960s. The bedrooms are generous in size and have balconies. Most of them have twin beds and a sleek and contemporary bathroom, with a shower stall and enough space to spread out your stuff.

Calle Clemenceau 4, Condado, San Juan, PR 00907. © 800/533-2649 or 787/722-5058. Fax 787/723-8590. www.canariohotels.com. 40 units. Winter $145 double; off-season $95–$105 double. Rates include continental breakfast and morning newspaper. AE, DISC, MC, V. Bus: B21 or C10. **Amenities:** Access to health club; tour desk; laundry. *In room:* A/C, TV, safe.

INEXPENSIVE

Arcade Inn *(Value*   This inn, originally built as a private home in 1943 and transformed into a simple hotel in 1948, didn't become well known until the late 1960s, when its reasonable rates began to attract families with children and college students traveling in groups. It's a stucco-covered building with vaguely Spanish colonial detailing on a residential street lined with similar structures. Each unit has simple, slightly battered furniture and a small shower-only bathroom. There's no pool and few amenities on-site, but the beach is only a 5-minute walk away.

Calle Taft 8, Condado, San Juan, PR 00911. © 787/725-0668. Fax 787/728-7524. 19 units (shower only). Winter $70–$80 double, $130 suite; off-season $60–$70 double, $110 suite. MC, V. Free parking. Bus: A5 or B21. **Amenities:** Bar; babysitting. *In room:* A/C, TV, fridge.

Atlantic Beach Hotel   This is the most famous gay hotel in Puerto Rico. Housed in a five-story building with vaguely Art Deco styling, the hotel is best known for its ground-floor indoor/outdoor bar—the most visibly gay bar in Puerto Rico. It extends from the hotel lobby onto a wooden deck about 15 feet above the sands of Condado Beach. The units are simple cubicles with stripped-down but serviceable and clean decor. Some of the rooms are smaller than others, but few of the short-term guests seem to mind—maybe because the place can have the spirit of a house party. Each unit has a small, shower-only bathroom with plumbing that might not always be in prime condition. There's a whirlpool on the rooftop; an on-again, off-again in-house restaurant; and the above-mentioned bar. The top floor is devoted to a duplex penthouse with a soaring pyramid-shaped ceiling. The space was originally conceived as a disco that thrived in the 1970s and early 1980s.

Several readers have written in to complain about the restrictive policy of not allowing a guest to take a visitor back to the bedrooms. One disgruntled patron wrote, "Lighten up, folks! We're big boys and can decide for ourselves who we want to bring up to our room. If you're going with a lover, fine. If you want to play with the locals, stay in another hotel."

Calle Vendig 1, Condado, San Juan, PR 00907. **☎ 787/721-6900.** Fax 787/721-6917. www.atlanticbeachhotel.net. 35 units (shower only). Winter $100–$135 double; off-season $70–$100 double. AE, DC, MC, V. Bus: A7. **Amenities:** Restaurant; bar; whirlpool; laundry/dry cleaning. *In room:* A/C, TV, safe.

At Wind Chimes Inn ☆ *Kids*   This restored and renovated Spanish manor, 1 short block from the beach and 3½ miles (5.5km) from the airport, is one of the best guesthouses on the Condado. Upon entering a tropical patio, you'll find tile tables surrounded by palm trees and bougainvillea. There's plenty of space on the deck and a covered lounge for relaxing, socializing, and eating breakfast. Dozens of decorative wind chimes add melody to the daily breezes. The good-sized rooms offer a choice of size, beds, and kitchens; all contain ceiling fans and air-conditioning. Beds are comfortable and come in four sizes, ranging from twin to king. The shower-only bathrooms, though small, are efficiently laid out. Families like this place not only because of the accommodations and the affordable prices but because they can also prepare light meals here, cutting down on food costs.

Av. McLeary 1750, Condado, San Juan, PR 00911. **☎ 800/946-3244** or 787/727-4153. Fax 787/728-0671. www.atwindchimesinn.com. 17 units (shower only). Winter $80–$129 double, $125–$140 suite; off-season $65–$110 double, $120 suite. Rates include continental breakfast. AE, DISC, MC, V. Parking $5. Bus: B21 or A5. **Amenities:** Pool. *In room:* A/C, TV, kitchen.

Casa del Caribe *Value*   Don't expect the Ritz, but if you're looking for a bargain on the Condado, this is it. This renovated guesthouse was built in the 1940s, later expanded, and then totally refurbished with tropical decor in 1995. A very Puerto Rican ambience has been created, with emphasis on Latin hospitality and comfort. On a shady side street just off Ashford Avenue, behind a wall and garden, you'll discover Casa del Caribe's wraparound veranda. The small but cozy guest rooms have ceiling fans and air conditioners, and most feature original Puerto Rican art. The bedrooms are inviting, with comfortable furnishings and efficiently organized shower-only bathrooms. The front porch is a social center for guests, and you can also cook out at a barbecue area. The beach is a 2-minute walk away, and the hotel is also within walking distance of some megaresorts, with their glittering casinos.

Calle Caribe 57, San Juan, PR 00907. ✆ 877/722-7139 or 787/722-7139. Fax 787/723-2575. 13 units (shower only). Winter $75–$130 double; off-season $55–$99 double. Rates include continental breakfast. AE, DISC, MC, V. Parking $5. Bus–B21. **Amenities:** Babysitting; laundry/dry cleaning. *In room:* A/C, TV.

4 Miramar

Miramar, a residential neighborhood, is very much a part of metropolitan San Juan, and a brisk 30-minute walk will take you where the action is. Regrettably, the beach is at least half a mile (1km) away.

Hotel Excelsior   Handsome accommodations and good service are offered at this family-owned and -operated hotel. Some of the bedrooms have been refurbished; many have fully equipped kitchenettes, and each has two phones (one in the bathroom), marble vanities, and a tub-and-shower combo. Included in the rates are shoeshines and transportation to the nearby beach, as well as parking in the underground garage or the adjacent parking lot. A lot of your reaction to this hotel will depend on your room assignment. Some units on the same floor can vary in quality. If possible, ask to see the room before checking in. One disgruntled reader called the Excelsior "an overexaggerated dump."

Av. Ponce de León 801, San Juan, PR 00907. ✆ 800/298-4274 or 787/721-7400. Fax 787/723-0068. 140 units. Winter $195–$215 double, $259 suite; off-season $165–$199 double, $229 suite. Children 9 and under stay free in parent's room; cribs free. AE, DC, MC, V. Free parking. Bus: B1 or A5. **Amenities:** 2 restaurants; pool; gym; room service; babysitting; laundry/dry cleaning. *In room:* A/C, TV, hair dryer.

5 Santurce & Ocean Park

Less fashionable (and a bit less expensive) than their nearest neighbors Condado (to the west) and Isla Verde (to the east), Santurce and Ocean Park are wedged into a modern, not particularly beautiful neighborhood that's bisected with lots of roaring traffic arteries and commercial enterprises. Lots of *Sanjuaneros* come here to work in the district's many offices and to eat in its many restaurants. The coastal subdivision of Ocean Park is a bit more fashionable than landlocked Santurce, but with the beach never more than a 20-minute walk away, few of Santurce's residents seem to mind.

MODERATE

Hosteria del Mar 🍸   Lying a few blocks from the Condado casinos and right on the beach are the white walls of this distinctive landmark. It's in a residential seaside community that's popular with locals looking for beach action on weekends. The hotel boasts medium-sized ocean-view rooms. Those on the second floor have balconies; those on the first floor open onto patios. The guest-room decor is invitingly tropical, with wicker furniture, good beds, pastel prints, and ceiling fans, plus small but efficient bathrooms, some with shower, some with tub only. The most popular unit is no. 208, with a king-size bed, private balcony, kitchenette, and a view of the beach; it's idyllic for a honeymoon. There's no pool, but a full-service restaurant here is known for its vegetarian, macrobiotic, and Puerto Rican plates, all freshly made. The place is simple, yet with its own elegance, and the hospitality is warm.

Calle Tapía 1, Ocean Park, San Juan, PR 00911. ✆ **877/727-3302** or 787/727-3302. Fax 787/268-0772. hosteria@caribe.net. 8 units. Winter $75–$125 double without ocean view, $165–$185 double with ocean view, $195–$240 apt; off-season $75–$90 double without ocean view, $120–$130 double with ocean view, $185–$195 apt. Children 11 and under stay free in parent's room. AE, DC, DISC, MC, V. Bus: A5. **Amenities:** Restaurant; room service; babysitting; laundry/dry cleaning. *In room:* A/C, TV, kitchenette in 3 units, coffeemaker in some, safe.

L'Habitation Beach Guesthouse   This small hotel sits on a tranquil tree-lined street with a sandy beach right in its backyard. Located only a few blocks from the Condado, this inn has a laid-back atmosphere. The good-sized and well-maintained bedrooms have ceiling fans, comfortable beds, and fairly simple furnishings. The most spacious rooms are nos. 8 and 9, which also open onto ocean views. Each unit has a small, tiled, shower-only bathroom. Chairs and beverage service are provided in a private beach area, and guests can enjoy breakfast alfresco. You can also eat or drink on the breezy patio overlooking the sea. Ask for one of the bar's special margaritas.

Calle Italia 1957, Ocean Park, San Juan, PR 00911. ✆ **787/727-2499.** Fax 787/727-2599. www.habitationbeach.com. 10 units (shower only). Winter $75–$96 double; off-season $60–$83 double. Extra person $15. Rates include continental breakfast. AE, DISC, MC, V. Free parking. Bus: T1. **Amenities:** Laundry. *In room:* A/C, TV, coffeemaker, safe.

6 Isla Verde

Beach-bordered Isla Verde is closer to the airport than the Condado and Old San Juan. The hotels here are farther from Old San Juan than those in Miramar, Condado, and Ocean Park. It's a good choice if you don't mind the isolation and want to be near fairly good beaches.

VERY EXPENSIVE

Inter-Continental San Juan Resort & Casino $\mathcal{R}$ Thanks to an extensive $15.2 million restoration, this resort on the beach now competes with Wyndham El San Juan Hotel next door, but it still doesn't overtake it. You'll get the sense of living in a sophisticated beach resort rather than a hotel where the sun rises and sets around the whims of high-rolling gamblers.

Most of the comfortable, medium-sized rooms have balconies and terraces and tasteful furnishings with a lot of pizzazz. Top-floor rooms are the most expensive, even though they lack balconies. Each bathroom has a power showerhead, a deep tub, and a scale. The most desirable units are in the Plaza Club, a mini-hotel within the hotel that sports a private entrance, concierge service, complimentary food and beverage buffets, and suite/spa and beach facilities. Dining within any of this hotel's six restaurants merits attention, although the choice is vaster at the neighboring Wyndham El San Juan Hotel. Even if you're not a guest, consider a visit to the Inter-Continental, to Ruth's Chris Steak House, which serves the best steaks in San Juan. Momoyama is also worth a trek across town, and its sushi bar is the finest along the beachfront. However, we find the Market Cafe, with its made-to-order foods and snacks, overrated.

Av. Isla Verde 5961, Isla Verde, PR 00937. © **800/443-2009** or 787/791-6100. Fax 787/253-2510. www.interconti.com. 400 units. Winter $269–$489 double, $409–$1,699 suite; off-season $199–$339 double, $279–$450 suite. Children 15 and under stay free in parent's room. AE, DC, DISC, MC, V. Self-parking $10; valet parking $15. Bus: M7. **Amenities:** 6 restaurants; 3 bars; the Caribbean's largest free-form pool; gym; scuba diving; limousine service; business center; room service (6am–2pm and 5pm–2am); massage; babysitting; laundry/dry cleaning. *In room:* A/C, TV, coffeemaker, hair dryer, iron, safe.

Ritz-Carlton San Juan Hotel, Spa & Casino $\mathcal{R}\mathcal{R}\mathcal{R}$ This is one of the most spectacular deluxe hotels in the Caribbean. Set on 8 acres of prime beachfront, within a 5-minute drive of the airport, it appeals to both business travelers and vacationers. The decor reflects Caribbean flavor and the Hispanic culture of the island, with art-work from prominent local artists. More visible, however, is an emphasis on continental elegance. Some of the most opulent public areas anywhere, these include wrought-iron balustrades and crystal chandeliers.

Beautifully furnished guest rooms open onto ocean views or the gardens of nearby condos. Rooms are very large, with excellent furnishings and fine linen. The bathrooms are exceptionally plush, with tub-and-shower combos, scales, bathrobes, and deluxe toiletries. Some rooms are accessible for guests with disabilities. Preferred accommodations are in the 9th-floor Ritz-Carlton Club, which has a private lounge and personal concierge staff.

The scope and diversity of dining here is second only to that at the Wyndham El San Juan, and for top-shelf dining venues, the Ritz-Carlton has no equal. The Vineyard Room is one of the finest restaurants in San Juan (p. 102). The hotel has the Caribbean's largest casino (p. 133).

Av. de los Gobernadores (State Rd.) 6961, no. 187, Isla Verde, PR 00979. ℂ **800/ 241-3333** or 787/253-1700. Fax 787/253-0700. www.ritzcarlton.com. 414 units. Winter $279–$399 double; off-season $199–$299 double. Year-round from $975 suite. AE, DC, DISC, MC, V. Valet parking $15. Bus: A7, M7, or T1. **Amenities:** 3 restaurants; 3 bars; nightclub; Caribbean's largest casino; 7,200-sq.-ft. pool; 2 tennis courts; gym; children's program; salon; 24-hr. room service; babysitting; laundry/dry cleaning. *In room:* A/C, TV, dataport, minibar, hair dryer, iron, safe.

The Water Club ☀☀☀
A refreshing change from the mega-chain resorts of San Juan, this ultrachic hotel is hip and contemporary. It's the city's only "boutique hotel" on a beach. We find much to praise at this small and exclusive hotel because of its highly personalized and well-trained staff. Although avant-garde, the design is not daringly provocative. Behind glass are "waterfalls," even on the elevators, and inventive theatrical-style lighting is used to bring the outdoors inside. The one-of-a-kind glass art doors are from Murano, the fabled center of glassmaking outside Venice. The hotel overlooks Isla Verde's best beach area, and all the bedrooms are spacious, opening onto views of the water and containing custom-designed beds positioned to face the ocean. Bathrooms are tiled and elegant, with tub-and-shower combinations. Unique features are the open-air 11th-floor exotic bar, with the Caribbean's only rooftop fireplace. The pool is a level above; it's like swimming in an ocean in the sky.

Calle José M. Tartak 2, Isla Verde, Puerto Rico 00979. ℂ **888/265-6699** or 787/253-0100. Fax 787/253-0220. www.waterclubsanjuan.com. Winter $395–$485 double, $995 suite; off-season $205–$310 double, $825 suite. AE, DC, MC, V. Bus: T1 or A5. **Amenities:** Restaurant; 2 bars; rooftop pool; fitness center; Jacuzzi; room service; babysitting; laundry/dry cleaning. *In room:* A/C, TV, minibar, hair dryer, safe.

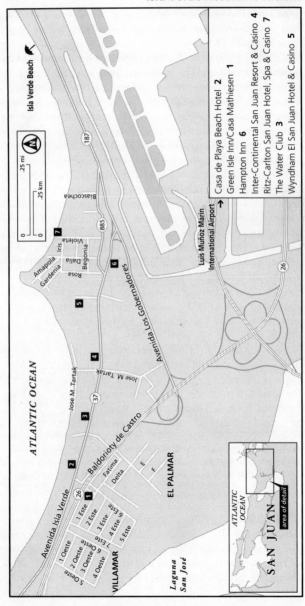

Isla Verde Accommodations

Casa de Playa Beach Hotel **2**
Green Isle Inn/Casa Mathiesen **1**
Hampton Inn **6**
Inter-Continental San Juan Resort & Casino **4**
Ritz-Carlton San Juan Hotel, Spa & Casino **7**
The Water Club **3**
Wyndham El San Juan Hotel & Casino **5**

ATLANTIC OCEAN

Isla Verde Beach

.25 mi
.25 km

Biascochea

Luis Muñoz Marín
International Airport

Violeta
Iris
Begonia
Dalia
Amapola
Gardenia
Rosa

Avenida Los Gobernadores

Jose M. Tartak

Baldorioty de Castro

Avenida Isla Verde

VILLAMAR

5 Oeste
4 Oeste
3 Oeste
6 Oeste
2 Oeste
1 Oeste

5 Este
4 Este
3 Este
6 Este
2 Este
1 Este

Fatima
Delta
E
F

EL PALMAR

Laguna
San José

ATLANTIC
OCEAN

area of detail

SAN JUAN

Wyndham El San Juan Hotel & Casino ✫✫✫ *(Kids)*   One of the best hotels in Puerto Rico, this place evokes Havana in its heyday. Built in the 1950s, it was restored with an infusion of millions in the 1990s. It's a great choice for (well-to-do) families, with lots of activities for children. The beachfront hotel is surrounded by 350 palms, century-old banyans, and gardens. Its 700-yard-long sandy beach is the finest in the San Juan area. The hotel's river pool, with currents, cascades, and lagoons, evokes a jungle stream, and the lobby is the most opulent and memorable in the Caribbean. Entirely sheathed in red marble and hand-carved mahogany paneling, the public rooms stretch on almost endlessly.

The large, well-decorated rooms have intriguing touches of high-tech; each contains three phones and a VCR. Bedrooms are the ultimate in luxury in San Juan, with honey-hued woods and rattans and king or double beds. Bathrooms have all the amenities and tub-and-shower combos; a few feature Jacuzzis. About 150 of the units, designed as comfortable bungalows, are in the outer reaches of the garden. Known as *casitas,* they include Roman tubs, atrium showers, and access to the fern-lined paths of a tropical jungle a few steps away. A 17-story, $60 million wing with 120 suites, all oceanfront, was completed in 1998. The ultra-luxury tower features 103 one- or two-bedroom units, 8 garden suites, 5 governor's suites, and 4 presidential suites.

No other hotel in the Caribbean offers such a rich diversity of dining options and such high-quality food. Japanese, Italian, Mexican, and 24-hour American/Caribbean restaurants are just a few of the options. (See chapter 5 for reviews of Back Street Hong Kong, La Piccola Fontana, Yamato, and The Ranch.)

Av. Isla Verde 6063, San Juan, PR 00979. ℂ 800/WYNDHAM or 787/791-1000. Fax 787/791-0390. www.wyndham.com. 389 units. Winter $415–$565 double, from $625 suite; off-season $145–$495 double, from $515 suite. AE, DC, DISC, MC, V. Self-parking $10; valet parking $15. Bus: M7. **Amenities:** 8 restaurants; 3 bars; 2 pools; tennis courts; health club and spa; steam room; sauna; watersports; children's program; 24-hr. room service; massage; babysitting; dry cleaning. *In room:* A/C, TV/VCR, minibar, coffeemaker, hair dryer, safe.

MODERATE

Hampton Inn *(Kids)*   Opened in 1997, this chain hotel is set across the busy avenue from Isla Verde's sandy beachfront, far enough away to keep costs down but within a leisurely 10-minute walk of the casinos and nightlife. Two towers, with four and five floors, hold the well-maintained, well-furnished, and comfortable bedrooms. There's no restaurant on the premises, no real garden; other than a

> ## (Kids) Family-Friendly Accommodations
>
> **Wyndham El San Juan Hotel & Casino** (p. 80)   This hotel, although expensive, offers more programs for children than any other hotel in Puerto Rico. Its supervised Kids' Klub provides daily activities—ranging from face painting to swimming lessons—for children 5 to 12 years of age. See "Especially for Kids" in chapter 6.
>
> **Hampton Inn** (p. 80)   For families seeking the kind of lodging values found on the mainland, this new hotel is highly desirable, as many of its rooms have two double beds. There's also a beautiful swimming pool in a tropical setting. Suites have microwaves and refrigerators.
>
> **Condado Plaza Hotel & Casino** (p. 70)   For the family seeking an upmarket resort with lots of facilities, this is the best choice along the Condado. Its Camp Taíno is guided by experts and occupies children under 12 throughout the day for a fee.
>
> **At Wind Chimes Inn** (p. 74)   Families like this hotel not only because of the accommodations and the affordable prices but because they can prepare meals here, cutting down on food costs.

whirlpool and a swimming pool with a swim-up bar, there are very few facilities or amenities. Because of its reasonable prices and location, however, this Isla Verde newcomer could be a good choice. Families are especially fond of staying here, despite the fact that there are no special children's programs; many of the rooms have two double beds and suites have microwaves and refrigerators.

Av. Isla Verde 6530, Isla Verde, PR 00979. (C) **800/HAMPTON** or 787/791-8777. Fax 787/791-8757. 201 units. Winter $179 double, $199 suite; off-season $129 double, $149 suite. Rates include breakfast bar. AE, DC, MC, V. Free parking. Bus: A5 or C45. **Amenities:** Bar; pool; gym; whirlpool; babysitting; laundry/dry cleaning. *In room:* A/C, TV, minibar in suites, fridge in suites, coffeemaker, hair dryer, iron, microwave in suites.

INEXPENSIVE

Casa de Playa Beach Hotel (Finds)   Jutting out over the sand on the mile-long (1.5km) Isla Verde beach, this bargain oasis is a find. If you're less interested in being in the center of San Juan than you are in spending time on the beach, check out this modest choice.

The hotel consists of two two-story buildings, with a porch around the second floor and a small garden in front. Furnishings are modest and functional but comfortable nonetheless. Each room has a tidily maintained, small bathroom with a tiled shower. Standard but inexpensive Italian food is served at a beach bar and restaurant. The hotel doesn't have everything—no pool, no room service—but the price is hard to beat in Isla Verde.

Av. Isla Verde 4851, San Juan, PR 09979. © **800/916-2272** or 787/728-9779. Fax 787/727-1334. 21 units. Winter $90 double, $175 suite; off-season $80 double, $120 suite. Children 9 and under stay free in parents' room. Rates include continental breakfast. AE, DC, DISC, MC, V. Free parking. Bus: A5. **Amenities:** Restaurant; bar; babysitting. *In room:* A/C, TV, fridge in some, coffeemaker in suites, safe.

Green Isle Inn/Casa Mathiesen   Across the busy avenue from the larger and much more expensive San Juan Grand Beach Resort & Casino, this is really two hotels in one. They stand side by side and charge the same prices. Both of them are equally comfortable, though modest. The beach is a 5-minute walk away, and each of the hotels has a pool. There are 25 rooms at the Green Isle. Casa Mathiesen is only slighter larger, with 29 units. The furnishings are summery, simple, and comfortable. Each has a tiled tub-and-shower bathroom.

Calle Uno 36, Villamar, Isla Verde, PR 00979. © **800/677-8860** or 787/726-8662. Fax 787/268-2415. www.greenisleinn.com. 54 units. Winter $79–$84 double; off-season $73–$82 double. AE, MC, V. Free parking. Bus: A5. **Amenities:** Restaurant; bar; 2 small pools; laundry. *In room:* A/C, TV, kitchenette (in some), safe.

5

Where to Dine in San Juan

San Juan has the widest array of restaurants in the Caribbean. You can enjoy fine continental, American, Italian, Chinese, Mexican, and Japanese cuisines, to name a few. In recent years, many restaurants have shown a greater appreciation for traditional Puerto Rican cooking, and local specialties now appear on the menus of numerous restaurants. When possible, many chefs enhance their dishes with native ingredients.

Many of San Juan's best restaurants are in the resort hotels along the Condado and at Isla Verde. There has been a restaurant explosion in San Juan in the past few years, but many of the newer ones are off the beaten tourist path, and some have not yet achieved the quality found at many of the older, more traditional restaurants.

Local seafood is generally in plentiful supply, but no restaurant guarantees that it will have fresh fish every night, especially during winter, when the sea can be too turbulent for fishing. In those cases, the chef relies on fresh or frozen fish flown in from Miami. If you want fresh fish caught in Puerto Rican waters, ask your server about the catch of the day. Make sure he or she can guarantee that the fish was recently caught rather than resting for a while in the icebox.

1 Best Bets

- **Best Caribbean Chef**   Reigning supreme as chef of the year, Jeremie Cruz holds forth at **La Belle Epoque,** an elegant Condado setting in the Casabella Building, Av. Magdalena 1400 (© 787/977-1765), with a superb blend of French and fusion cuisine. The service is peerless, and top-quality ingredients are used to fashion noble dishes. See p. 94.
- **Best Classic Creole Cooking**   In its new location in Old Town's Museum of Art of Puerto Rico, Chef Wilo Benet at **Pikayo,** Av. José de Diego 299 (© 787/721-6194), holds forth. He's a master specialist in the *criolla* cooking of the colonial age, emphasizing the Spanish, Indian, and African elements in his unusual recipes. See p. 99.

- **Best Wine List**   The luxurious **Vineyard Room** in the dazzling Ritz-Carlton, 6961 State Road #187, Isla Verde (© 787/ 253-1700), serves a refined California/Mediterranean cuisine, but we'd go there just for the wine list. The countries best represented on the wine *carte* are France, Australia, Germany, Italy, Spain, and even South Africa. The California selection will make you think you're back in the Napa Valley. There is also a good selection of the increasingly fashionable wines from Chile. See p. 102.

- **Best Classic French Cuisine**   If you like classic French food, then head to **La Chaumière,** Calle Tetuán 367 (© 787/722-3330), in San Juan's Old Town. In back of the Tapía Theater, this two-story restaurant is intimate and inviting. The cuisine follows time-tested recipes of which Escoffier might have approved: onion soup, oysters Rockefeller, scallops Provençal, and a perfectly prepared rack of baby lamb Provençal. See p. 86.

- **Best Nuevo Latino Cuisine**   **Parrot Club,** Calle Fortaleza 363 (© 787/725-7370), wows tastebuds with its modern interpretation of Puerto Rican specialties. Even San Juan's mayor and the governor have made it their favorite. Husband-and-wife team Emilio Figueroa and Gigi Zafero borrow from a repertoire of Puerto Rican and Spanish recipes, and they also use Taíno and African influences in their cuisine. Their ceviche is the best in town, and their Creole-style flank steak is worth the trek from Condado Beach. See p. 86.

- **Best Burgers**   Patrons freely admit that **El Patio de Sam,** Calle San Sebastián 102 (© 787/723-1149), is not always on target with its main dishes. But they agree on one thing: The hamburgers are the juiciest and most delectable in San Juan. The Old Town atmosphere is also intriguing—you almost expect to encounter Bogey and Bacall. See p. 89.

- **Best Spanish Cuisine**   You'd have to go all the way to Madrid to find Spanish food as well prepared as it is at **Ramiro's,** Av. Magdalena 1106 (© 787/721-9049). The chefs take full advantage of fresh island produce to create an innovative cuisine. In fact, the style is New Creole, although its roots are firmly planted in Spain. Their fresh fish and chargrilled meats are succulent, and any dessert with the strawberry-and-guava sauce is a sure palate pleaser. See p. 95.

- **Best Local Cuisine**   Devoted to *la cocina criolla,* the term for the often starchy local cuisine, **Ajili Mójili,** Av. Ashford 1052

(© 787/725-9195), features food that islanders might have enjoyed in their mama's kitchens. Try such specialties as *mofongos* (green plantains stuffed with veal, chicken, shrimp, or pork) or the most classic *arroz con pollo* (stewed chicken with saffron rice) in town. See p. 94.

- **Best Italian Restaurant** In Wyndham El San Juan Hotel & Casino, **La Piccola Fontana**, Av. Isla Verde 6063 (© 787/ 791-0966), takes you on a culinary tour of sunny Italy. Plate after plate of delectable northern Italian food is presented nightly—everything from grilled filets of fresh fish to succulent pastas. Service is first-rate, the welcome warm. See p. 101.

- **Best Sunday Brunch** Both locals and American visitors flock to **Palmera** at the Caribe Hilton, Calle Los Rosales (© 787/721-0303), for its delectable all-you-can-eat Sunday brunch. Good food, glamour, and live music are combined here. The freshly prepared seafood alone is worth the set price, which includes champagne. See p. 92.

- **Best Drinks** Even when we're just in San Juan waiting for plane connections and have time available, we take a taxi to **Maria's**, Calle del Cristo 204 (© 787/721-1678), in Old San Juan, for the coolest and most original drinks in the city. On a hot day, there is no finer place to enjoy a mixed-fruit frappé; a banana, pineapple, or chocolate frost; or an orange, papaya, or lime freeze. See p. 131.

2 Old San Juan

EXPENSIVE

Il Perugino ⚂ TUSCAN/UMBRIAN This is one of the most elegant Italian restaurants in San Juan, with a courtyard containing covered tables. It's located in a 270-year-old town house, a short walk uphill from Catedral de San Juan. The entrance is filled with dozens of photographs of owner/chef Franco Seccarelli with friends and well-known patrons, the most notable being Luciano Pavarotti. Dishes and flavors are perfectly balanced. Examples include shrimp salad (usually a mundane dish, but quite special here), scallop salad, perfectly marinated fresh salmon, veal entrecôte with mushrooms, and medallions of beef flavored with balsamic vinegar. In season, there's an emphasis on black and white truffles, although these ingredients can raise the dish price substantially. Want something adventurous? Try the black pasta with crayfish and baby eels.

Calle del Cristo 105. ℂ **787/722-5481.** Reservations required. Main courses $18–$39. AE, MC, V. Daily 6:30–11pm. Bus: Old Town trolley.

La Chaumière 𝔸𝔸 CLASSIC FRENCH   The classic cuisine here has a loyal following of foodies. Just steps from the famous Tapía Theater, this restaurant has cafe-style decor in a greenhouse setting. You might begin with a Marseilles-style fish soup or a hearty country paté, then follow with a perfectly prepared rack of baby lamb Provençal, filet mignon with béarnaise sauce, magret of duckling, or Dover sole meunière. Or you might choose the tender chateaubriand for two. Old standbys include chitterling sausage with red-wine sauce, veal Oscar, and oysters Rockefeller.

Calle Tetuán 367. ℂ **787/722-3330.** Reservations required. Main courses $25–$32. AE, DC, MC, V. Mon–Sat 6pm–midnight. Closed July–Aug. Bus: Old Town trolley.

Parrot Club 𝔸𝔸𝔸 NUEVO LATINO   Parrot Club is the hottest restaurant in Old San Juan. This bistro and bar serves Nuevo Latino cuisine that blends traditional Puerto Rican cookery with Spanish, Taíno, and African influences. It's set in a stately looking 1902 building that was originally a hair-tonic factory. Today you'll find a cheerful-looking dining room where San Juan's mayor and the governor of Puerto Rico can sometimes be spotted, and a verdantly landscaped courtyard where tables for at least 200 diners are scattered amid potted ferns, palms, and orchids. Live music, either Brazilian, salsa, or Latino jazz, is offered nightly, as well as during the popular Sunday brunches.

Menu items are updated interpretations of old Puerto Rican specialties. They include ceviche of halibut, salmon, tuna, and mahimahi; delicious crab cakes; criolla-style flank steak; and pan-seared tuna served with a sauce made from dark rum and essence of oranges. Everybody's favorite drink is a "Parrot Passion," made from lemon-flavored rum, triple sec, oranges, and passion fruit.

Calle Fortaleza 363. ℂ **787/725-7370.** Reservations not accepted. Main courses $17–$29 at dinner, $12–$20 at lunch. AE, DC, MC, V. Mon–Fri 11:30am–3pm; Sat noon–3pm; Sun noon–4pm and 6–11pm; Fri–Sat 6pm–midnight. Closed 2 weeks in July. Bus: Old Town trolley.

MODERATE

Amadeus 𝔸𝔸 CARIBBEAN   Housed in a brick-and-stone building that was constructed in the 18th century by a wealthy merchant, Amadeus offers Caribbean ingredients with a nouvelle twist. The appetizers alone are worth the trip here, especially the Amadeus

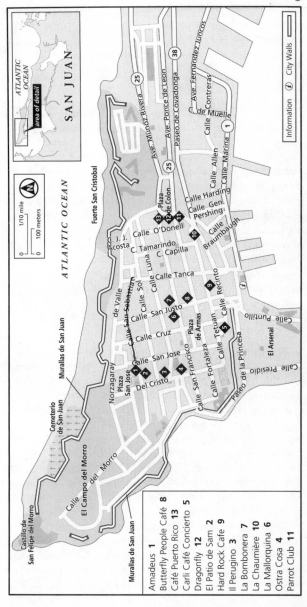

Amadeus **1**
Butterfly People Café **8**
Café Puerto Rico **13**
Carli Café Concierto **5**
Dragonfly **12**
El Patio de Sam **2**
Hard Rock Cafe **9**
Il Perugino **3**
La Bombonera **7**
La Chaumière **10**
La Mallorquina **6**
Ostra Cosa **4**
Parrot Club **11**

Information ⓘ   ▭ City Walls

dumplings with guava sauce and arrowroot fritters. And try the smoked-salmon-and-caviar pizza. One zesty specialty is pork scaloppine with sweet-and-sour sauce.

Calle San Sebastián 106 (across from the Iglesia de San José). ℂ 787/722-8635. Reservations recommended. Main courses $8.75–$13 lunch, $12–$26 dinner. AE, MC, V. Mon 6pm–2am; Tues–Sun noon–2am (kitchen closes at midnight). Bus: Old Town trolley.

Carli Café Concierto ℱ INTERNATIONAL This stylish restaurant is owned by Carli Muñoz. The gold discs hanging on the walls attest to Carli's success in his previous role as a pianist for The Beach Boys. Nowadays, Carli entertains his dinner guests nightly with a combination of standards, romantic jazz, and original material on his grand piano. Diners can sit outside on the Plazoleta, where they can enjoy a panoramic view of the bay, or they can eat inside against a backdrop of a tasteful decor of terra-cotta walls and black marble tables. The chef tempts visitors with an imaginative international menu, including such delights as quail rockettes stuffed with dried fruits and sage. The filet of salmon and a mouth-watering rack of lamb are among the finest main dishes. The bar, with its mahogany and brass fittings, is an ideal spot to chill out.

Edificio Banco Popular, Calle Tetuán 206, off Plazoleta Rafael Carrión. ℂ 787/ 725-4927. Reservations recommended. Main courses $17–$29. AE, MC, V. Mon–Thurs 4–11:30pm; Fri–Sat 4pm–1:30am. Bus: M2 or M3.

Dragonfly ℱℱℱ LATIN/ASIAN This is San Juan's hottest new restaurant. The decor has been compared to that of a bordello in Old San Francisco. You pass through the beaded curtains into a world of red ceilings, fringed lamps, and gilded mirrors. The restaurant lies right across the street from the Parrot Club, and these two dining enclaves have put the newly named SoFo district (south of Calle Fortaleza in Old Town) on the culinary map. In the bar the drink of choice is a Cosmopolitan, the preferred cigarette Marlboro, and the most popular drink, a lethal "Dragon Punch." Night after night Dragonfly is the fun party place in town, unlike the more staid Parrot Club. Along with the latest gossip, you can enjoy live Latin jazz as background music.

This new-generation San Juan restaurant offers sexy cookery, such as seafood ceviche scooped up with yucca, and plantain chips, *chicharrónes* (pork rinds), spicy crab cakes, and a host of other dishes, such as marinated grilled meats. We applaud the chefs for their use of root vegetables such as yucca. The red snapper and grouper are excellent, and we love the pumpkin and beans of every type. The barbecued lamb shanks are very hearty and filling. Ravioli, timbales, confits, cassoulets—it's a dizzy array of taste temptations.

Calle Fortaleza 364. © 787/977-3886. Reservations required. Main courses $8–$21. AE, MC, V. Mon–Wed 6:30–10:30pm; Thurs–Sat 6:30pm–midnight. Bus: A5 or T1.

El Patio de Sam AMERICAN/PUERTO RICAN   Established in 1953, this joint has survived several generations of clients, who came here for booze, fantastic juicy burgers, Puerto Rican food, and dialogue. The setting includes an exterior space with tables that overlook a historic statue of Ponce de León and a well-known church, and a labyrinth of dark, smoked-stained inner rooms with high-beamed ceilings and lots of potted plants. The menu includes paella, grilled chicken and steak, black-bean soup, calamari, and codfish croquettes.

Calle San Sebastián 102 (across from the Iglesia de San José). © 787/723-1149. Sandwiches, burgers, and salads $9–$9.50; platters $13–$33. AE, DC, DISC, MC, V. Daily 11am–midnight. Bus: Old Town trolley.

La Mallorquina 𝒜 PUERTO RICAN   This is San Juan's oldest restaurant, founded in 1848, and it has been run by the Rojos family since 1900. If you look carefully at the floor adjacent to the old-fashioned mahogany bar, you'll see the building's original gray-and-white marble flooring, which the owners are laboriously restoring, square foot by square foot, to its original condition. Lunches here tend to attract local office workers; dinners are more cosmopolitan and more leisurely, with many residents of the Condado and other modern neighborhoods selecting this place specifically because of its old-fashioned, old-world charm.

The food has changed little here over the decades, with special emphasis on asopao made with rice and either chicken, shrimp, or lobster and shrimp. Arroz con pollo is almost as popular. Begin with either garlic soup or gazpacho, end with flan, and you'll have eaten a meal that's authentically Puerto Rican.

Calle San Justo 207. © 787/722-3261. Reservations not accepted at lunch, recommended at dinner. Dinner main courses $15–$36 (highest price is for lobster). AE, MC, V. Mon–Sat noon–10pm. Closed Sept. Bus: Old Town trolley.

Ostra Cosa 𝒜𝒜 *Finds* ECLECTIC   This is the most artfully promoted restaurant in San Juan, with a growing clientele who swear that the ambience here is one of the most sensual and romantic in Old San Juan. It was created by a former advertising executive, Alberto Nazario, a lifestyle guru who mingles New Age thinking with good culinary techniques to promote love, devotion, and a heightened sexuality. Couples dine beneath a massive quenepe tree—waiters will tell you to hug the tree and make a wish—in a colonial courtyard surrounded by a 16th-century building that was once the home of the colony's governor. The atmosphere, enhanced by domesticated quail and chirping tree frogs, will make you feel far removed from the cares of the city. Featured foods are high in phosphorus, zinc, and flavor, designed to promote an "eat-up, dress-down experience." The ceviche is superb, as are the grilled prawns. But it is the conch, known as Caribbean Viagra, that rates "Wow!!" or "Ay Ay Ay!!!"

Calle del Cristo 154. ℭ 787/722-2672. Reservations recommended. Main courses $12–$25. AE, MC, V. Aug–Sept Mon–Fri 6–10pm, Sat–Sun noon–10pm. Oct–July daily noon–10pm. Bus: Old Town trolley.

INEXPENSIVE

Butterfly People Café *Kids* CONTINENTAL/AMERICAN This rather cramped restaurant is on the second floor of a restored mansion, next to the world's largest gallery devoted to butterflies. Wherever you look, thousands of framed butterflies will delight or horrify you. You can dine at one of the tables inside the cafe, which overlooks a courtyard. This is among the most kid-welcoming place in town, and most children take delight in eating in a setting surrounded by the framed butterflies, viewing it as a sort of fantasy world. The cuisine is tropical and light European fare, made with fresh ingredients appealing to children, as opposed to the more heavy-handed Puerto Rican cuisine offered at nearby dining spots. You might begin with gazpacho or vichyssoise, follow with quiche or one of the daily specials, and finish with chocolate mousse or the tantalizing raspberry chiffon pie with fresh raspberry sauce. A full bar offers tropical specialties such as piña coladas, fresh-squeezed Puerto Rican orange juice, and Fantasia, a frappé of seven fresh fruits.

Calle Fortaleza 152. ℭ 787/723-2432. Salads, sandwiches, and quiches $4–$8. AE, MC, V. Mon–Wed and Fri–Sat 10am–5pm. Bus: Old Town trolley.

Café Puerto Rico CREOLE/PUERTO RICAN On the Plaza de Colón, this restaurant offers balconies overlooking one of the most charming of Old Town squares. The setting is colonial, with beamed ceilings and tile floors, and with ceiling fans whirling overhead. The menu features hearty regional fare. Tasty options include fried fish filet, paella, and lobster cooked as you like it. Eggplant parmagiana is an excellent vegetarian option, and you might also order eye round stuffed with ham in Creole sauce. On weekends live bands play here, and the sound of romantic boleros or salsa fill the air. The cafe is an especially good value then because you get your food and entertainment for just the price of dinner.

Calle O'Donnell 208. ☎ **787/724-2281.** Main courses $9–$20. AE, MC, V. Daily 11:30am–11pm (bar open till 2am Thurs–Sat). Bus: Old Town trolley.

Hard Rock Cafe *Kids* AMERICAN   This is San Juan's most blatant example of gringo-derived cultural imperialism. Set near the cruise-ship terminals on a historic avenue in the Old Town, it's loaded with rock 'n' roll memorabilia and permeated with an engaging friendliness. One dining room is devoted to the Beatles, complete with symbol-rich murals that only the most fervent fans can interpret. Standard menu items include barbecued ribs and pork sandwiches, chicken and rib combos, smoked pork chops, pastas, steaks, fiery chili, and a selection of well-stuffed sandwiches. On days when cruise ships pull into port (usually Tues and Sun), the place is likely to be mobbed.

Calle Recinto Sur 253. ☎ **787/724-7625.** Burgers, sandwiches, and platters $7–$22. AE, DC, DISC, MC, V. Daily 11am–11pm. Bus: Old Town trolley.

La Bombonera *Value* PUERTO RICAN   This place offers exceptional value in its homemade pastries, well-stuffed sandwiches, and endless cups of coffee—and it has done so since 1902. Its atmosphere evokes turn-of-the-20th-century Castille transplanted to the New World. The food is authentically Puerto Rican, homemade, and inexpensive, with regional dishes such as rice with squid, roast leg of pork, and seafood asopao. For dessert, you might select an apple, pineapple, or prune pie, or one of many types of flan. Service is polite, if a bit rushed, and the place fills up quickly at lunchtime.

Calle San Francisco 259. ☎ **787/722-0658.** Reservations recommended. American breakfast $4–$8; main courses $7–$15. AE, DISC, MC, V. Daily 7:30am–8pm. Bus: Old Town trolley.

3 Puerta de Tierra

Invernino *ITALIAN*   Presenting a tempting array of foodstuff from all the major culinary zones of Italy, this restaurant has already become a hit since its opening in late 2001. It received worldwide fame as the setting of the wedding of Oscar de la Hoya to Millie Corretijer. The restaurant is named for a sculpture in its foyer that was created in 1790 by the Italian artist Sau Frilli. The ambience is one of the most sophisticated and inviting in San Juan;

the restaurant is filled with paintings and stainless-steel sculptures. A former warehouse, Invernino has been transformed into an up-market restaurant that serves some of the Caribbean's finest Italian cuisine, made with top-quality ingredients handpicked by the chefs. Chef Gerard Cribbin, known in the past for his pasta and steak restaurants, likes diners to "taste every ingredient in a particular dish." Nothing he serves is overpowered with sauces, including succulent steaks such as filet mignon and pastas such as striped lobster ravioli. The fettuccine with fresh clams merits a prize, and the tiramisu is the best in San Juan. A much-frequented watering hole is the cigarette bar on the second floor, where live piano music is played.

Atlantic View Building, Av. Ponce de León 162. ℂ **787/724-2166.** Reservations required. Main courses $18–$34. AE, MC, V. Mon–Fri 11:30am–3pm; Mon–Sat 5–11pm. Bus: B21.

Morton's of Chicago 𝒦𝒦 STEAK   When it comes to steaks, Ruth's Chris Steak House in Isla Verde enjoys a slight edge, but otherwise Morton's is king of the steaks and other choice meats. The chain of gourmet steakhouses was founded in 1978 by Arnie Morton, former executive vice president of the *Playboy* empire. Beef lovers, from Al Gore to Liza Minnelli, know they'll get quality meats perfectly cooked at Morton's. Carts laden with your selection, ranging from prime Midwestern beefsteaks to succulent lamb or veal chops, are wheeled around for your selection. And Morton's has the island's best prime rib. This is a place where the bartenders make stiff drinks, and the waiters tempt you with their fresh fish, lobster, and chicken dishes. The vegetables here are among the freshest in the area. The house specialty is a 24-ounce porterhouse. Appetizers include perfectly cooked jumbo shrimp with cocktail sauce and smoked Pacific salmon. For dessert, we always gravitate to one of the soufflés, such as raspberry or Grand Marnier.

In the Caribe Hilton, Calle Los Rosales. ℂ **787/977-6262.** Reservations required. Main courses $20–$40. AE, DC, MC, V. Mon–Sat 5:30–11pm; Sun 5–10pm. Bus: B21.

Palmera 𝒦 𝒦𝒾𝒹𝓈 INTERNATIONAL   Every Sunday the Hilton's brunch captivates the imagination of island residents and U.S. visitors with its combination of excellently prepared food, glamour, and entertainment. There's a clown to keep the children amused, as well as live music on the bandstand for anyone who cares to dance. Champagne is included in the price. Food is arranged at several different stations: Puerto Rican dishes, seafood, paella, ribs, cold cuts,

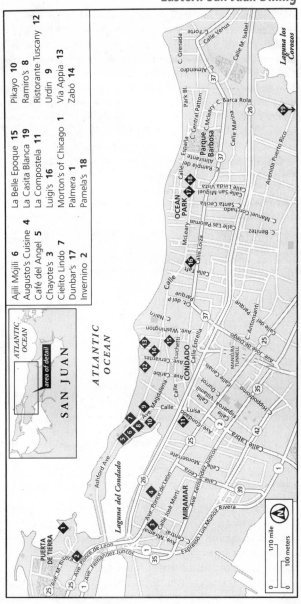

Ajili Mójili **6**
Augusto's Cuisine **4**
Café del Angel **5**
Chayote's **3**
Cielito Lindo **7**
Dunbar's **17**
Invernino **2**

La Belle Epoque **15**
La Casita Blanca **19**
La Compostela **11**
Luigi's **16**
Morton's of Chicago **1**
Palmera **1**
Pamela's **18**

Pikayo **10**
Ramiro's **8**
Ristorante Tuscany **12**
Urdin **9**
Via Appia **13**
Zabó **14**

steaks, pastas, and salads. Afterward, you might like to stroll amid the boutiques and seafront facilities of this famous hotel. In the evening you can order from a standard international menu. However, we recommend this restaurant mainly for its buffet. If you're visiting the Hilton for the evening for dining and entertainment, we'd recommend the cuisine at Morton's (see above) over Palmera.

In the Caribe Hilton, Calle Los Rosales. ℂ **787/721-0303.** Reservations recommended. All-you-can-eat buffet brunch $39 for adults, half price for children under 7; main courses $14–$20. AE, DC, MC, V. Sun buffet 12:30–4pm; daily 6am–midnight. Bus: B21.

4 Condado

EXPENSIVE

Ajili Mójili 𝕽𝕽 PUERTO RICAN/CREOLE This restaurant is devoted exclusively to *la cucina criolla,* the starchy, down-home cuisine that developed on the island a century ago. Though the building housing it is quite modern, you can see artful replicas of the kind of crumbling brick walls you'd expect in Old San Juan and a bar that evokes Old Spain. The staff will willingly describe menu items in colloquial English. Locals come here for a taste of the food they enjoyed at their mother's knee, like *mofongos* (green plantains stuffed with veal, chicken, shrimp, or pork), arroz con pollo, *medallones de cerdo encebollado* (pork loin sautéed with onions), *carne mechada* (beef rib-eye stuffed with ham), and *lechon asado con maposteado* (roast pork with rice and beans). Wash it all down with an ice-cold bottle of local beer.

Av. Ashford 1052 (at the corner of Calle Joffre). ℂ **787/725-9195.** Reservations recommended. Main courses $16–$35; children's menu $6. AE, MC, V. Mon–Fri 11:30am–3pm; Mon–Sat 6–10pm; Sun 12:30–4pm and 6–10pm. Bus: B21.

La Belle Epoque 𝕽𝕽𝕽 FUSION/FRENCH Twice in recent years, master chef Jeremie Cruz has been voted "Caribbean Chef of the Year," and he currently reigns supreme as Puerto Rico's greatest talent in the kitchen. Expect spectacular dining at this elegant enclave of exquisitely prepared cuisine. The Condado setting is one of Murano chandeliers, hand-painted custom-made plates, and Italian damask tablecloths. In addition to two exquisite dining rooms, there is a Smoker Terrace with a wide collection of fine cigars, plus a cozy wine cellar with a selection of more than 1,000 vintage bottles. Even a basic onion soup for an appetizer is prepared with flair, although you can order more luxurious concoctions such as lobster bisque. Another starter might be in seafood mousse resting under a brown potato crust or perhaps a watercress and arugula salad studded with walnuts and savory bits of blue cheese. For a main course, opt for the poached salmon with "lobster potatoes," one of the best dishes we've ever sampled here. Other options might include a classic coq au vin, given added dimension by the use of wild mushrooms, or seared bay scallops with spinach and saffron-laced mussel sauce. Between courses a palate cleanser is served, a refreshing fermented cider with frozen white grapes. Desserts are among the most unusual, delicious, and imaginative on the island—try the lemon-grass soup with sorbet, pieces of fresh fruit, and candied carrots.

Casabella Building, Av. Magdalena 1400. ✆ **787/977-1765.** Reservations required. Main courses $12–$25 lunch, $17–$29 dinner. AE, MC, V. Mon–Sat noon–3pm and 5–11pm. Bus: B21.

La Compostela ✺ INTERNATIONAL   This restaurant offers formal service from a battalion of well-dressed waiters. Established by a Galician-born family, the pine-trimmed restaurant has gained a reputation as one of the best in the capital. The chef made his name on the roast peppers stuffed with salmon mousse. Equally delectable are duck with orange and ginger sauce and baby rack of lamb with fresh herbs. The shellfish grilled in brandy sauce is a sure winner. The chef also makes two different versions of paella, both savory. The wine cellar, comprising some 10,000 bottles, is one of the most impressive in San Juan.

Av. Condado 106. ✆ **787/724-6088.** Reservations required. Main courses $24–$39. AE, MC, V. Mon–Fri noon–2:30pm; Mon–Sat 6:30–10:30pm. Bus: M2.

Ramiro's ✺✺ SPANISH/INTERNATIONAL   This restaurant boasts the most imaginative menu on the Condado. Its refined "New Creole" cooking is a style pioneered by owner and chef Jesús Ramiro. You might begin with breadfruit mille-feuille with local crabmeat and avocado. For your main course, any fresh fish or meat can be chargrilled on request. Some recent menu specialties have included paillard of lamb with spiced root vegetables and guava sauce, charcoal-grilled black Angus steak with shiitake mushrooms, and grilled striped sea bass with citrus sauce. Among the many homemade desserts are caramelized mango on puff pastry with strawberry-and-guava sauce, and "four seasons" chocolate.

Av. Magdalena 1106. ✆ **787/721-9049.** Reservations recommended off-season, required in winter. Main courses $23–$40. AE, DC, MC, V. Sun–Fri 6–10pm; Sat 6–11pm. Bus: A7, T1, or M2.

Ristorante Tuscany ★★★ NORTHERN ITALIAN This is the showcase restaurant of one of the most elaborate hotel reconstructions in the history of Puerto Rico, and the kitchen continues to rack up culinary awards. Notable entrees include grilled veal chops with shallots and glaze of Madeira, and grilled chicken breast in cream sauce with chestnuts, asparagus, and brandy, surrounded with fried artichokes. The seafood selections are excellent, especially the fresh red snapper sautéed in olive oil, garlic, parsley, and lemon juice. The risottos prepared al dente in the traditional northern Italian style are the finest on the island, especially the one made with seafood and herbs. The cold and hot appetizers are virtual meals unto themselves, with such favorites as grilled polenta with sausages or fresh clams and mussels simmered in herb-flavored tomato broth.

In the San Juan Marriott Resort, Av. Ashford 1309. ℂ 787/722-7000. Reservations recommended. Main courses $20–$34. AE, DC, DISC, MC, V. Daily 6–11pm. Bus: B21.

MODERATE

Most main courses in the restaurants below are at the low end of the price scale. These restaurants each have only two or three dishes that are expensive, almost invariably involving shellfish.

Luigi's ★★ ITALIAN/GENOVESE There's a formal and even romantic atmosphere here at night. When chef-owner Luigi Sanguineti came to Puerto Rico from Genoa in the late 1980s, he liked the place so much he decided to bring "a little bit of Genoa" to the old town. After gaining a reputation as one of the island's foremost European chefs, Luigi finally opened his own place in 2000. Since then he's been delighting the palates of locals and visitors with high-quality Italian cuisine. Try the gnocchi with pesto or the eggplant lasagna, and perhaps start with a savory antipasto prepared by Luigi himself. His lobster ravioli is San Juan's finest, and another dish we like a lot is the shrimp risotto.

104 Diez de Andino. ℂ 787/977-0134. Reservations recommended. Main courses $10–$22. AE, MC, V. Mon–Sat noon–10pm; Sun noon–5pm. Bus: B5.

Urdin ★★ PUERTO RICAN/INTERNATIONAL Urdin is proud of its reputation as one of the capital's bright young restaurants. It occupies a low-slung, stucco-covered house set near a slew of competitors. Inside, a fanciful decor of postmodern, Caribbean-inspired accents and metal sculptures brings a touch of Latino New York. Popularity has brought an unexpected development to this highly visible restaurant: The bar is almost more popular than the food. Consequently, you're likely to find the bar area jam-packed every day between 6 and 10pm. Cliquish, heterosexual, and fashionable, some of this crowd eventually gravitates toward the tables. Yes, that was Ricky Martin we spotted here one evening. Filled with authentic Spanish flavor that's not necessarily geared to the palates of timid diners, the food is innovative, flavorful, strong, and earthy. For starters, there are baby eels Bilbaina style and Castilian lentil soup. Main courses include fresh filet of salmon in mustard sauce, filet of fish "Hollywood style" (with onions, raisins, and mango slices, served in white-wine sauce), and rack of lamb with orange sauce. One always-pleasing dish is piquillo peppers stuffed with seafood mousse and black-olive sauce. Savvy locals finish their meal with a slice of sweet-potato cheesecake. The staff can put a damper on (if they're sulky) or enhance (if they're welcoming) a meal here.

Av. Magdalena 1105. © 787/724-0420. Reservations recommended. Main courses $14–$27. AE, MC, V. Mon–Sat noon–3pm and 6–11pm. Bus: A7.

Zabó 🍴 INTERNATIONAL   This restaurant enjoys citywide fame, thanks to its blend of bucolic charm and superb innovative food. It's set in a dignified villa that provides some low-rise dignity in a sea of skyscraping condos. The creative force here is owner and chef/culinary director Paul Carroll, who built the place from its origins as a simple deli into one of the most sought-after restaurants on the Condado. Menu items fuse the cuisines of the Mediterranean, the Pacific Rim, and the Caribbean into a collection that includes dishes such as blinis stuffed with medallions of lobster with ginger, thyme, and beurre blanc; carpaccio of salmon with mesclun salad and balsamic vinegar; and baked chorizo stuffed with mushrooms, sherry, paprika, and cheddar. The black-bean soup is among the very best in Puerto Rico, served with parboiled cloves of garlic marinated in olive oil that melt in your mouth like candy.

Calle Candina 14 (entrance is via an alleyway leading from Av. Ashford between avs. Washington and Cervantes). © 787/725-9494. Reservations recommended. Main courses $8.75–$29 at lunch, $20–$29 at dinner. AE, MC, V. Tues–Wed 6–10pm; Thurs–Sat 6–11pm; Fri noon–3pm. Bus: A7.

INEXPENSIVE

Café del Angel CREOLE/PUERTO RICAN   Don't come here for the decor. The juice bar up front looks like it was transported from Miami's Flagler Street in 1950, and the plastic green furniture won't compel you to get *Architectural Digest* on the phone. If indeed there is an "angel," as the cafe's name suggests, it is in the kitchen. The chef serves remarkably good food at affordable prices. The place has been in operation for more than a decade. Paintings and figures of its namesake angels decorate the dining room. Some 100 hungry diners can be fed here at one time, in a relaxed atmosphere that is welcoming and friendly. The service is also efficient. Prepare for some real island flavor, as in the traditional *mofongo relleno con camarones,* which is sautéed, mashed plantain with shrimp. You can order a generous helping of tender beefsteak sautéed with onions and peppers or a perfectly grilled chicken. *Pastel,* a kind of creamy polenta of cornmeal, is served with many dishes, and the fresh garlic bread is complimentary.

Av. Ashford 1106. ℭ 787/643-7594. Reservations not necessary. Breakfast $4; main courses $7–$20. MC, V. Wed–Mon 10am–10pm. Bus: 21.

Cielito Lindo *Value* MEXICAN   One of the most likable things about this restaurant is the way it retains low prices and an utter lack of pretension, despite the expensive Condado real estate that surrounds it. Something about it might remind you of a low-slung house in Puebla, Mexico, home of owner Jaime Pandal, who maintains a vigilant position from a perch at the cash register. Walls are outfitted with an intriguing mix of Mexican arts and crafts and ads for popular tequilas and beer. None of the selections has changed since the restaurant was founded, a policy that long-term clients find reassuring. The place is mobbed, especially on weekends, with those looking for heaping portions of well-prepared, standardized Mexican food. Examples include fajitas of steak or chicken; strips of filet steak sautéed with green peppers and onions, covered with tomatoes and spicy gravy; enchiladas of chicken or cheese, covered with cheese and served with sour cream; and several kinds of tacos.

Av. Magdalena 1108. ℭ 787/723-5597. Reservations recommended for dinner. Main courses $8–$17. AE, MC, V. Mon–Sat 11am–10:30pm. Bus: B21 or C10.

Via Appia *G* PIZZA/ITALIAN   A favorite of *Sanjuaneros* visiting Condado for the day, Via Appia offers food that's sometimes praiseworthy. Its pizzas are the best in the neighborhood. The chef's signature pizza, Via Appia, is a savory pie made with sausages, onions, mushrooms, pepperoni, green peppers, cheese, and spices. Vegetarians also have a pizza to call their own (made with whole-wheat dough, eggplant, mushrooms, green peppers, onions, tomatoes, and cheese). There's even a pizza with meatballs. Savory pasta dishes, including baked ziti, lasagna, and spaghetti, are also prepared with several of your favorite sauces. All of this can be washed down with sangria. During the day, freshly made salads and sandwiches are also available.

Av. Ashford 1350. ℭ 787/725-8711. Pizza and main courses $9–$16. AE, MC, V. Mon–Fri 11am–11pm; Sat–Sun 11am–midnight. Bus: A5.

5 Miramar

Augusto's Cuisine ★★★ FRENCH/INTERNATIONAL   With its European flair, this is one of the most elegant and glamorous restaurants in Puerto Rico. Austrian-born owner/chef Augusto Schreiner, assisted by a partly French-born staff, operates from a gray-and-green dining room set on the lobby level of a 15-story hotel in Miramar. Menu items are concocted from strictly fresh ingredients, including such dishes as lobster risotto; rack of lamb with aromatic herbs and fresh garlic; an oft-changing cream-based soup of the day (one of the best is corn and fresh oyster soup); and a succulent version of medallions of veal Rossini style, prepared with foie gras and Madeira sauce. The wine list is one of the most extensive on the island.

In the Hotel Excelsior, Av. Ponce de León 801. ✆ **787/725-7700.** Reservations recommended. Main courses $24–$36. AE, MC, V. Tues–Fri noon–3pm; Tues–Sat 7–9:30pm. Bus: B1 or A5.

Chayote's ★ PUERTO RICAN/INTERNATIONAL   The cuisine of this restaurant is among the most innovative in San Juan. It draws local business leaders, government officials, and celebs like Sylvester Stallone and Melanie Griffith. It's an artsy, modern, basement-level bistro in a surprisingly obscure hotel (the Olimpo). The restaurant changes its menu every three months, but you might find appetizers like a yucca turnover stuffed with crabmeat and served with mango and papaya chutney, or ripe plantain stuffed with chicken and served with fresh tomato sauce. For a main dish, you might try red snapper filet with citrus vinaigrette made of passion fruit, orange, and lemon. An exotic touch appears in the pork filet seasoned with dried fruits and spices in tamarind sauce and served with green banana and taro root timbale. To finish off your meal, there's nothing better than the mango flan served with macerated strawberries.

In the Olimpo Hotel, Av. Miramar 603. ✆ **787/722-9385.** Reservations recommended. Main courses $21–$28. AE, MC, V. Tues–Fri noon–2:30pm; Tues–Sat 7–10:30pm. Bus: B5.

6 Santurce & Ocean Park

VERY EXPENSIVE

Pikayo ★★★ PUERTO RICAN/CAJUN   This is an ideal place to go for the new generation of Puerto Rican cookery, with a touch of Cajun thrown in for spice and zest. This place not only keeps up with the latest culinary trends, but it often sets them, thanks to the inspired guidance of owner and celebrity chef Wilo Benet. Formal but not stuffy, and winner of more culinary awards than virtually any other restaurant in Puerto Rico, Pikayo is a specialist in the criolla cuisine of the colonial age, emphasizing the Spanish, Indian, and African elements in its unusual recipes. Appetizers include a dazzling array of taste explosions: Try shrimp spring rolls with peanut sofrito sauce; crab cake with aioli; or perhaps a ripe plantain, goat cheese, and onion tart. Main course delights feature charred rare yellowfin tuna with onion *escabeche* and red snapper filet with sweet potato purée served with foie gras butter. Our favorite remains the grilled shrimp with polenta and barbecue sauce made with guava.

Museum of Art of Puerto Rico, Av. José de Diego 299. © 787/721-6194. Reservations recommended. Main courses $29–$34; fixed-price menus $65. AE, DC, MC, V. Tues–Sun noon–3pm; Tues–Sat 6–11pm. Closed 2 weeks in Dec–Jan. Bus: M2, A7, or T1.

EXPENSIVE

Pamela's ℛ CARIBBEAN FUSION   A sense of cachet and style is very pronounced at this restaurant, a fact that's somewhat surprising considering its out-of-the-way location. Part of its allure derives from a sophisticated blend of Caribbean cuisines that combines local ingredients with Puerto Rican flair and a sense of New York style. Menu items include a salad that marries vine-ripened and oven-roasted tomatoes, each drizzled with a roasted-garlic–and-cilantro vinaigrette; club sandwiches stuffed with barbecued shrimp and cilantro-flavored mayonnaise; plantain-encrusted crab cakes with a spicy tomato-herb emulsion; and grilled island-spiced pork loin served with guava glaze and fresh local fruits. Beer and any of a wide array of party-colored drinks go well with this food.

In the Número 1 Guest House, Calle Santa Ana 1, Ocean Park. © 787/726-5010. Reservations recommended. Sandwiches and salads at lunch $10–$14; main course platters $20–$29. AE, MC, V. Daily noon–3pm and 7–10:30pm. Bus: A5.

INEXPENSIVE

Dunbar's INTERNATIONAL   Sprawling over at least five distinctly different dining and drinking areas, this is the busiest, most active, and most legendary bar and pub in Ocean Park. Painted an arresting shade of tangerine, it was established in 1982. The best way to navigate the labyrinth of Dunbar's is to wander through its various spaces: A large-screen TV room on the second floor attracts a macho, mostly North American crowd; a ground-floor pool room appeals to a deceptively affluent crowd of Spanish-speaking lawyers and doctors; and the various bars and cubbyholes ripple with possibilities for making friends or influencing your romantic destiny. Well-prepared menu items, each conceived by California-born veteran chef Trent Eichler, pour out of the busy kitchens. Examples include thick sandwiches (Spanish chorizo sausage with roasted peppers is an ongoing favorite), omelets, pastas, and juicy steaks. French fries are made from vitamin-rich yams and conventional potatoes. Favorite drinks include (what else?) Sex on the Beach and lots of margaritas. Dunbar's was named, incidentally, after a particularly eccentric character in Joseph Heller's *Catch-22*.

Av. McLeary 1954. ℂ **787/728-2920.** Reservations required Fri and Sun. Burgers and sandwiches $8.50–$13; main courses $11–$24. AE, DC, MC, V. Mon–Thurs 11:30am–midnight; Fri 11:30am–1am; Sat 5pm–1am; Sun 10am–2pm. Bus: A5 or A7.

7 Near Ocean Park

La Casita Blanca ✫ *(Finds)* CREOLE/PUERTO RICAN   Island politicians are said to have the best noses for good home cooking. We don't know if that is true or not, but one of their favorite places is this eatery. Governors or governor wannabes also come here to order excellent regional fare. This is a converted family home that opened its door to diners in the mid-1980s, and it's been a favorite of locals from all walks of Puerto Rican society ever since. In a popular barrio, it is off the tourist trail and best reached by taxi. You'll need to make a reservation for lunch but should have no trouble finding a table at dinner. The traditional Creole menu includes such delights as *guisado y arroz con gandule* (beef stew with rice and small beans), or *bacalao* (salt codfish with yucca). Guaranteed to put hair on your chest is *patita* (pigs' trotters in a Creole sauce). Veal with sautéed onions is popular, as is grilled red snapper or the chicken fricassee. A typical chicken asopao, a soupy rice stew, is also served. Fried plantains, rice, and beans come with most dishes.

Calle Tapía 351. ℂ **787/726-5501.** Reservations recommended at lunch. Main courses $7–$17; Sun buffet $10–$12. MC, V. Mon–Thurs 11:30am–7pm; Fri–Sat 11:30am–10pm; Sun noon–5pm. Bus: C11.

8 Isla Verde

VERY EXPENSIVE

La Piccola Fontana ✫✫✫ NORTHERN ITALIAN   Right off the luxurious Palm Court in the Wyndham El San Juan Hotel, this restaurant takes classic northern Italian cuisine seriously and delivers plate after plate of delectable food nightly. From its white linen to its classically formal service, it enjoys a fine reputation. The food is straightforward, generous, and extremely well prepared. You'll dine in one of two neo-Palladian rooms whose wall frescoes depict Italy's ruins and landscapes. Menu items range from the appealingly simple—such as grilled filets of fish or grilled veal chops—to more elaborate dishes—such as *tortellini San Daniele,* made with veal, prosciutto, cream, and sage; and *linguine scogliere,* with shrimp, clams, and other seafood. Grilled medallions of filet mignon are served with braised arugula, Parmesan cheese, and balsamic vinegar.

In Wyndham El San Juan Hotel & Casino, Av. Isla Verde 6063. ⓒ **787/791-0966.** Reservations required. Main courses $29–$40. AE, DC, MC, V. Daily 6–11pm. Bus: M7.

The Vineyard Room ⓖⓖⓖ CALIFORNIA/MEDITERRANEAN Within the realm of haute cuisine served with impeccable European credentials, this is the finest restaurant in San Juan. The Vineyard Room duplicates the gourmet citadels of Italy and France more accurately than any other restaurant in Puerto Rico, thanks to a staff of culinary luminaries spearheaded by Philippe Trosch, a prize catch that Ritz-Carlton worked hard to get. The waitstaff is the best trained in Puerto Rico. The wine-tasting menus, either four or five courses, are the best on the island. The wine list is superb, with both whites and reds from the Continent, as well as a strong emphasis on California wines. For the exotic, there are bottles from Chile, South Africa, and Australia. You can select innovative appetizers like potato cannelloni filled with Caribbean lobster risotto, or a summer salad of cavallion melon, serrano ham, mozzarella, and olive pesto with ciabatta toast. The main courses are equally appealing: Try Nantucket sea bass with barley tapenade and black olive sabayon, or apple-smoked rabbit with cannellini bean mash. You might precede (or end) an experience here at the bar, where the dark paneling and deep leather seats emulate an Edward-ian-era men's club in London.

In the Ritz-Carlton San Juan Hotel, Spa & Casino, 6961 State Rd. 187, Isla Verde, Carolina. ⓒ **787/253-1700.** Reservations required. Main courses $34–$37. Fixed-price menus $45, $55, $65, $75. AE, DC, MC, V. Daily 6–10pm. Bus: M7.

EXPENSIVE
Back Street Hong Kong ⓖ MANDARIN/SZECHUANHU-NAN To reach this restaurant, you head down a re-creation of a backwater street in Hong Kong—disassembled from its original home at the 1964 New York World's Fair, and rebuilt here with its original design intact. A few steps later, you enter one of the best Chinese restaurants in the Caribbean, serving consistently good

Isla Verde Dining

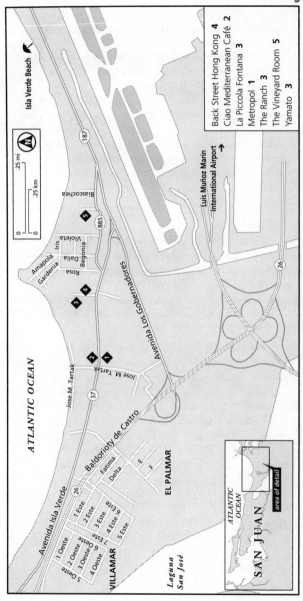

Back Street Hong Kong **4**
Ciao Mediterranean Café **2**
La Piccola Fontana **3**
Metropol **1**
The Ranch **3**
The Vineyard Room **5**
Yamato **3**

(Kids) **Family-Friendly Restaurants**

Palmera (p. 92) The Sunday brunch here—which is half price for children—is an all-you-can-eat buffet. There's even a clown on hand to keep the kids entertained.

Hard Rock Cafe (p. 91) The local branch of this international chain is a sure-fire hit with kids. The burgers are pretty good.

Butterfly People Café (p. 90) Children love eating lunch in this fantasy world of mounted butterflies. A favorite drink is the Fantasia—a frappé made from seven fresh fruits.

food, filled with fragrance and flavor. Beneath a soaring redwood ceiling, you can enjoy pineapple fried rice served in a pineapple, scallops with orange sauce, Szechuan beef with chicken, or Dragon and Phoenix (lobster with shrimp).

In Wyndham El San Juan Hotel & Casino, Av. Isla Verde 6063. ℂ **787/791-1000,** ext. 1758. Reservations recommended. Main courses $18–$29. AE, MC, V. Mon–Sat 5pm–midnight; Sun 1pm–midnight. Bus: M7.

Yamato ℛ JAPANESE The artfully simple decor at Yamato shows the kind of modern urban minimalism that you might expect in an upscale California restaurant. Separate sections offer conventional seating at tables; at a countertop within view of a sushi display; or at seats around a hot grill where chefs shake, rattle, and sizzle their way through a fast but elaborate cooking ritual. Many visitors include at least some sushi with an entree such as beef sashimi with tataki sauce, shrimp tempura with noodle soup, filet mignon or chicken with shrimp or scallops, or several kinds of rice and noodle dishes.

In Wyndham El San Juan Hotel & Casino, Av. Isla Verde 6063. ℂ **787/791-1000.** Reservations recommended. Sushi $2.25–$3 per piece; sushi and teppanyaki dinners $24–$40. AE, MC, V. Daily 6pm–midnight. Bus: M7.

MODERATE
The Ranch AMERICAN/STEAK When the very posh Wyndham El San Juan Hotel carved out a space for this irreverent, tongue-in-cheek eatery on its top (10th) floor, it was viewed as a radical departure from an otherwise grand collection of in-house restaurants. The result is likely to make you smile, especially if you

have roots anywhere west of Ohio. You'll be greeted with a hearty "Howdy, partner" and the jangling of spurs from a crew of denim-clad cowboys as you enter a replica of a corral in the North American West. Banquettes and barstools are upholstered in faux cowhide; the decor is appropriately macho and rough-textured, and even the cowgirls on duty are likely to lasso anyone they find particularly appealing. The cowboys sing as they serve your steaks, barbecued ribs, country-fried steaks, Tex-Mex fajitas, and enchiladas. Food that's a bit less beefy includes seared red snapper with a cilantro-laced pico de gallo sauce. Especially succulent are soft-shell crabs layered in a pyramid with blue and yellow tortillas. And if you want to buy a souvenir pair of cowboy spurs, you'll find an intriguing collection of western accessories and uniforms for sale outside. Consider beginning your meal with any of 20 kinds of tequila cocktails at the Tequila Bar, which lies a few steps away, on the same floor.

In Wyndham El San Juan Hotel & Casino, Av. Isla Verde 6063. ℃ **787/791-1000.** Reservations recommended at dinner Fri–Sat, otherwise not necessary. Main courses $16–$34. AE, DC, DISC, MC, V. Sun–Thurs 5:30–11pm; Fri–Sat 5:30pm–midnight. Bus: M7.

INEXPENSIVE

Ciao Mediterranean Café ✸✸ 🄺𝒾𝒹𝓈 MEDITERRANEAN   This is the most charming restaurant in Isla Verde, and it is one of our enduring favorites. It's draped with bougainvillea and set directly on the sands, attracting both hotel guests and locals wandering in barefoot from the beach. The visual centerpiece is an open-air kitchen set within an oval-shaped bar. A crew of cheerfully animated chefs mingle good culinary technique with Latino theatricality.

Pizzas and pastas are popular here, and even more appealing are such dishes as seafood salad, wherein shrimp, scallops, calamari, peppers, onions, and lime juice create something you might expect in the south of Italy. *Kalamarakia tiganita* (Greek-style squid), consisting of battered and deep-fried squid served with ratatouille and spicy marinara sauce; rack of lamb with ratatouille, polenta, and Provençal herbs; and a mixed grill of seafood are evocative of what you'd expect in Marseilles, thanks to the roe-enhanced aioli and couscous. Compared to most of the restaurants around here, this cafe serves lighter fare that kids go for, especially in its selection of pizzas and pastas. The desserts are also some of the most luscious at Isla Verde, especially the ice cream.

Inter-Continental San Juan Grand Resort & Casino, Av. Isla Grande 187. ℃ **787/ 791-5000.** Reservations recommended for dinner. Breakfast $5–$8; pizzas and salads $8–$17; main courses $16–$25. AE, MC, V. Daily 6:30am–10pm. Bus: M7.

Metropol CUBAN/PUERTO RICAN/INTERNATIONAL
This is part of a restaurant chain known for serving the island's best
Cuban food, although the chefs prepare a much wider range of
dishes. Metropol is the happiest blend of Cuban and Puerto Rican
cuisine we've ever had. The black-bean soup is among the island's
finest, served in the classic Havana style with a side dish of rice and
chopped onions. Endless garlic bread accompanies most dinners,
including Cornish game hen stuffed with Cuban rice and beans or
perhaps marinated steak topped with a fried egg (reportedly Castro's
favorite). Smoked chicken and chicken fried steak are also heartily
recommended; portions are huge. Plantains, yucca, and all that
good stuff accompany most dishes. Finish with a choice of thin or
firm custard. Most dishes are at the low end of the price scale.

Av. Isla Verde. ℭ **787/791-4046.** Main courses $7–$29. AE, MC, V. Daily
11:30am–10:30pm. Bus: C41, B42, or A5.

6

Exploring San Juan

The Spanish began to settle in the area now known as Old San Juan around 1521. At the outset, the city was called Puerto Rico ("Rich Port"), and the whole island was known as San Juan.

The streets are narrow and teeming with traffic, but a walk through Old San Juan—in Spanish, *El Viejo San Juan*—is like a stroll through 5 centuries of history. You can do it in less than a day. In this historic 7-square-block area of the western side of the city, you can see many of Puerto Rico's chief sightseeing attractions and do some shopping along the way.

On the other hand, you might want to plop down on the sand with a drink or get outside and play. "Diving, Fishing, Tennis & Other Outdoor Pursuits," later in this chapter, describes the beaches and sports in the San Juan area.

1 Seeing the Sights

SUGGESTED ITINERARIES

In case you would like to drag yourself away from the beach, here are some suggestions for how to see San Juan.

If You Have 1 Day

To make the most of a short stay, head straight for Old San Juan for an afternoon of sightseeing and shopping. Definitely schedule a visit to El Morro Fortress. Try to spend 2 hours at Condado Beach. Enjoy a Puerto Rican dinner at a local restaurant, listen to some salsa music, and enjoy a rum punch before retiring for the night.

If You Have 2 Days

On your first day, spend the morning shopping and sightseeing in Old San Juan. Schedule visits to El Morro and San Juan Cathedral, and then relax on Condado Beach for the rest of the day. Enjoy a Puerto Rican dinner and some local music before retiring.

On your second day, spend the morning exploring El Yunque rain forest, a lush 28,000-acre site east of San Juan.

3 hours at nearby Luquillo Beach, the finest
o Rico. Buy lunch from an open-air kiosk.
San Juan for the evening, and attend either a folk-
culture show (if available) or a Las Vegas–style revue. Visit the
casinos for some action before retiring.

FORTS

Castillo de San Felipe del Morro *(Kids)* Called "El Morro,"
this fort stands on a rocky promontory dominating the entrance to
San Juan Bay. Constructed in 1540, the original fort was a round
tower, which can still be seen deep inside the lower levels of the cas-
tle. More walls and cannon-firing positions were added, and by
1787, the fortification attained the complex design you see today.
This fortress was attacked repeatedly by both the English and the
Dutch.

The U.S. National Park Service protects the fortifications of Old
San Juan, which have been declared a World Heritage Site by the
United Nations. With some of the most dramatic views in the
Caribbean, you'll find El Morro an intriguing labyrinth of dun-
geons, barracks, vaults, lookouts, and ramps. Historical and back-
ground information is provided in a video in English and Spanish.
The nearest parking is the underground facility beneath the Quin-
centennial Plaza at the Ballajá barracks (Cuartel de Ballajá) on Calle
Norzagaray. Sometimes park rangers lead hour-long tours for free,
although you can also visit on your own. With the purchase of a
ticket here, you don't have to pay the admission for Fort San
Cristóbal (see below) if you visit during the same day.

At the end of Calle Norzagaray. ℂ 787/729-6960. Admission $2 adults, $1 ages
13–17, free for children 12 and under. Daily 9am–5pm. Bus: A5, B21, or B40.

Fort San Cristóbal This huge fortress, begun in 1634 and
reengineered in the 1770s, is one of the largest ever built in the
Americas by Spain. Its walls rise more than 150 feet above the sea—
a marvel of military engineering. San Cristóbal protected San Juan
against attackers coming by land as a partner to El Morro, to which
it is linked by a half-mile (1km) of monumental walls and bastions
filled with cannon-firing positions. A complex system of tunnels
and dry moats connects the center of San Cristóbal to its "out-
works," defensive elements arranged layer after layer over a 27-acre
site. You'll get the idea if you look at the scale model on display. Like
El Morro, the fort is administered and maintained by the National
Park Service. Be sure to see the Garita del Diablo (the Devil's Sen-
try Box), one of the oldest parts of San Cristóbal's defenses, and

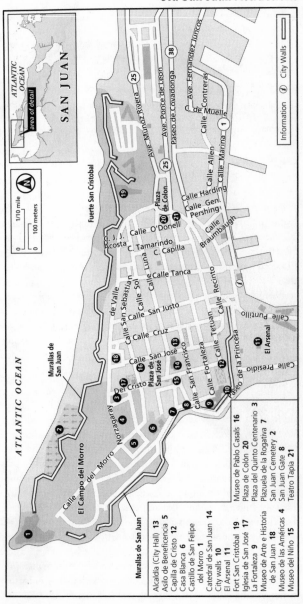

Old San Juan Attractions

ATLANTIC OCEAN

ATLANTIC OCEAN

SAN JUAN

area of detail

Muralles de San Juan

Fuerte San Cristóbal

1/10 mile

100 meters

N

El Campo del Morro

Calle del Campo del Morro

Calle del Morro

Norzagaray

Del Cristo

de Valle

Calle San Sebastián

Calle Sol

Calle Luna

C. J. J. Acosta

C. Tamarindo

C. Capilla

Calle O'Donell

Plaza de Colón

Calle Harding

Calle Gen. Pershing

Calle Allen

Calle Contreras

Calle Marina

C. de Muelle

Ave. Fernández Juncos

Ave. Ponce de León

Ave. Muñoz Rivera

Paseo de Covadonga

Calle Braumbaugh

Calle Tanca

Calle San Justo

Calle Cruz

Calle de San José

Plaza de San José

Calle San Francisco

Calle Recinto

Calle Tetuán

Calle Fortaleza

Calle Presidio

Calle Puntilla

El Arsenal

Paseo de la Princesa

Calle San José

Muralles de San Juan

38

25

25

1

Alcaldía (City Hall) **13**
Asilo de Beneficencia **5**
Capilla de Cristo **12**
Casa Blanca **6**
Castillo de San Felipe del Morro **1**
Catedral de San Juan **14**
City walls **10**
El Arsenal **11**
Fort San Cristóbal **19**
Iglesia de San José **17**
La Fortaleza **9**
Museo de Arte e Historia de San Juan **18**
Museo de las Américas **4**
Museo del Niño **15**
Museo de Pablo Casals **16**
Plaza de Colón **20**
Plaza del Quinto Centenario **3**
Plazuela de la Rogativa **7**
San Juan Cemetery **2**
San Juan Gate **8**
Teatro Tapia **21**

Information ⓘ   City Walls

famous in Puerto Rican legend. The devil himself, it is said, would snatch away sentinels at this lonely post at the edge of the sea. In 1898 the first shots of the Spanish-American War in Puerto Rico were fired by cannons on top of San Cristóbal during an artillery duel with a U.S. Navy fleet. Sometimes park rangers lead hour-long tours for free, and you can also visit on your own.

In the northeast corner of Old San Juan (uphill from Plaza de Colón on Calle Norzagaray). 𝄐 **787/729-6960.** Admission $2 adults, $1 ages 13–17, free for children 12 and under. Daily 9am–5pm. Bus: A5, B21, or B40; then the free trolley from Covadonga station to the top of the hill.

CHURCHES

Capilla de Cristo   Cristo Chapel was built to commemorate what legend says was a miracle. In 1753 a young rider lost control of his horse in a race down this very street during the fiesta of St. John's Day and plunged over the precipice. Moved by the accident, the secretary of the city, Don Mateo Pratts, invoked Christ to save the youth, and he had the chapel built when his prayers were answered. Today it's a landmark in the old city and one of its best-known historical monuments. The chapel's gold and silver altar can be seen through its glass doors. Because the chapel is open only 1 day a week, most visitors have to settle for a view of its exterior.

Calle del Cristo (directly west of Paseo de la Princesa). 𝄐 **787/722-0861.** Free admission. Tues 10am–2pm. Bus: Old Town trolley.

Catedral de San Juan   This, the spiritual and architectural centerpiece of Old San Juan, as you see it in its present form, was begun in 1540 as a replacement for a thatch-roofed chapel that was blown apart by a hurricane in 1529. Chronically hampered by a lack of funds and a recurring series of military and weather-derived disasters, it slowly evolved into the gracefully vaulted, Gothic-inspired structure you see today. Among the many disasters to hit this cathedral are the following: In 1598 the Earl of Cumberland led the British Navy in a looting spree, and in 1615 a hurricane blew away its roof. In 1908 the body of Ponce de León was disinterred from the nearby Iglesia de San José and placed in a marble tomb near the transept, where it remains today. The cathedral also contains the wax-covered mummy of St. Pio, a Roman martyr persecuted and killed for his Christian faith. The mummy has been encased in a glass box ever since it was placed here in 1862. To the right of the mummy is a bizarre wooden replica of Mary with four swords stuck in her bosom. After all the looting and destruction over the centuries, the cathedral's great treasures, including gold and silver, are long gone, although many beautiful stained-glass windows remain. The cathedral faces Plaza de las Monjas (the Nuns' Square), a shady spot where you can rest.

Calle del Cristo 153 (at Caleta San Juan). ℂ 787/722-0861. Free admission. Daily 8:30am–4pm. Bus: Old Town trolley.

Iglesia de San José   Initial plans for this church were drawn in 1523, and Dominican friars supervised its construction in 1532. Both the church and its monastery were closed by decree in 1838, and the property was confiscated by the royal treasury. Later, the Crown turned the convent into a military barracks. The Jesuits restored the badly damaged church. This was the place of worship for Ponce de León's descendants, who are buried here, under the family's coat of arms. The conquistador, killed by a poisoned arrow in Florida, was interred here until his removal to the Catedral de San Juan in 1908.

Although it was badly looted, the church still has some treasures, including *Christ of the Ponces,* a carved crucifix presented to Ponce de León, four oils by José Campeche, and two large works by Francisco Oller. Campeche was the leading Puerto Rican painter of the 18th century, and Oller was Puerto Rico's stellar artist of the late 19th and early 20th centuries. Many miracles have been attributed to a painting in the **Chapel of Belém,** a 15th-century Flemish work called *Virgin of Bethlehem.*

Plaza de San José, Calle del Cristo. ℂ 787/725-7501. Free admission. Church and Chapel of Belém, Mon–Wed and Fri 7am–3pm; Sat 8am–1pm. Bus: Old Town trolley.

MUSEUMS
Many of the museums in Old San Juan close for lunch between 11:45am and 2pm, so schedule your activities accordingly if you intend to museum-hop.

Museo de Arte 𝒜𝒜   Puerto Rico's most important gallery, which opened in 2000 and was constructed at a cost of $55 million, is a state-of-the-art showcase for the island nation's rich cultural heritage, as reflected mainly through its painters. Housed in a former city hospital in Santurce, the museum features both a permanent collection and temporary exhibitions. Prominent local artists are the star—for example, Francisco Oller (1833–1917), who brought a touch of Cézanne or Camille Pissarro to Puerto Rico (Oller actually studied in France with both of these Impressionists). Another leading star of the permanent collection is José Campeche, a late-18th-century classical painter. The museum is like a living textbook of

Puerto Rico, beginning with its early development and going on to showcase camp aspects, such as the poster art created here in the mid–20th century. All the important modern island artists are also presented, including the best known, the late Angel Botello, and also such contemporaries as Rafael Tufiño and Arnaldo Roche Rabell.

299 Av. José de Diego, Santurce. ℭ 787/977-6277. Admission $5 adults, $3 children under age 12. Tues and Thurs–Sat 10am–5pm; Wed 10am–8pm; Sun 11am–6pm. Bus: A5.

Museo de Arte e Historia de San Juan   Located in a Spanish colonial building at the corner of Calle MacArthur, this cultural center was the city's main marketplace in the mid–19th century. Local art is displayed in the east and west galleries, and audiovisual materials reveal the history of the city. Sometimes major cultural events are staged in the museum's large courtyard. English- and Spanish-language audiovisual shows are presented Monday through Friday every hour on the hour from 9am to 4pm.

Calle Norzagaray 150. ℭ 787/724-1875. Free admission. Tues–Sun 9am–4pm. Bus: B21 to Old San Juan terminal; then a trolley from the terminal to the museum.

Museo de las Américas ⊛   This museum showcases the artisans of North, South, and Central America, featuring everything from carved figureheads from New England whaling ships to dugout canoes carved by Carib Indians in Dominica. It is unique in Puerto Rico and well worth a visit. Also on display is a changing collection of paintings by artists from throughout the Spanish-speaking world, some of which are for sale, and a permanent collection called "Puerto Rican *Santos*," donated by Dr. Ricardo Alegría.

Cuartel de Ballajá. ℭ 787/724-5052. Free admission. Tues–Sun 10am–4pm. Bus: Old Town trolley.

Museo de Pablo Casals   This museum is devoted to the memorabilia left to the people of Puerto Rico by the musician Pablo Casals. The maestro's cello is here, along with a library of videotapes (which can be played upon request) of some of his festival concerts. This small 18th-century house also contains manuscripts and photographs of Casals. The annual Casals Festival draws worldwide interest and internationally known performing artists; it's held during the first 2 weeks of June.

Plaza San José, Calle San Sebastián 101. ℭ 787/723-9185. Admission $1 adults, 50¢ children. Tues–Sat 9:30am–5pm. Bus: Old Town trolley.

HISTORIC SIGHTS

In addition to the forts and churches listed above, you might want to see the sites described below.

San Juan Gate, Calle San Francisco and Calle Recinto Oeste, built around 1635, just north of La Fortaleza, several blocks downhill from the cathedral, was the main point of entry into San Juan if you arrived by ship in the 17th and 18th centuries. The gate is the only one remaining of the several that once pierced the fortifications of the old walled city. For centuries it was closed at sundown to cut off access to the historic old town. Bus: B21.

Plazuela de la Rogativa, Caleta de las Monjas, is a little plaza with a statue of a bishop and three women, commemorating one of Puerto Rico's most famous legends. In 1797, from across San Juan Bay at Santurce, the British held the Old Town under siege. That same year they mysteriously sailed away. Later, the commander claimed he feared that the enemy was well prepared behind those walls; he apparently saw many lights and believed them to be reinforcements. Some people believe that those lights were torches carried by women in a *rogativa,* or religious procession, as they followed their bishop. Bus: T1.

The **city walls** around San Juan were built in 1630 to protect the town against both European invaders and Caribbean pirates. The city walls that remain today were once part of one of the most impregnable fortresses in the New World and even today are an engineering marvel. Their thickness averages 20 feet at the base and 12 feet at the top, with an average height of 40 feet. At their top, notice the balconied buildings that served for centuries as hospitals and also residences of the island's various governors. Between Fort San Cristóbal and El Morro, bastions were erected at frequent intervals. The walls come into view as you approach from San Cristóbal on your way to El Morro. Bus: Old Town trolley.

San Juan Cemetery, on Calle Norzagaray, officially opened in 1814 and has since been the final resting place for many prominent Puerto Rican families. The circular chapel, dedicated to Saint Magdalene of Pazzis, was built in the 1860s. Aficionados of old graveyards can wander among marble monuments, mausoleums, and statues, marvelous examples of Victorian funereal statuary. Because there are no trees, or any other form of shade here, it would be best not to go exploring in the noonday sun. In any case, be careful—the cemetery is often a venue for illegal drug deals and can be dangerous. Bus: Old Town trolley.

Alcaldía (City Hall)   The City Hall, with its double arcade flanked by two towers resembling Madrid's City Hall, was constructed in stages from 1604 to 1789. Still in use, this building today contains a tourist-information center downstairs plus a small art gallery on the first floor.

Calle San Francisco. ℂ **787/724-7171**, ext. 2391. Free admission. Mon–Fri 8am–4pm. Closed holidays. Bus: Old Town trolley.

Casa Blanca   Ponce de León never lived here, although construction of the house—built in 1521, 2 years after his death—is sometimes attributed to him. The work was ordered by his son-in-law, Juan García Troche. The parcel of land was given to Ponce de León as a reward for services rendered to the Crown. Descendants of the explorer lived in the house for about 2½ centuries, until the Spanish government took it over in 1779 for use as a residence for military commanders. The U.S. government also used it as a home for army commanders. On the first floor, the **Juan Ponce de León Museum** is furnished with antiques, paintings, and artifacts from the 16th through the 18th centuries. In back is a garden with spraying fountains, offering an intimate and verdant respite.

Calle San Sebastián 1. ℂ **787/724-5477**. Admission $2. Tues–Sat 9am–noon and 1–4:30pm. Bus: Old Town trolley.

El Arsenal   The Spaniards used a shallow craft to patrol the lagoons and mangroves in and around San Juan. Needing a base for these vessels, they constructed El Arsenal in the 19th century. It was at this base that they staged their last stand, flying the Spanish colors until the final Spaniard was removed in 1898, at the end of the Spanish-American War. Changing art exhibitions are held in the building's three galleries.

La Puntilla. ℂ **787/723-3068**. Free admission. Wed–Sun 8:30am–4:30pm. Bus: Old Town trolley.

La Fortaleza   The office and residence of the governor of Puerto Rico is the oldest executive mansion in continuous use in the Western Hemisphere, and it has served as the island's seat of government for more than 3 centuries. Its history goes back even further than that, to 1533, when construction began on a fortress to protect San Juan's Spanish settlers during raids by Carib tribesmen and pirates. The original medieval towers remain, but as the edifice was subsequently enlarged into a palace, other modes of architecture and ornamentation were also incorporated, including baroque, Gothic, neoclassical, and Arabian. La Fortaleza has been designated a national historic site by the U.S. government. Informal but proper attire is required.

Calle Fortaleza, overlooking San Juan Harbor. ✆ **787/721-7000**, ext. 2211. Free admission. 30-min. tours of the gardens and building (conducted in English and Spanish) given Mon–Fri, every hour 9am–3:30pm. Bus: Old Town trolley.

Teatro Tapía Standing across from the Plaza de Colón, this is one of the oldest theaters in the Western Hemisphere, built about 1832. In 1976 a restoration returned the theater to its original appearance. Much of Puerto Rican theater history is connected with the Tapía, named after the island's first prominent playwright, Alejandro Tapía y Rivera (1826–82). Various productions—some musical—are staged here throughout the year, representing a repertoire of drama, dance, and cultural events.

Av. Ponce de León. ✆ **787/721-0169**. Access limited to tickets holders at performances (see "San Juan After Dark," later in this chapter). Bus: B8 or B21.

HISTORIC SQUARES

In Old San Juan, **Plaza del Quinto Centenario (Quincentennial Plaza)** overlooks the Atlantic from atop the highest point in the city. A striking and symbolic feature of the plaza, which was constructed as part of the 1992/1993 celebration of the 500th anniversary of the discovery of the New World, is a sculpture that rises 40 feet from the plaza's top level. The monumental sculpture in black granite and ceramics symbolizes the earthen and clay roots of American history and is the work of Jaime Suarez, one of Puerto Rico's foremost artists. From its southern end, two needle-shaped columns point skyward to the North Star, the guiding light of explorers. Placed around the plaza are fountains, other columns, and sculpted steps that represent various historic periods in Puerto Rico's 500-year heritage.

Sweeping views extend from the plaza to El Morro Fortress at the headland of San Juan Bay and to the Dominican Convent and San José Church, a rare New World example of Gothic architecture. Asilo de Beneficencia, a former indigents' hospital dating from 1832, occupies a corner of El Morro's entrance and is now the home of the Institute of Puerto Rican Culture. Adjacent to the plaza is the Cuartel de Ballajá, built in the mid–19th century as the Spanish army headquarters and still the largest edifice in the Americas constructed by Spanish engineers; it houses the Museum of the Americas.

Centrally located, Quincentennial Plaza is one of modern Puerto Rico's respectful gestures to its colorful and lively history. It is a perfect introduction for visitors seeking to discover the many rich links with the past in Old San Juan.

Once named St. James Square, or Plaza Santiago, **Plaza de Colón** in the heart of San Juan's Old Town is bustling and busy, reached along the pedestrian mall of Calle Fortaleza. The square was renamed Plaza de Colón to honor the 400th anniversary of the explorer's so-called discovery of Puerto Rico. Of course, it is more politically correct today to say that Columbus explored or came upon an already inhabited island. He certainly didn't discover it. But when a statue here, perhaps the most famous on the island, was erected atop a high pedestal, it was clearly to honor Columbus, not to decry his legacy.

SIGHTSEEING TOURS

If you want to see more of the island but you don't want to rent a car or manage the inconveniences of public transportation, perhaps an organized tour is for you.

Castillo Sightseeing Tours & Travel Services, 2413 Calle Laurel, Punta La Marias, Santurce (𝄢 787/791-6195), maintains offices at some of the capital's best-known hotels, including the Caribe Hilton and San Juan Marriott Resort. Using six of their own air-conditioned buses, with access to others if demand warrants it, the company's tours include pickups and drop-offs at hotels as an added convenience.

One of the most popular half-day tours departs most days of the week between 8:30 and 9am, lasts 4 to 5 hours, and costs $35 per person. Leaving from San Juan, it tours along the northeastern part of the island to El Yunque. The company also offers a city tour of San Juan that departs daily around 1pm. The 4-hour trip costs $32 per person and includes a stop at the Bacardi Rum Factory. The company also operates full-day snorkeling tours to the reefs near the coast of a deserted island off Puerto Rico's eastern edge aboard one of two sail- and motor-driven catamarans. With lunch, snorkeling gear, and piña coladas included, the full-day (7:45am–5pm) excursion goes for $69 per person.

Few cities of the Caribbean lend themselves so gracefully to walking tours. You can embark on these on your own, stopping and shopping en route.

ESPECIALLY FOR KIDS

Puerto Rico is one of the most family-friendly islands in the Caribbean, and many hotels offer family discounts. Programs for children are also offered at a number of hotels, including day and night camp activities and babysitting services. Trained counselors at these camps supervise children as young as 3 in activities ranging from nature hikes to tennis lessons, coconut carving, and sand-sculpture contests.

Teenagers can learn to hip-hop dance Latino-style with special salsa and merengue lessons, learn conversational Spanish, indulge in watersports, take jeep excursions, or scuba-dive in some of the best diving locations in the world.

The best kiddies program is offered at **Wyndham El San Juan Hotel & Casino** (p. 80), where camp activities are presented to children between the ages of 5 and 13. Counselors design activities according to the interests of groups of up to 10 children. Kids Klub members receive a T-shirt, membership card, and three Sand Dollars for use in the game room or at a poolside restaurant. The daily fee of $28 includes lunch.

Museo del Niño (Children's Museum) *Kids*   In the late 1990s, the city of San Juan turned over one of the most desirable buildings in the colonial zone—a 300-year-old villa directly across from the city's cathedral—to a group of sociologists and student volunteers. Jointly, they created the only children's museum in Puerto Rico. Through interactive exhibits, children learn simple lessons, such as the benefits of brushing teeth or recycling aluminum cans, or the value of caring properly for pets. Staff members include lots of student volunteers who play either one-on-one or with small groups of children. Nothing here is terribly cerebral, and nothing will necessarily compel you to return. But it does provide a play experience that some children will remember for several weeks.

Calle del Cristo 150. ℂ **787/722-3791**. Admission $3. Tues–Thurs 9am–3:30pm; Fri 9am–5pm; Sat–Sun 12:30–5pm. Bus: Old Town trolley.

2 Diving, Fishing, Tennis & Other Outdoor Pursuits

Active vacationers have a wide choice of things to do in San Juan, from beaching to windsurfing. The beachside hotels, of course, offer lots of watersports activities (see the hotel listings in chapter 4).

THE BEACHES

Some public stretches of shoreline around San Juan are over-crowded, especially on Saturday and Sunday; others are practically deserted. If you find that secluded, hidden beach of your dreams, proceed with caution. On unguarded beaches you'll have no way to protect yourself or your valuables should you be approached by a robber or mugger, which has been known to happen. For more

The Cathedral of Rum

Called "the Cathedral of Rum," the **Bacardi Distillery** at Route 888, km 2.6 at Cataño (© **787/788-1500**), is the largest of its kind in the world. Reached by taking a 20-minute ferry ride across San Juan Bay (50¢ each way), the distillery produces 100,000 gallons of rum daily. Free 45-minute guided tours take place Monday through Saturday from 8:30am to 4:30pm. Complimentary rum drinks are offered at the beginning of the tour, and a gift shop sells a wide assortment of handsome items, from T-shirts to duffel bags. Naturally, you can purchase Bacardi rums here, at prices that are slightly more reasonable than those at home. Some rums available here are not sold on the U.S. mainland and make unusual gifts.

Upon entering the first floor, you'll get a glimpse of what rum production was like a century ago, including oak barrels used in the aging process and an old sugar-cane wagon. On the fifth floor you'll enter the Hall of Rum with a collection of beverages made by the corporation over a period of years. You'll then witness "the birth of rum"—the fermentation processes of molasses (it takes 100 gal. of molasses to produce one barrel of rum).

At the end of the tour, you'll visit the Bacardi Family Museum, documenting the family's history, and you can watch a short video about the bottling process. Afterward, you can stroll through the beautiful grounds overlooking Old San Juan.

information about the island's many beaches, call the **Department of Sports and Recreation** at © 787/728-5668.

All beaches on Puerto Rico, even those fronting the top hotels, are open to the public. Public bathing beaches are called *balnearios* and charge for parking and for use of facilities, such as lockers and showers. Public beaches shut down on Monday; if Monday is a holiday, the beaches are open for the holiday but close the next day. Beach hours are from 9am to 5pm in winter, to 6pm off-season. Major public beaches in the San Juan area have changing rooms and showers.

Famous with beach buffs since the 1920s, **Condado Beach** 🐾🐾 put San Juan on the map as a tourist resort. Backed up by high-rise hotels, it seems more like Miami Beach than any other beach in the Caribbean. From parasailing to sailing, all sorts of watersports can be booked at kiosks along the beach or at the activities desk of the hotels. There are also plenty of outdoor bars and restaurants. People-watching is a favorite sport along these golden strands.

A favorite of *Sanjuaneros* themselves, **Isla Verde Beach** ✿✿ is also ideal for swimming, and it, too, is lined with high-rise resorts a la Miami Beach. Many luxury condos are on this beachfront. Isla Verde has picnic tables, so you can pick up the makings of a lunch and make it a day at the beach. This strip is also good for snorkeling because of its calm, clear waters, and many kiosks will rent you equipment. Isla Verde Beach extends from the end of Ocean Park to the beginning of a section called Boca Cangrejos. The best beach at Isla Verde is at the Wyndham Hotel El San Juan. Most sections of this long strip have separate names, such as El Alambique, which is often the site of beach parties, and Punta El Medio, bordering the new Ritz-Carlton, also a great beach and very popular, even with the locals. If you go past the luxury hotels and expensive condos behind the Luís Muñoz Marín International Airport, you arrive at the major public beach at Isla Verde. Here you'll find parking, showers, fast-food joints, and watersports equipment. The sands here are whiter than those of the Condado, and they are lined with coconut palms, sea-grape trees, and even almond trees, all of which provide shade from the fierce noonday sun.

One of the most attractive beaches in the Greater San Juan area is **Ocean Park Beach** ✿✿, a mile of fine gold sand in a neighborhood east of Condado. This beach attracts both young people and a big gay crowd. Access to the beach at Ocean Park has been limited recently, but the best place to enter is from a section called El Ultimo Trolley. This area is ideal for volleyball, paddleball, and other games. The easternmost portion, known as Punta Las Marias, is best for windsurfing. The waters at Ocean Park are fine for swimming, although they can get rough at times.

Rivaling Condado and Isla Verde beaches, **Luquillo Beach** is the grandest in Puerto Rico and one of the most popular. It's 30 miles (48km) east of San Juan, near the town of Luquillo (see chapter 7).

SPORTS & OTHER OUTDOOR PURSUITS

BIKE RENTALS   Much favored by the dozens of holidaymakers pedaling up and down the Condado, **Condado Bicycles,** Av. Ashford 1024 (✆ **787/722-6288**), rents big-geared mountain bikes for $20 a day. Fortunately for the neighborhood's noise pollution, they don't rent mopeds or motor scooters. The best places to bike are along Avenida Ashford (in Condado), Calle Loiza (between Condado and Ocean Park), and Avenida Baldorioty de Castro (in Santurce). Other streets in this area may be too congested. Similarly, because of the traffic, biking in Old San Juan is not recommended.

DEEP-SEA FISHING 🐟 Deep-sea fishing is top-notch here. Allison tuna, white and blue marlin, sailfish, wahoo, dolphin (mahimahi), mackerel, and tarpon are some of the fish that can be caught in Puerto Rican waters, where 30 world records have been broken. Charter arrangements can be made through most major hotels and resorts.

Capt. Mike Benitez, who has chartered out of San Juan for more than 40 years, is one of the most qualified sport-fishing captains in the world. (Past clients include Jimmy Carter.) **Benitez Fishing Charters** can be contacted directly at P.O. Box 9066541, Puerto de Tierra, San Juan, PR 00906 (© **787/723-2292** until 6pm). The captain offers a 45-foot air-conditioned deluxe Hatteras called the *Sea Born*. Fishing tours for parties of up to six cost $490 for a half-day excursion and $850 for a full day, with beverages and all equipment included.

GOLF A 45-minute drive east from San Juan on the northeast coast takes you to Palmer and its 6,145-yard **Westin Rio Mar Golf Course** 🐟 (© **787/888-6000**). Inexperienced golfers prefer this course to the more challenging and more famous courses at Dorado (see chapter 7), even though trade winds can influence your game along the holes bordering the water, and occasional fairway flooding can present some unwanted obstacles. Greens fees are $160 for hotel guests, $185 for nonguests. A gallery of 100 iguanas also adds spice to your game at Rio Mar.

SCUBA DIVING In San Juan, the best outfitter is **Caribe Aquatic Adventures**, P.O. Box 9024278, San Juan Station, San Juan, PR 00902 (© **787/281-8858**), which operates a dive shop in the rear lobby of the Normandie Hotel that's open daily from 8am to 4pm. The company offers diving certification from both PADI and NAUI as part of 40-hour courses priced at $465 each. A resort course for first-time divers costs $100. Also offered are local daily dives in the waters close to San Juan, as well as the option of traveling farther afield into waters near the reefs of Puerto Rico's eastern shore. If time permits, we recommend a full-day dive experience; if time is limited, try one of the many worthy dive sites that lie closer to San Juan and can be experienced in a half day.

SNORKELING Snorkeling is better in the outlying portions of the island than in overcrowded San Juan. But if you don't have time to explore greater Puerto Rico, you'll find that most of the popular beaches, such as Luquillo and Isla Verde, have pretty good visibility and kiosks that rent equipment. Snorkeling equipment generally rents for $15. If you're on your own in the San Juan area, one of the best places is the San Juan Bay marina near the Caribe Hilton.

Watersports desks at the big San Juan hotels at Isla Verde and Condado can generally make arrangements for instruction and equipment rental and can also lead you to the best places for snorkeling, depending on where you are in the sprawling metropolis. If your hotel doesn't offer such services, you can contact **Caribe Aquatic Adventures** (see "Scuba Diving," above), which caters to both snorkelers and scuba divers. You can also rent equipment from **Caribbean School of Aquatics,** Taft No. 1, Suite 10F, San Juan (© **787/728-6606**).

WINDSURFING A favorite spot for windsurfing is the sheltered waters of the Condado Lagoon in San Juan. Throughout the island, many of the companies that feature snorkeling and scuba diving also offer windsurfing equipment and instruction, and dozens of hotels offer facilities on their own premises. Another good spot is at the Radisson Normandie Hotel, where **Caribe Aquatic Adventures** has its main branch (see "Scuba Diving," above). Board rentals cost $25 to $30 per hour; lessons cost $45.

3 Shopping

Because Puerto Rico is a U.S. commonwealth, U.S. citizens don't pay duty on items brought back to the mainland. And you can still find great bargains on Puerto Rico, where the competition among shopkeepers is fierce. Even though the U.S. Virgin Islands are duty-free, you can often find far lower prices on many items in San Juan than on St. Thomas.

The streets of Old Town, such as Calle San Francisco and Calle del Cristo, are the major venues for shopping. Malls in San Juan are generally open Monday through Saturday from 9am to 9pm, Sunday from 11am to 5pm. Regular stores in town are usually open Monday through Saturday from 9am to 6pm. In Old San Juan many stores are open on Sunday, too.

Native handicrafts can be good buys, including needlework, straw work, ceramics, hammocks, and papier-mâché fruits and vegetables, as well as paintings and sculptures by Puerto Rican artists. Among these, the carved wooden religious idols known as *santos* (saints) have been called Puerto Rico's greatest contribution to the plastic arts and are sought by collectors. For the best selection of santos, head for Galería Botello (see "Art," below), Olé, or Puerto Rican Arts & Crafts (see "Gifts & Handicrafts," later in this chapter).

Puerto Rico's biggest and most up-to-date shopping mall is **Plaza Las Américas,** in the financial district of Hato Rey, right off the Las Américas Expressway. This complex, with its fountains and modern architecture, has more than 200 mostly upscale shops. The variety of goods and prices is roughly comparable to that of large stateside malls.

Unless otherwise specified, the following stores can be reached via the Old Town trolley.

ART

Butterfly People   Butterfly People is a gallery and cafe (p. 90) in a handsomely restored building in Old San Juan. Butterflies, sold here in artfully arranged boxes, range from $20 for a single mounting to thousands of dollars for whole-wall murals. The butterflies are preserved and will last forever. The dimensional artwork is sold in limited editions and can be shipped worldwide. Most of these butterflies come from farms around the world, some of the most beautiful hailing from Indonesia, Malaysia, and New Guinea. Tucked away within the same premises is **Malula Antiques.** Specializing in tribal art from the Moroccan sub-Sahara and Syria, it contains a sometimes-startling collection of primitive and timeless crafts and accessories. Calle Fortaleza 152. ✆ **787/723-2432.**

Galería Botello   A contemporary Latin American art gallery, Galería Botello is a living tribute to the late Angel Botello, one of Puerto Rico's most outstanding artists. Born after the Spanish Civil War in a small village in Galicia, Spain, he fled to the Caribbean and spent 12 years in Haiti. His paintings and bronze sculptures, evocative of his colorful background, are done in a style uniquely his own. This galería is his former colonial mansion home, which he restored himself. Today it displays his paintings and sculptures, showcases the works of many outstanding local artists, and offers a large collection of Puerto Rican antique santos. Calle del Cristo 208. ✆ **787/723-2879.**

Galería Palomas   This and the also-recommended Galería Botello are the two leading art galleries of Puerto Rico. Here you can find works by some of the leading painters in Latin America. Prices range from $75 to $35,000, and exhibits are rotated every 2 to 3 weeks. The setting is a 17th-century colonial house. Of special note are works by such local artists as Homer, Moya, and Alicea. Calle del Cristo 207. ✆ 787/725-2660.

Sun 'n Sand   This is the best store in San Juan for Haitian art and artifacts. Its walls are covered with framed versions of primitive Haitian landscapes, portraits, crowd scenes, and whimsical visions of jungles where lions, tigers, parrots, and herons take on quasi-human personalities and forms. Most paintings range from $35 to $350, although you can usually bargain them down a bit. Look for the brightly painted wall hangings crafted from sheets of metal. Also look for satirical metal wall hangings, brightly painted, representing the *tap-taps* (battered public minivans and buses) of Port-au-Prince. They make amusing and whimsical souvenirs of a trip to the Caribbean. Calle Fortaleza 152. ✆ 787/722-1135.

BOOKS

Bell, Book & Candle   For travel guides, maps, and beach-reading material, head here. It is a large, general-interest bookstore that carries fiction and classics in both Spanish and English, plus a huge selection of postcards. Av. José de Diego 102, Santurce. ✆ 787/728-5000. Bus: A5.

Libreria Cronopios   This is the leading choice in the Old Town, with the largest selection of titles. It sells a number of books on Puerto Rican culture as well as good maps of the island. Calle San José 255. ✆ 787/724-1815.

CARNIVAL MASKS

La Calle   Every Puerto Rican knows that the best, and cheapest, place to buy brightly painted carnival masks (*caretas*) is in Ponce, where the tradition of making them from papier-mâché originated. But if you can't spare the time for a side excursion to Ponce, this store in Old San Juan stocks one of the most varied inventories of vegigantes in the Puerto Rican capital. Depending on their size and composition (some include coconut shells, gourds, and flashy metal trim), they range from $12 to $2,400 each. Side-by-side with the pagan-inspired masks, you'll find a well-chosen selection of paintings by talented local artists, priced from $250 to $2,000 each. Calle Fortaleza 105. ✆ 787/725-1306.

CIGARS

Club Jibarito   This is the retail outlet of a Puerto Rican–based manufacturer of genuinely excellent cigars. You can select from the Jibarito cigars that are proudly displayed within one of the best-designed humidors in town. Overall it's our favorite cigar emporium in San Juan, with a polite staff and lots and lots of class. 202 Calle Cristo. ✆ 787/724-7797.

CLOTHING & BEACHWEAR

Casa Marriot *Finds*   For more than 50 years, businessmen of San Juan have been coming here for a wide selection of mostly English, tropical-weight fabrics. For a suit, most North American men require from 3½ to 4 yards of fabric, priced from $13 to $110 a yard, plus another 2½ yards of lining, priced around $5 a yard. The helpful staff can direct you to any of several local tailors, who will charge from $250 to $350 to whip that fabric into a suit. Calle Tanca 255. ✆ 787/722-0444.

Mrs. and Miss Boutique   The most visible article available within this shop is "the magic dress," for $115. Crafted in Morocco of a silky-looking blend of rayon and cotton, it comes in 10 different colors or patterns and can be worn 11 different ways. (A saleswoman will show you how.) The shop also stocks sarongs for $10 and long dresses, sometimes from Indonesia, that begin at only $25. Calle Fortaleza 154. ✆ 787/724-8571.

Nono Maldonado   Named after its owner, a Puerto Rico–born designer who worked for many years as the fashion editor of *Esquire* magazine, this is one of the most fashionable and upscale haberdashers in the Caribbean. Selling both men's and women's clothing, it contains everything from socks to dinner jackets, as well as ready-to-wear versions of Maldonado's twice-a-year collections. Both ready-to-wear and couture are available here. Although this is the designer's main store (midway between the Condado Plaza and the Ramada Hotel), there is also a Maldonado boutique in Wyndham El San Juan Hotel in Isla Verde. Av. Ashford 1051. ✆ 787/721-0456. Bus: A7.

COFFEE & SPICES

Spicy Caribbee   This shop has the best selection of Puerto Rican coffee, which is gaining an increasingly good reputation among aficionados. Alto Grande is the grandest brand. Other favorite brands of Puerto Rican coffee are Café Crema, Café Rico, Rioja, and Yaucono—in that order. The shop also has Old Town's best array of hot spicy sauces of the Caribbean. Calle Cristo 154. ✆ 787/725-4690.

DEPARTMENT STORES

Marshalls   This store, part of the U.S. discount chain, is one of our favorite department stores in the whole Caribbean. Thousands of *Sanjuaneros* also consider it their favorite shopping expedition as well. A few dedicated born-to-shop advocates pop in virtually every day to see what new items have gone on sale. At Plaza de Armas, across from the City Hall, expect to see a massive array—at cut-rate prices—of designer clothes, housewares, home furnishings, and shoes, plus a variety of other merchandise. Calle Rafael Cordero 154. ℂ 787/722-3020.

GIFTS & HANDICRAFTS

Bared & Sons (Value)   Now in its fourth decade, this is the main outlet of a chain of at least 20 upper-bracket jewelry stores on Puerto Rico. It has a worthy inventory of gemstones, gold, diamonds, and wristwatches on the street level, which does a thriving business with cruise-ship passengers. But the real value of this store lies one floor up, where a monumental collection of porcelain and crystal is on display in claustrophobic proximity. It's a great source for hard-to-get and discontinued patterns (priced at around 20% less than at equivalent stateside outlets) from Christofle, Royal Doulton, Wedgwood, Limoges, Royal Copenhagen, Lalique, Lladró, Herend, Baccarat, and Daum. Calle Fortaleza 65 (at the corner of Calle San Justo). ℂ 787/724-4811.

Bóveda   This long, narrow space is crammed with exotic jewelry, clothing, greeting cards with images of life in Puerto Rico, some 100 handmade lamps, antiques, Mexican punched tin and glass, and Art Nouveau reproductions, among other items. Calle del Cristo 209. ℂ 787/725-0263.

Centro Nacional de Artes Populares y Artesanias   This store, a superb repository of native crafts, sells crafts of high-quality work. Centro Nacional scans the islands for artisans who still practice time-treasured crafts and do so with considerable skill. The prices aren't cheap, but the work merits the tab. At Calle del Cristo. ℂ 787/721-6866.

El Artesano   If your budget doesn't allow for an excursion to the Andes, head for this shop. You'll find Mexican and Peruvian icons of the Virgin Mary; charming depictions of fish and Latin American birds in terra cotta and brass; all kinds of woven goods; painted cupboards, chests, and boxes; and mirrors and Latin dolls. Calle Fortaleza 314. ℂ 787/721-6483.

Libreria y Tienda de Artesania del Instituto de Cultura Puertorriqueña   This store, next to the Convento de los Dominicos, has not only a collection of books on Puerto Rico, but a good display of crafts in the Old Town, including santos, Indian artifacts, carnival masks (many from Ponce), and baskets. All pieces are said to be made in Puerto Rico, rather than in places such as Taiwan, as is so often the case. Calle Norzagaray 98. ℰ 787/721-6866.

Olé   Browsing this store is a learning experience. Even the standard Panama hat takes on new dimensions. Woven from fine-textured *paja* grass and priced from $20 to $1,000, depending on the density of the weave, the hats are all created the same size, then blocked—by an employee on-site—to fit the shape of your head. Dig into this store's diverse inventory to discover a wealth of treasures—hand-beaten Chilean silver, Peruvian Christmas ornaments, Puerto Rican santos— almost all from Puerto Rico or Latin America. Calle Fortaleza 105. ℰ 787/724-2445.

Puerto Rican Arts & Crafts   Set in a 200-year-old colonial building, this unique store is one of the premier outlets on the island for authentic artifacts. Of particular interest are papier-mâché carnival masks from Ponce, whose grotesque and colorful features were originally conceived to chase away evil spirits. Taíno designs inspired by ancient petroglyphs are incorporated into most of the sterling silver jewelry sold here. There's an art gallery in back, with silk-screened serigraphs by local artists. The outlet has a gourmet Puerto Rican food section with items like coffee, rum, and hot sauces for sale. A related specialty of this well-respected store involves the exhibition and sale of modern replicas of the Spanish colonial tradition of santos, which are carved and sometimes polychromed representations of the Catholic saints and the infant Jesus. Priced from $44 to $225 each, and laboriously carved by artisans in private studios around the island, they're easy to pack in a suitcase because the largest one measures only 12 inches from halo to toe. Calle Fortaleza 204. ℰ 787/725-5596.

JEWELRY

Barrachina's   The birthplace, in 1963, of the piña colada (an honor co-claimed by the staff at the Caribe Hilton), Barrachina's is a favorite of cruise-ship passengers. It offers one of the largest selections of jewelry, perfume, cigars, and gifts in San Juan. There's a patio for drinks where you can order (what else?) a piña colada. There is also a Bacardi rum outlet (bottles cost less than stateside but cost the same as at the Bacardi distillery), a costume jewelry department, a gift shop, and a section for authentic silver jewelry, plus a restaurant. Calle Fortaleza 104 (between Calle del Cristo and Calle San José). ℰ 787/725-7912.

Gaston Bared Jewelry   This is an offshoot of the above-recommended Bared & Sons, but with a more contemporary inventory. This shop also has a branch at Calle Fortaleza 208 (same phone) that sells Murano crystal, Hummel and Lladró figurines, watches (including Omega, Seiko, and Tissot), and colored gemstones, such as amethysts, set into gold and silver settings. Calle Fortaleza 154 (at Calle San José). ✆ 787/722-2172.

Joyería Riviera   This emporium of 18-karat gold and diamonds is the island's leading jeweler. Adjacent to Plaza de Armas, the shop has an impeccable reputation. Its owner, Julio Abislaiman, stocks his store from such diamond centers as Antwerp, Tel Aviv, and New York. This is the major distributor of Rolex watches on Puerto Rico. Prices in the store range from $150 into the tens of thousands of dollars—at these prices, it's a good thing you can get "whatever you want," according to the owner. Calle La Cruz 205. ✆ 787/725-4000.

R. Kury   This is the factory outlet for the oldest jewelry factory on Puerto Rico, the Kury Company. Most of the output is shipped stateside. Don't expect a top-notch jeweler here: Many of the pieces are produced in endless repetition. But don't overlook this place for 14-karat-gold ornaments. Some of the designs are charming, and prices are about 20% less than those at retail stores on the U.S. mainland. Plaza los Muchachos, Calle Fortaleza 201. ✆ 787/724-3102.

LACE & LINENS

Linen House   This unpretentious store specializes in table linens, bed linens, and lace and has the island's best selection. Some of the most delicate pieces are expensive, but most are moderate in price. Inventories include embroidered shower curtains that sell for around $35 each, and lace doilies, bun warmers, place mats, and tablecloths that seamstresses took weeks to complete. Some astonishingly lovely items are available for as little as $30. The aluminum/pewter serving dishes have beautiful Spanish-colonial designs. Prices here are sometimes 40% lower than those on the North American mainland. Calle Fortaleza 250. ✆ 787/721-4219.

MALLS

El Convento Shopping Arcade   Some of the finest merchandise in Old Town is displayed in various shops at the El Convento hotel. Come here for a selection of eclectic jewelry, timepieces, fine china, luxury gift and home-furnishing items, cigars, tobacco, and other items. For example, at the Old City Cigar Emporium, a walk-in humidor contains a collection of the finest tobaccos in the

Caribbean. The Oggetti Outlet Store features several bargains in crystal, china, and gift items for the home, and the Oggetti Alessi Boutique carries the renowned Milanese designer line of colorful home accessories. Shop at Oggetti offers an exclusive collection of objets d'art, designer-crafted furnishings, and selected items from Tiffany. Calle Cristo 100. ✆ 787/723-2877.

4 San Juan After Dark

San Juan nightlife comes in all varieties. From the vibrant performing-arts scene to street-level salsa and the casinos, discos, and bars, there's plenty of entertainment available almost any evening.

As in a Spanish city, nightlife begins very late, especially on Friday and Saturday nights. Hang out until the late, late afternoon on the beach, have dinner around eight o'clock (nine would be even more fashionable), and then the night is yours. The true party animal will rock until the broad daylight.

Qué Pasa?, the official visitor's guide to Puerto Rico, lists cultural events, including music, dance, theater, film, and art exhibits. It's distributed free by the tourist office.

THE PERFORMING ARTS

Centro de Bellas Artes   In the heart of Santurce, the Performing Arts Center is a 6-minute taxi ride from most of the Condado hotels. It contains the Festival Hall, Drama Hall, and the Experimental Theater. Some of the events here will be of interest only to Spanish speakers; others attract an international audience. Av. Ponce de León 22. ✆ 787/724-4747, or 787/725-7334 for the ticket agent. Tickets $13–$65; 50% discounts for seniors. Bus: 1.

Teatro Tapía   Standing across from Plaza de Colón and built about 1832, this is one of the oldest theaters in the Western Hemisphere (see "Historic Sights," earlier in this chapter). Productions, some musical, are staged throughout the year and include drama, dances, and cultural events. You'll have to call the box office (open Mon–Fri 9am–6pm) for specific information. Av. Ponce de León. ✆ 787/721-0169. Tickets $25–$30, depending on the show. Bus: B8 or B21.

THE CLUB & MUSIC SCENE

Babylon   Modeled after an artist's rendition of the once-notorious city in Mesopotamia, this nightclub is designed in the form of a circle, with a central dance floor and a wraparound balcony where onlookers and voyeurs—a 25-to-45-year-old age group—can observe the activities on the floor below. As one patron put it,

"Here's where gringos can shake their bon-bons with San Juan's old guard." Equipped with one of the best sound systems in the Caribbean, its location within the most exciting hotel in San Juan allows guests the chance to visit the hotel's bars, its intricately decorated lobby, and its casino en route. Open Thursday through Saturday from 10pm to 3am. In Wyndham El San Juan Hotel & Casino, Av. Isla Verde 6063, Isla Verde. ℭ **787/791-1000**. Cover $10, free for residents of El San Juan Hotel. Bus: M7.

Club Laser   Set in the heart of the old town, this disco is especially crowded when cruise ships pull into town. Once inside, you can wander over the three floors of its historic premises, listening to whatever music happens to be hot in New York at the time, with lots of additional Latino merengue and salsa thrown in as well. Depending on the night, the age of the crowd varies, but in general it's the 20s, 30s, and even 40s set. Hours are usually Thursday through Sunday from 8pm to 4am. Calle del Cruz 251 (near the corner of Calle Fortaleza). ℭ **787/725-7581**. Cover $8–$10 (free cover for women after midnight on Sat). Bus: Old Town trolley.

Lupi's   You can hear some of the best Spanish rock at this Mexican pub and restaurant. It is a current hot spot, with typical South of the Border decoration and such familiar dishes as fajitas, nachos, and burritos. A wide range of people of all ages are attracted to the place, although after 10pm patrons in their 20s and 30s predominate. Live rock groups perform after 11pm. In addition to the nightly rock bands, Caribbean music is also played on Friday and karaoke on Sunday. Open daily from 11am to 2am. Carretera 187, km 1.3, Isla Verde. ℭ **787/253-1664**. No cover. Bus: A5.

Rumba   This bar and pub is one of Old San Juan's hot spots, and it's the best place in Puerto Rico to go for salsa dancing. Hot, hot music is played by live bands. This is where the Puerto Ricans go themselves, leaving the tourists salsa dancing at such hotels as the Wyndham El San Juan or the Marriott on the Condado. The average age is 18 to 28. The club also spins African-tinged bomba favorites for its young patrons. Open daily from 7pm to closing (no set time). Calle San Sebastián 152. ℭ **787/725-4407**. Bus: Old Town trolley.

San Juan Chateau *Finds*   This is the best venue in the city for merengue and salsa. The cover charge depends on what group is appearing. (You no longer get Ricky Martin here, incidentally.) On Friday and Saturday, live Latin groups perform, but Sunday night the club goes gay, with drag shows and the like. The club attracts a wide age range from late teenagers to the middle-aged. Open Friday from 5pm to closing (no set time), and Saturday and Sunday from 9pm to closing. Av. Chardon 9, Hato Rey. ✆ 787/751-2000. Cover $8–$20. Bus: B21.

Unplugged Café *(Finds)* This trendy hot spot is the place to go to hear live music. Attracting an under-35 crowd, it is also a good choice for island cuisine, so you can dine here and make a whole evening of it. The main lounge is upstairs, with a friendly bar to one side. The repertoire here is called a "musical magazine"—jazz bands on Tuesday, blues and R&B on Wednesday, rock on Thursday and Friday, and local Spanish rock bands or international musicians on the weekends. Sunday afternoons see comedy shows and international music. From 6 to 9pm on Thursday nights you can hear (or participate in) karaoke. Friday night is the best time for dancing to a salsa beat. In between the music, you can order such dishes as breaded shark with mango sauce, which tastes better than your mother's version. Open Tuesday and Wednesday 11am to 12:30am, Thursday and Friday 11am to 2am, Saturday 4pm to 2am, and Sunday 3pm to midnight. Av. José de Diego 365, Santurce. ✆ 787/723-1423. Cover Wed–Sat $3–$5. Bus: 1.

THE BAR SCENE

Unless otherwise stated, there is no cover charge at the following bars.

Café Tabac If you're in Old Town and would like to sip a good glass of port or smoke a stogie, head for this sector's best-loved cigar bar. The establishment also serves light meals. Open Sunday through Thursday from 5pm to midnight, and Friday through Saturday from 5pm to 2am. Calle Fortaleza 262. ✆ 787/725-6785. Bus: Old Town trolley.

Cigar Bar The Palm Court Lobby at the elegant Wyndham El San Juan boasts an impressive cigar bar, with a magnificent repository of the finest stogies in the world. Although the bar is generally filled with visitors, some of San Juan's most fashionable men—and women, too—can be seen puffing away in this chic rendezvous while sipping cognac. Open daily from 6pm to 3am. Wyndham El San Juan Hotel & Casino, Av. Isla Verde 6063, Isla Verde. ✆ 787/791-1000. Bus: A5.

El Patio de Sam Except for the juicy burgers, we're not so keen on the food served here anymore (and neither are our readers), but we still like to visit Old Town's best-known watering hole, one of the most popular late-night joints with a good selection of beers. Live entertainment is presented here Monday through Saturday. This is a fun joint—that is, if you dine somewhere else before coming here. Open daily from 11am to midnight. Calle San Sebastian 102. ✆ 787/ 723-1149. Bus: Old Town trolley.

Fiesta Bar   This bar lures a healthy mixture of local residents and hotel guests, usually the post-35 set. The margaritas are appropriately salty, the rhythms are hot and Latin, and the free admission usually helps you forget any losses you might have suffered in the nearby casinos. From Thursday to Sunday nights you can hear some of the best salsa and merengue music in San Juan here. Open Thursday through Sunday from 6pm to 2am. In the Condado Plaza Hotel & Casino, Av. Ashford 999. ✆ 787/721-1000. Bus: C10.

Maria's   Forget the tacky decorations. This is the town's most enduring bar, a favorite local hangout and a prime target for Old Town visitors seeking Mexican food and sangria. The atmosphere is fun, and the tropical drinks include piña coladas and frosts made of banana, orange, and strawberry, as well as the Puerto Rican beer Medalla. Open daily from 10:30am to 3am. Calle del Cristo 204. ✆ 787/ 721-1678. Bus: Old Town trolley.

Ñapa   In Puerto Rico the nickname for this place in slang means "something extra." That's what the owner, Luis Moscoso, had in mind when he took over a broken-down film house and restored it into a fancy bar/restaurant with marble and lighting designed to flatter. The club enjoys a waterfront location on the Condado. You can come here to drink and party, but the menu of fusion cuisine is good enough that you might want to dine here as well, as it's far better than the routine club fare. Live music is also a nightly presentation. Open daily from 11:30am to 2:30 pm and from 6 to 11pm (Sat–Sun until 2am or later). Av. Ashford 1018. ✆ 787/724-3686. Bus: B21.

Palm Court   This is the most beautiful bar on the island—perhaps in the entire Caribbean. Most of the patrons are hotel guests, but well-heeled locals make up at least a quarter of the business at this fashionable rendezvous. Set in an oval wrapped around a sunken bar area, amid marble and burnished mahogany, it offers a view of one of the world's largest chandeliers. After 7pm on Monday through Saturday, live music, often salsa and merengue, emanates from an adjoining room (El Chico Bar). Open daily from 6pm to 3am. In Wyndham El San Juan Hotel & Casino, Av. Isla Verde 6063, Isla Verde. ✆ 787/791-1000. Bus: A5.

Violeta's   Stylish and comfortable, Violeta's occupies the ground floor of a 200-year-old beamed house. Because of its location in the

Old Town, the bar draws an equal mix of visitors and locals, usually in their 20s and 30s. Sometimes a pianist performs at the oversized grand piano. An open courtyard out back provides additional seating for sipping margaritas or other drinks. Open daily from 5pm to 1am. Calle Fortaleza 56 (2 blocks from the El Convento). ℂ 787/723-6804. Old Town trolley.

Wet Bar/Liquid   Two chic new drinking spots operate out of San Juan's finest boutique hotel, The Water Club. The main bar, Liquid, is a large area downstairs at the hotel. It's quickly become one of San Juan's most fashionable hangouts for both chic locals and a medley of visitors in all age groups. With its glass walls overlooking the ocean, it features Latino music. The best bar for watching the sun set over San Juan is the Wet Bar on the 11th floor, featuring jazz music and the Caribbean's only rooftop fireplace for those nippy nights in winter when you want to drink outside. The sensuous decor here includes striped zebra-wood stools, futons, pillowy sofas, and hand-carved side tables. The walls feature Indonesian carved teak panels. Wet Bar open Thursday through Saturday 7pm to 1am; Liquid Bar open Thursday through Saturday 6pm to 1am. In the Water Club, Calle José M. Tartak 2. ℂ 787/728-3666. Bus: A5.

HOT NIGHTS IN GAY SAN JUAN

Straight folks are generally welcome in each of these gay venues, and many local couples show up for the hot music and dancing. Local straight boys who show up to cause trouble are generally ushered out quickly. Unless otherwise stated, there is no cover.

Beach Bar   This is the site of a hugely popular Sunday afternoon gathering, which gets really crowded beginning around 4pm and stretches into the wee hours. There's an open-air bar protected from rain by a sloping rooftop and a space atop the seawall with a panoramic view of the Condado beachfront. Drag shows on Sunday take place on the terrace. Open daily 11am to 1am or later. On the ground floor of the Atlantic Beach Hotel, Calle Vendig 1. ℂ 787/721-6900. Bus: A7.

Cups   Set in a Latino tavern, this place is valued as the only place in San Juan that caters almost exclusively to lesbians. Men of any sexual persuasion aren't particularly welcome. The scene reminds many lesbians of a tropical version of one of the bars they left behind at home. Entertainment such as live music or cabaret is presented

Wednesday at 9pm and Friday at 10pm. Open Wednesday through Saturday from 7pm to 4am. Calle San Mateo 1708, Santurce. ℂ 787/ 268-3570. Bus: B21.

Eros This two-level nightclub caters exclusively to the city's growing gay population. Patterned after the dance emporiums of New York, but on a smaller scale, the club has cutting-edge music and bathrooms that are among the most creative in the world. Here, wall murals present fantasy-charged, eroticized versions of ancient Greek and Roman gods. Regrettably, only one night a week (Wed) is devoted to Latino music; on other nights, the music is equivalent to what you'd find in the gay discos of either Los Angeles or New York City. Open Wednesday through Sunday from 10pm to 3 or 4am. Av. Ponce de León 1257, Santurce. ℂ 787/722-1131. Cover $5. Bus: 1.

CASINOS

Many visitors come to Puerto Rico on package deals and stay at one of the posh hotels at the Condado or Isla Verde just to gamble.

Nearly all the large hotels in San Juan/Condado/Isla Verde offer casinos, and there are other large casinos at some of the bigger resorts outside the metropolitan area. The atmosphere in the casinos is casual, but still you shouldn't show up in bathing suits or shorts. Most of the casinos open around noon and close at 2, 3, or 4am. Guest patrons must be at least 18 years old to enter.

The casino generating all the excitement today is the 18,500-square-foot **Ritz-Carlton Casino,** 6961 State Rd., Isla Verde (ℂ 787/ 253-1700), the largest casino in Puerto Rico. It combines the elegant decor of the 1940s with tropical fabrics and patterns. This is one of the plushest and most exclusive entertainment complexes in the Caribbean. You almost expect to see Joan Crawford—beautifully frocked, of course—arrive on the arm of Clark Gable. It features traditional games such as blackjack, roulette, baccarat, craps, and slot machines.

One of the splashiest of San Juan's casinos is at the **Wyndham Old San Juan Hotel & Casino,** Calle Brumbaugh 100 (ℂ 787/ 721-5100), where five-card stud competes with some 240 slot machines and roulette tables. You can also try your luck at the **Wyndham El San Juan Hotel & Casino** (one of the most grand), Av. Isla Verde 6063 (ℂ 787/791-1000), or the **Condado Plaza Hotel & Casino,** Av. Ashford 999 (ℂ 787/721-1000). You do not have to flash passports or pay any admission fees.

7

Near San Juan

Within easy reach of San Juan's cosmopolitan bustle are superb attractions and natural wonders. With San Juan as your base, you can explore the island by day and return in time for a final dip in the ocean and an evening on the town. Other places near San Juan, such as the Hyatt resorts at Dorado, are destinations unto themselves.

About 90 minutes west of San Juan is the world's largest radar/radio-telescope, **Arecibo Observatory.** After touring this awesome facility, you can travel west to nearby **Río Camuy,** for a good look at marvels below ground. Here you can plunge deep into the subterranean beauty of a spectacular cave system carved over eons by one of the world's largest underground rivers.

Prefer to stay closer to San Juan? Virtually on the city's doorstep, only 18 miles (29km) to the west, is the **Dorado resort,** home of the famed Hyatt Dorado and Hyatt Regency Cerromar Beach hotels. Both properties open onto beautiful white sandy beaches. If you want to avoid the congestion of the Condado's high-rise hotels, consider a beach holiday here. Both Hyatts are family-friendly.

Just 35 miles (56km) east of San Juan is the Caribbean National Forest, the only tropical rain forest in the U.S. National Park System. Named by the Spanish for its anvil-shaped peak, **El Yunque** receives more than 100 billion gallons of rainfall annually. If you have time for only one side trip, this is the one to take. Waterfalls, wild orchids, giant ferns, towering tabonuco trees, and sierra palms make El Yunque a photographer's and hiker's paradise. Pick up a map and choose from dozens of trails graded by difficulty, including El Yunque's most challenging—the 6-mile (9.5km) El Toro Trail to the peak. At El Yunque is El Portal Tropical Center, with 10,000 square feet of exhibit space, plazas, and patios. This facility greatly expands the recreational and educational programs available to visitors. La Coca Falls and an observation tower are just off Route 191.

Visitors can combine a morning trip to El Yunque with an afternoon of swimming and sunning on tranquil **Luquillo Beach.** Soft white sand, shaded by coconut palms and the blue sea, makes this

Puerto Rico's best and best-known beach. Take a picnic or, better yet, sample local specialties from the kiosks.

1 Arecibo & Camuy ✶

68 to 77 miles (190km–124km) W of San Juan

GETTING THERE

Arecibo Observatory lies a 1¼-hour drive west of San Juan, outside the town of Arecibo. From San Juan head west along four-lane Route 22 until you reach the town of Arecibo. At Arecibo, head south on Route 10; the 20-mile (32km) drive south on this four-lane highway is almost as interesting as the observatory itself. From Route 10, follow the signposts along a roller-coaster journey on narrow two-lane roads. Still following the signposts, you take routes 626 and 623, crossing the lush Valley of Río Tanamá until you reach Route 625, which will lead you to the entrance to the observatory.

On the same day you visit the Arecibo Observatory, you can also visit the Río Camuy caves. The caves also lie south of the town of Arecibo. Follow Route 129 southwest from Arecibo to the entrance of the caves, which are at km 18.9 along the route, north of the town of Lares. Like the observatory, the caves lie approximately 1½ hours west of San Juan.

EXPLORING THE AREA

Dubbed "an ear to heaven," **Observatorio de Arecibo** ✶ (© 787/ 878-2612; www.naic.edu) contains the world's largest and most sensitive radar/radio-telescope. The telescope features a 20-acre dish, or radio mirror, set in an ancient sinkhole. It's 1,000 feet in diameter and 167 feet deep, and it allows scientists to monitor natural radio emissions from distant galaxies, pulsars, and quasars, and to examine the ionosphere, the planets, and the moon using powerful radar signals. Used by scientists as part of the Search for Extraterrestrial Intelligence (SETI), this is the same site featured in the movie *Contact* with Jodie Foster. This research effort speculates that advanced civilizations elsewhere in the universe might also communicate via radio waves. The 10-year, $100 million search for life in space was launched on October 12, 1992, the 500-year anniversary of the New World's discovery by Columbus.

Unusually lush vegetation flourishes under the giant dish, including ferns, wild orchids, and begonias. Assorted creatures like mongooses, lizards, and dragonflies have also taken refuge there.

Suspended in outlandish fashion above the dish is a 600-ton platform that resembles a space station.

This is not a site where you'll be launched into a *Star Wars* journey through the universe. You are allowed to walk around the platform, taking in views of this gigantic dish. At the Angel Ramos Foundation Visitor Center, you are treated to interactive exhibitions on the various planetary systems and introduced to the mystery of meteors and educated about intriguing weather phenomena.

Tours are available at the observatory Wednesday through Friday from noon to 4pm, Saturday and Sunday from 9am to 4pm. The cost is $4 for adults, $2 for children and seniors. There's a souvenir shop on the grounds. Plan to spend about 1½ hours at the observatory.

Parque de las Cavernas del Río Camuy (Río Camuy Caves) ⊛⊛⊛ (© 787/898-3100) contains the third-largest underground river in the world. It runs through a network of caves, canyons, and sinkholes that have been cut through the island's limestone base over the course of millions of years. Known to the pre-Columbian Taíno peoples, the caves came to the attention of speleologists in the 1950s; they were led to the site by local boys already familiar with some of the entrances to the system. The caves were opened to the public in 1986. Visitors should allow about 1½ hours for the total experience.

Visitors first see a short film about the caves, then descend into the caverns in open-air trolleys. The trip takes you through a 200-foot-deep sinkhole and a chasm where tropical trees, ferns, and flowers flourish, along with birds and butterflies. The trolley then goes to the entrance of Clara Cave of Epalme, one of 16 caves in the Camuy caves network, where visitors begin a 45-minute walk, viewing the majestic series of rooms rich in stalagmites, stalactites, and huge natural "sculptures" formed over the centuries.

Tres Pueblos Sinkhole, located on the boundaries of the Camuy, Hatillo, and Lares municipalities, measures 65 feet in diameter, with a depth of 400 feet—room enough to fit all of El Morro Fortress in San Juan. In Tres Pueblos, visitors can walk along two platforms—one on the Lares side, facing the town of Camuy, and the other on the Hatillo side, overlooking Tres Pueblos Cave and the Río Camuy.

The caves are open Wednesday through Sunday from 8am to 3:45pm. Tickets cost $10 for adults, $7 for children 2 to 12, and $5 for seniors. Parking is $2. For more information, phone the park.

2 Dorado ✶

18 miles (29km) W of San Juan

Dorado—the name itself evokes a kind of magic—is a world of luxury resorts and villas that unfolds along the north shore of Puerto Rico. The elegant **Hyatt Dorado Beach Resort & Country Club** and the newer, larger **Hyatt Regency Cerromar Beach Hotel** sit on the choice white-sand beaches here.

The site was originally purchased in 1905 by Dr. Alfred T. Livingston, a Jamestown, N.Y., physician, who developed it as a 1,000-acre grapefruit-and-coconut plantation. Dr. Livingston's daughter, Clara, widely known in aviation circles as a friend of Amelia Earhart, owned and operated the plantation after her father's death. It was she who built the airstrip here.

GETTING THERE

If you're driving from San Juan, take Highway 2 west to Route 693 north to Dorado (trip time: 40 min.). Otherwise, call **Dorado Transport Corp.,** which occupies an office on the site shared by the Hyatt hotels (✆ **787/796-1234**). Using 18-passenger minibuses, they offer frequent shuttle service between the Hyatt Hotels and the San Juan airport. They operate at frequent intervals, daily between 11am and 10pm. The fare is $20 per person, but a minimum of three passengers must make the trip in order for the bus to operate.

Once you're in Dorado, you can get around via the shuttle bus that travels between the two hotels every 30 minutes during the day.

SPORTS & OTHER OUTDOOR PURSUITS

GOLF The Robert Trent Jones, Sr.–designed courses at the **Hyatt Regency Cerromar** and the **Hyatt Dorado Beach** ✶✶ match the finest anywhere. The two original courses, known as east and west (✆ 787/796-8961 for tee times), were carved out of a jungle and offer tight fairways bordered by trees and forests, with lots of ocean holes. The somewhat newer and less noted north and south courses (✆ 787/796-8915 for tee times) feature wide fairways with well-bunkered greens and an assortment of water traps and tricky wind factors. Each is a par-72 course. The longest is the south course, at 7,047 yards. Guests of the Hyatt hotels get preferred tee times and pay lower fees than nonguests. On the north and south courses, guests pay $70 to $90, and nonguests pay $85 to $115. On the east and west courses guests pay $126 to $145, and nonguests pay from $151 to $181. Golf carts at any of the courses rent for $25, whether you play 9 or 18 holes. There are two pro shops—one for the north and south courses and one for the east and west courses, each with a bar and snack-style restaurant. Both are open daily from 7am until dusk.

WINDSURFING & OTHER WATERSPORTS   The best place for watersports on the island's north shore is along the well-maintained beachfront of the Hyatt Dorado Beach Resort & Country Club, near the 10th hole of the east golf course. Here, **Penfield Island Adventures** (© **787/382-4631,** ext. 3262, or 787/796-2188) offers 90-minute **windsurfing lessons** for $80 each; board rentals cost $50 per half day. Well-supplied with a wide array of Windsurfers, including some designed specifically for beginners and children, the school benefits from the almost-uninterrupted flow of the north shore's strong, steady winds and an experienced crew of instructors. A **kayaking/snorkeling** trip (© **787/796-4645**), departing daily at 9:15am and 11:45am and lasting 2 hours, costs $69. Two-tank boat **dives** go for $95 per person. **Waverunners** can be rented for $60 per half-hour for a single rider or $75 for two riders. A **Sunfish** rents for $50 for 1 hour, $68 for 2 hours.

WHERE TO STAY

Embassy Suites Dorado del Mar Beach & Golf Resort 🏌
This new beachfront property in Dorado lies less than 2 miles (3km) from the center of Dorado and within easy access from the San Juan airport. It is the only all-suite resort in Puerto Rico, and it has been a success since its opening in 2001. The sparkling new property offers two-room suites with balconies and 55 two-bedroom condos.

The suites are spread over seven floors, each spacious and furnished in a Caribbean tropical motif, with artwork and one king-size bed or two double beds. Most of them have ocean views of the water. Each condo has a living room, kitchen, whirlpool, and balcony.

Although the accommodations are suites or condos, one bedroom in a condo can be rented as a double room (the rest of the condo is shut off). Likewise, it's also possible for two people to rent one bedroom in a condo, with the living room and kitchen facilities available (the other bedroom is closed off). Because condos contain two bedrooms, most of them are rented to parties of four.

The hotel attracts many families because of its very spacious accommodations. It also attracts golfers because of its Chi Chi Rodriguez signature par-72 18-hole golf course set against a panoramic backdrop of mountains and ocean.

210 Dorado del Mar Blvd., Dorado, PR 00646. © **787/796-6125.** Fax 787/796-6145. www.embassysuitesdorado.com. 229 units. Year-round $139–$195

DORADO **139**

double, $165–$259 suite, $205–$299 1-bedroom condo, $315–$440 2-bedroom condo. AE, DC, MC, V. **Amenities:** 2 restaurants; pool and bar grill; pool; golf; 24-hr. business center; room service; babysitting; laundry. *In room:* A/C, TV, dataport, kitchenette, hair dryer, iron, safe.

Hyatt Dorado Beach Resort & Country Club ✿✿ *Kids*   Hyatt

has spent millions on improvements here. This is the more elegant and subdued of the two Hyatt properties, the Cerromar attracting more families and rowdy conventions bent on having a good time. The renovated guest rooms have marble bathrooms and terra-cotta floors throughout. Accommodations are available on the beach or in villas tucked in and around the lushly planted grounds. They're fairly spacious, and bathrooms have everything from tubs to bathrobes, deluxe toiletries to power showers. The casitas are a series of private beach or poolside houses.

Dinner is served in a three-tiered main dining room where you can watch the surf. Hyatt Dorado chefs have won many awards, and the food at the hotel restaurants is among the most appealing in Puerto Rico.

Highway 693, Dorado, PR 00646. ✆ **800/233-1234** or 787/796-1234. Fax 787/796-6560. www.hyatt.com. 298 units, 17 casitas. Winter $395–$595 double, from $705 casita for 2; off-season $175-$365 double, from $375 casita for 2. MAP (mandatory in winter) $70 extra per day for adults, $35 extra per day for children. AE, DC, DISC, MC, V. **Amenities:** 3 restaurants; 2 bars; 2 pools; 2 18-hole championship golf courses; 7 Laykold tennis courts; spa; windsurfing school; children's camp; 24-hr. room service; babysitting; laundry/dry cleaning. *In room:* A/C, minibar, hair dryer, iron, safe.

Hyatt Regency Cerromar Beach Hotel ✿✿ *Kids*   The name

Cerromar is a combination of two Spanish words—*cerro* (mountain) and *mar* (sea)—and true to its name, this resort is surrounded by mountains and ocean. Approximately 22 miles (35km) west of San Juan, the high-rise hotel shares the 1,000-acre former Livingston estate with the more elegant Dorado, so guests can enjoy the Robert Trent Jones, Sr., golf courses and other facilities at the hotel next door.

All rooms have first-class appointments and are well maintained; most have private balconies. The floors throughout are tiled and the furnishings are casual tropical, in soft colors and pastels. Many units are wheelchair accessible, and some are reserved for nonsmokers. Bathrooms are equipped with tubs and power showers; the Regency Club units also have robes and hair dryers.

Even if you're trapped at your resort every night because of the isolation of Dorado itself, you'll find a wide variety of cuisine here, ranging from Asian to Italian. The fare is relatively standard but adequate. The water playground contains the world's longest freshwater swimming pool: a 1,776-foot-long fantasy pool with a river-like current in five connected free-form pools. It takes 15 minutes to float from one end of the pool to the other. There are also 14 waterfalls, tropical landscaping, a subterranean Jacuzzi, water slides, walks, bridges, and a children's pool. A full-service spa and health club provides services for all manner of body and skin care, including massages.

Highway 693, Dorado, PR 00646. ☎ 800/233-1234 or 787/796-1234. Fax 787/796-4647. www.hyatt.com. 506 units. Winter $375–$535 double, from $805 suite; spring and fall $255–$350 double, from $600 suite; summer $200–$250 double, from $455 suite. MAP (breakfast and dinner) $70 extra for adults, $35 extra for children. AE, DC, DISC, MC, V. **Amenities:** 4 restaurants; 3 bars; dance club; casino; world's longest freshwater pool; children's pool; 2 golf courses; 14 Laykold tennis courts (2 lit); spa and health club; snorkeling; children's programs; 24-hr. room service; babysitting; laundry/dry cleaning. *In room:* A/C, TV, minibar, safe.

DINING

El Malecón PUERTO RICAN　If you'd like to discover an unpretentious local place that serves good Puerto Rican cuisine, then head for El Malecón, a simple concrete structure that's minutes away from a small shopping center. It has a cozy family ambience and is especially popular on weekends. Some members of the staff speak English, and the chef is best with fresh seafood. The chef might also prepare a variety of items not listed on the menu. Most of the dishes are at the lower end of the price scale; only the lobster is expensive. On Wednesday and Friday a live band plays and patrons dance.

Rte. 693, km 8.2 Marginal Costa de Oro. ☎ 787/796-1645. Main courses $10–$37. AE, MC, V. Daily 11am–11pm.

Steak Co. ☆ STEAKS　This restaurant offers the best beef of the fine restaurants at the Hyatts. Frequented by an upscale, usually well-dressed clientele, it occupies a soaring, two-story room with marble and Italian-tile floors. Diners enjoy views of venerable trees draped in Spanish moss, a landscaped pond, and a waterfall while dining on well-conceived cuisine. The best steaks and prime ribs in this part of Puerto Rico are served here. Most dishes are at the lower end of the price scale. The most expensive main course—called "Sea and Earth"—consists of a tender filet mignon and a lobster tail. Most dishes are accompanied by large, perfectly baked potatoes and great sourdough bread. In the highly unlikely event that you have room for dessert, you'll be glad you do.

In the Hyatt Regency Cerromar. ☎ 787/796-1234, ext. 3240. Reservations required. Main courses $20–$48. AE, DC, DISC, MC, V. Daily 6–10pm.

Su Casa Restaurant 🏵🏵🏵 SPANISH/PUERTO RICAN   This is a restored version of the 19th-century Livingston family plantation home, and it offers the finest dining at all the Dorado Hyatt properties. It's an attractive setting—an old oceanfront hacienda with a red-tile roof, graceful staircases and a courtyard, and verandas in the Spanish style. Strolling musicians and candlelight add to the romantic ambience. The Rockefellers used to entertain their formally dressed guests at this posh Dorado beach hideaway, but today the dress is casual (but no shorts allowed). The chef produces innovative cuisine, using Puerto Rican fruits and vegetables whenever possible. Dining here is such an event that patrons make an evening of it. For a refreshing starter, try the white gazpacho with grapes or a tropical green salad with papaya, avocado, and Caribbean spices. The kitchen whips up a delectable seafood and chicken paella, or you can order mahimahi with a spicy corn sauce served with couscous and a spinach timbale. Meats are also savory, especially the roasted pork chops flavored with tamarind sauce.

In the Hyatt Dorado Beach Resort & Country Club. ✆ 787/796-1234. Reservations required. Main courses $27–$48. AE, DC, MC, V. Daily 6:30–10pm.

Zen Garden 🏵 ASIAN   Some of the best Asian food is found not in San Juan but in a Dorado Hyatt hotel. On the lower floor of this resort hotel, the chefs at Zen Garden roam Asia for all your favorite dishes, including both the Chinese and Japanese kitchens, with special attention paid to their very fresh sushi and sashimi collection. The restaurant also has an attractive bar and an elegantly decorated dining room. The larder has a delectable array of such delights as sea urchin, freshwater eel, and smoked salmon. Masters in the kitchen prepare delicious yellowtail, red snapper, octopus, and squid.

In the Hyatt Regency Cerromar Beach Resort & Casino, Dorado. ✆ 787/796-1234. Reservations required. Main courses $16–$25; sushi from $2.75 per order. AE, DC, MC, V. Daily 6–9pm.

3 El Yunque 🏵🏵🏵

25 miles (40km) E of San Juan

The El Yunque rain forest, a 45-minute drive east of San Juan, is a major attraction in Puerto Rico. Part of the Caribbean National Forest, this is the only tropical forest in the U.S. National Forest Service system. The 28,000-acre preserve was given its status by President Theodore Roosevelt. Today the virgin forest remains much as it was in 1493, when Columbus first sighted Puerto Rico.

GETTING THERE

From San Juan, road signs direct you to Route 3, which you follow east to the intersection of Route 191, a two-lane highway that heads south into the forest. Take 191 for 3 miles (5km), going through the village of Palmer. As the road rises, you will have entered the Caribbean National Forest. You can stop in at the El Portal Tropical Forest Center to pick up information (see below).

VISITOR INFORMATION

El Portal Tropical Forest Center, Route 191, Rio Grande (✆ 787/888-1880), an $18 million exhibition and information center, has 10,000 square feet of exhibition space. Three pavilions offer exhibits and bilingual displays. The actor Jimmy Smits narrates a documentary called "Understanding the Forest." The center is open daily from 9am to 5pm; it charges an admission of $3 for adults and $1.50 for children under 12.

El Yunque is the most popular spot in Puerto Rico for hiking; for a description of our favorite trails, see "Hiking Trails" below. The **Department of Natural Resources Forest Service** (✆ 787/724-8774) administers some aspects of the park, although for the ordinary hiker, more useful information may be available at **El Yunque Catalina Field Office,** near the village of Palmer, beside the main highway at the forest's northern edge (✆ 787/888-1880). The staff can provide material about hiking routes, and, with 10 days' notice, help you plan overnight tours in the forest. If you reserve in advance, the staff will also arrange for you to take part in 2-hour group tours. These tours are conducted Saturday through Monday every hour on the hour from 10:30am to 3:30pm; they cost $5 for adults and $3 for children under 12.

EXPLORING EL YUNQUE

Encompassing four distinct forest types, El Yunque is home to 240 species of tropical trees, flowers, and wildlife. More than 20 kinds of orchids and 50 varieties of ferns share this diverse habitat with millions of tiny tree frogs, whose distinctive cry of *coquí* (pronounced "ko-*kee*") has given them their name. Tropical birds include the lively, greenish blue, red-fronted Puerto Rican parrot, once nearly extinct and now making a comeback. Other rare animals include the Puerto Rican boa, which grows to 7 feet. (It is highly unlikely that you will encounter a boa. The few people who have are still shouting about it.)

El Yunque is the best of Puerto Rico's 20 forest preserves. The forest is situated high above sea level, with El Toro its highest peak. You can be fairly sure you'll be showered upon during your visit, since more than 100 billion gallons of rain fall here annually. However, the showers are brief and there are many shelters. On a quickie tour, many visitors reserve only a half day for El Yunque. But we think it's unique and deserves at least a daylong outing.

HIKING TRAILS   The best hiking trails in El Yunque have been carefully marked by the forest rangers. Our favorite, which takes 2 hours for the round-trip jaunt, is called **La Mina & Big Tree Trail,** and it is actually two trails combined. The La Mina Trail is paved and signposted. It begins at the picnic center adjacent to the visitor center and runs parallel to La Mina River. It is named for gold once discovered on the site. After you reach La Mina Falls, the Big Tree Trail begins (also signposted). It winds a route through the towering trees of Tabonuco Forest until it approaches Route 191. Along the trail you might spot such native birds as the Puerto Rican wood-pecker, the tanager, the screech owl, and the bullfinch.

Those with more time might opt for the **El Yunque Trail,** which takes 4 hours round-trip to traverse. This trail—signposted from El Caimitillo Picnic Grounds—takes you on a steep, winding path. Along the way you pass natural forests of sierra palm and *palo colorado* before descending into the dwarf forest of Mount Britton, which is often shrouded in clouds. Your major goal, at least for panoramic views, will be the lookout peaks of Roca Marcas, Yunque Rock, and Los Picachos. On a bright, clear day you can see all the way to the eastern shores of the Atlantic.

DRIVING THROUGH EL YUNQUE   If you're not a hiker but you appreciate rain forests, you can still enjoy En Yunque. You can drive through the forest on Route 191, which is a tarmac road. This trail goes from the main highway of Route 3, penetrating deep into El Yunque. You can see ferns that grow some 120 feet tall, and at any minute you expect a hungry dinosaur to peek between the fronds, looking for a snack. You're also treated to lookout towers offering panoramic views, waterfalls, picnic areas, and even a restaurant.

WHERE TO STAY

For the location of this parador, see the map "Paradores & Country Inns of Puerto Rico" on p. 45.

Ceiba Country Inn *(Finds)*   If you're looking for an escape from the hustle and bustle of everyday life, this is the place for you. This small, well-maintained bed-and-breakfast is located on the eastern-most part of Puerto Rico, near the Roosevelt Road's U.S. naval base (you must rent a car to reach this little haven in the mountains). El Yunque is only 15 miles (24km) away, and San Juan is 40 miles (64km) to the west. The rooms are on the bottom floor of a large, old family home, and each has a private shower-only bathroom. They are decorated in a tropical motif with flowered murals on the walls, painted by a local artist. For a quiet evening cocktail, you might want to visit the small lounge on the second floor.

Road no. 977, km 1.2 (P.O. Box 1067), Ceiba, PR 00735. ✆ 787/885-0471. Fax 787/885-0471. prinn@juno.com. 9 units (shower only). $75 double. Rate includes breakfast. AE, DISC, MC, V. Free parking. **Amenities:** Patio for outdoor entertainment; bar (guests only). *In room:* A/C, fridge.

WHERE TO DINE

We recommend the dining and drinking facilities at the Westin Rio Mar (see "Luquillo Beach" below), which sits very close to the entrance to El Yunque.

4 Luquillo Beach ✶✶✶

31 miles (50km) E of San Juan

Luquillo Beach is the island's best and most popular public stretch of sand. From here, you can easily explore El Yunque Rain Forest (see above). "Luquillo" is a Spanish adaptation of *Yukiyu,* the god believed by the Taínos to inhabit El Yunque.

GETTING THERE

If you are driving, pass the San Juan airport and follow the signs to Carolina. This leads to Route 3, which travels east toward the fishing town of Fajardo, where you'll turn north to Las Croabas. To reach the Westin, the area's major hotel, follow the signs to El Yunque, and then the signs to the Westin.

A hotel limousine (✆ 787/608-7666) from the San Juan airport costs $225 per carload to the Westin Rio Mar Beach Resort. A taxi costs approximately $70. Hotel buses make trips to and from the San Juan airport, based on the arrival times of incoming flights; the cost is $27.50 per person, each way, for transport to El Conquistador; $25 per person, each way, to the Westin.

HITTING THE BEACH

Luquillo Beach ✶✶✶, Puerto Rico's finest beach, is palm dotted and crescent-shaped, opening onto a lagoon with calm waters and a wide, sandy bank. It's very crowded on weekends but much better during the week. There are picnic tables and food stands that sell a sampling of the island's *frituras* (fried fare), especially cod fritters and tacos. The beach is open daily from 9am to 6pm.

You can also scuba dive and snorkel (see below) among the living reefs with lots of tropical fish. Offshore are coral formations and spectacular sea life—eels, octopuses, stingrays, tarpon, big puffer fish, turtles, nurse sharks, and squid, among other sea creatures.

SCUBA DIVING & SNORKELING

The best people to take you diving are at the **Dive Center** at the Westin Rio Mar Beach Resort, Country Club & Ocean Villas (© 787/888-6000). This is one of the largest dive centers in Puerto Rico, a PADI five-star facility with two custom-designed boats that usually take no more than 6 to 10 divers. Snorkeling and skin diving costs $65. The center also offers a full-day snorkeling trip, including lunch and drinks, for $89 per person. Boat tours are available daily from 9am to 4pm. For scuba divers, a two-tank dive costs $125.

WHERE TO STAY

Luquillo Beach Inn   This all-villa hotel has one-bedroom accommodations for up to four guests and two-bedroom villas that house six comfortably. Each unit has a full kitchen. By day the living room can be a social center, with the sofa bed converted to make it a bedroom in the evening. The inn is recommended for those who'd like to have a 2- or 3-day beach holiday at Luquillo, with visits to El Yunque. The room furnishings, although comfortable, evoke Miami motels in the 1950s. Units are spacious and graced with prints, but the aura is somewhat impersonal. The pool is small but is provided with chaise longues and tables. Because the beach is so close—and that's why guests flock here—the pool is little used. The hotel is ringed with balconies. Families are especially fond of the place because light meals can be prepared at any hour in the full kitchen in each unit.

Calle 701 Ocean Drive, Luquillo, PR 00773. © 787/889-3333. www.luquillobeach inn.com. 20 units. Year-round 1-bedroom apt for 2–4 persons $101 Sun–Thurs, $136 Fri–Sat; 2-bedroom apt for 4–6 persons $129 Sun–Thurs, $164 Fri–Sat. MC, V. **Amenities:** Summer snack bar; pool; babysitting; laundry. *In room:* A/C, TV, kitchen, coffeemaker, hair dryer.

Westin Rio Mar Beach Resort, Country Club, & Ocean Villas ★★★   Marking Westin's debut in the Caribbean, this $180 million, 481-acre resort lies on a relatively uncrowded neighbor (Rio Mar Beach) of the massively popular Luquillo Beach, a 5-minute drive away. It was designed to compete with the Hyatt hotels at Dorado and El Conquistador, with which it's frequently compared. It's the newest, freshest, and best property in the area.

Landscaping includes several artificial lakes situated amid tropical gardens. More than 60% of the guest rooms look out over palm trees to the Atlantic. Other units open onto the mountains and forests of nearby El Yunque (just a 15-min. drive away). Throughout, the style is Spanish hacienda with nods to the surrounding jungle, incorporating unusual art and sculpture that alternates with dark woods, deep colors, rounded archways, big windows, and tile floors. In the bedrooms, muted earth tones, wicker, rattan, and painted wood furniture add to the ambience. Bedrooms are spacious, with balconies or terraces, and good mattresses, plus tub-and-shower combos in the spacious bathrooms.

The resort encompasses the Rio Mar Country Club, site of two important golf courses. The older of the two, the Ocean Course, was designed by George and Tom Fazio as part of the original resort, and it has been a staple on Puerto Rico's professional golf circuit since the 1960s. In 1997 Westin opened the property's second 18-holer, the slightly more challenging River Course, the first Greg Norman–designed course in the Caribbean.

For diversity of cuisine, the only hotel in Puerto Rico that outpaces it is the Wyndham El Conquistador Resort (see chapter 10). The resort also has a 6,500-square-foot casino.

6000 Rio Mar Blvd. (19 miles/31km east of Luis Muñoz Marín International Airport, with entrance off Puerto Rico Hwy. 3), Rio Grande, PR 00745. © 800/WESTIN-1 or 787/888-6000. Fax 787/888-6600. www.westinriomar.com. 694 units. Year-round $395–$675 double, from $900 suite. AE, DC, DISC, MC, V. **Amenities:** 8 restaurants; 6 bars; casino; 13 tennis courts; health club and spa; deep-sea game fishing, sailing; children's programs; 24-hr. room service; laundry/dry cleaning; nearby horseback riding. *In room:* A/C, TV, minibar, coffeemaker, hair dryer, iron, safe.

WHERE TO DINE

Brass Cactus *Finds* AMERICAN   On a service road adjacent to Route 3 at the western edge of Luquillo, within a boxy-looking concrete building that's in need of repair, is one of the town's most popular bar/restaurants. Permeated with a raunchy, no-holds-barred spirit, this amiable spot has thrived since the early 1990s, when it was established by an Illinois-born bartender who outfitted the interior with gringo memorabilia. Drinks are stiff and the crowd looks tougher than it is, tending to calm down whenever food and drink are brought out. Menu items include king crab salad; tricolor tortellini laced with chicken and shrimp; several kinds of sandwiches and burgers; and platters of churrasco, T-bone steaks, chicken with tequila sauce, barbecued pork, and fried mahimahi.

In the Condominio Complejo Turistico, Rte. 3 Marginal. ℂ **787/889-5735.** Reservations not necessary. Sandwiches $7.50–$11; main courses $16–$24. MC, V. Sun–Thurs 11am–11pm; Fri–Sat 11am–midnight.

Palio ℛ ITALIAN   This richly decorated restaurant is the premier dining outlet of the region's largest and splashiest hotel. The Westin chain has poured time and energy into making this a showcase of the resort's creativity. Although most of the ingredients have to be flown in, the cuisine is excellent. A certain attachment to culinary tradition doesn't preclude a modern approach to the cookery. Dishes we've sampled have a superbly aromatic flavor and are beautifully presented and served. The sophisticated menu includes potato and sage gnocchi; rack of American lamb; fresh Maine lobster; center-cut veal chops stuffed with fresh mozzarella, tomatoes, and avocado and served with grappa-laced mashed potatoes; and baby free-range chicken, spit-roasted and served with rosemary jus.

In the Westin Rio Mar Beach Resort, Country Club & Ocean Villas. ℂ **787/ 888-6000.** Reservations recommended. Main courses $28–$38. AE, DC, MC, V. Nov–May daily 6–11pm; June–Oct Tues–Sat 6–11pm.

Sandy's Seafood Restaurant & Steak House ℛ *Value* SEAFOOD/STEAKS/PUERTO RICAN   The concrete-and-plate-glass facade is less obtrusive than that of other restaurants in town, and the cramped, Formica-clad interior is far from stylish. Nonetheless, Sandy's is one of the most famous restaurants in northeastern Puerto Rico, thanks to the wide array of luminaries—U.S. and Puerto Rican political figures, mainstream journalists, beauty pageant winners, and assorted slumming rich—who travel from as far away as San Juan to dine here. Set about a block from the main square of the seaside resort of Luquillo, it was founded in 1984 by Miguel Angel, aka Sandy.

Platters, especially the daily specials, are huge. The best examples include fresh shellfish, served on the half-shell; asopaos; four kinds of steak; five different preparations of chicken, including a tasty version with garlic sauce; four kinds of gumbos; paellas; a dozen preparations of lobster; and even jalapeño peppers stuffed with shrimp or lobster.

Calle Fernandez García 276. ℂ **787/889-5765.** Reservations recommended. Main courses $6–$20; lunch special Mon–Fri 11am–2:30pm $5. AE, DISC, MC, V. Daily 11am–between 9:30 and 11pm, depending on business.

8

Ponce & Mayagüez

For those who want to see a less urban side of Puerto Rico, Ponce, on the south shore, and Mayagüez, on the west coast, make good centers for sightseeing.

Founded in 1692, Ponce is Puerto Rico's second-largest city, and it has received much attention because of its inner-city restoration. Along with San Germán, Ponce is home to some of the finest Puerto Rican colonial architecture in the Caribbean. It is also contains the island's premier art gallery.

Puerto Rico's third-largest city, Mayagüez, is a port city on the west coast. It might not be as architecturally remarkable as Ponce, but it's a fine base for exploring and enjoying some very good beaches.

Mayagüez and Ponce also attract beach lovers. Playa de Ponce, for example, is far less crowded than the beaches along San Juan's coastal strip. The area also lures hikers to Puerto Rico's government national forest reserves, the best of which lie outside Ponce and include Guánica State Forest.

One of the biggest adventure jaunts in Puerto Rico, a trip to Mona Island, can also be explored from the coast near Mayagüez.

1 Ponce ★★

75 miles (121km) SW of San Juan

"The Pearl of the South," Ponce was named after Loíza Ponce de León, great-grandson of Juan Ponce de León. Founded in 1692, Ponce is today Puerto Rico's principal shipping port on the Caribbean. The city is well kept and attractive. A suggestion of a provincial Mediterranean town lingers in the air.

Timed to coincide with 1992's 500th anniversary celebration of Christopher Columbus's voyage to the New World, a $440 million renovation began to bring new life to this once-decaying city. The streets are lit with gas lamps and lined with neoclassical buildings, just as they were a century ago. Horse-drawn carriages clop by, and strollers walk along sidewalks edged with pink marble. Thanks to

Ponce

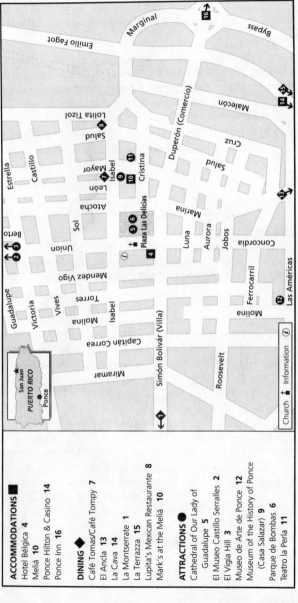

ACCOMMODATIONS ■
Hotel Bélgica **4**
Meliá **10**
Ponce Hilton & Casino **14**
Ponce Inn **16**

DINING ◆
Café Tomas/Café Tompy **7**
El Ancla **13**
La Cava **14**
La Montserrate **1**
La Terrazza **15**
Lupita's Mexican Restaurante **8**
Mark's at the Meliá **10**

ATTRACTIONS ●
Cathedral of Our Lady of
  Guadalupe **5**
El Museo Castillo Serralles **2**
El Vigia Hill **3**
Museo de Arte de Ponce **12**
Museum of the History of Ponce
  (Casa Salazar) **9**
Parque de Bombas **6**
Teatro la Perla **11**

the restoration, Ponce now recalls the turn of the 20th century, when it rivaled San Juan as a wealthy business and cultural center.

ESSENTIALS

GETTING THERE   Flying from San Juan to Ponce four times a day, **Cape Air** (© 800/352-0714), a small regional carrier, offers flights for $124 round-trip. Flight time is 35 minutes.

If you're driving, take Route 1 south to Highway 52, then continue south and west to Ponce. Allow at least 1½ hours.

GETTING AROUND   The town's inner core is small enough that everything can be visited on foot. Taxis provide the second-best alternative.

VISITOR INFORMATION   Maps and information can be found at the **tourist office,** Paseo del Sur Plaza, Suite 3 (© 787/843-0465). It's open Monday through Friday from 8am to 5pm.

SEEING THE SIGHTS
ATTRACTIONS IN PONCE

Most visitors go to Ponce to see the city's architectural restoration. Calle Reina Isabel, one of the city's major residential streets, is a virtual textbook of the different Ponceño styles, ranging from interpretations of European neoclassical to Spanish colonial. The neoclassical style here often incorporates balconies, as befits the warm climate, and an extensive use of pink marble. The "Ponce Créole" style, a term for Spanish colonial, includes both exterior and interior balconies. The interior balconies have a wall of tiny windows that allows sunlight into the patio.

With partial funding from the governments of Puerto Rico and Spain, Ponce has restored more than 600 of its 1,000 historic buildings. Many are on streets radiating from the stately **Plaza Las Delicias (Plaza of Delights).** On calles Isabel, Reina, Pabellones, and Lolita Tizol, electrical and telephone wires have been buried, replica 19th-century gas lamps have been installed, and sidewalks have been trimmed with the distinctive locally quarried pink marble. Paseo Atocha, one of Ponce's main shopping streets, is now a delightful pedestrian mall with a lively street festival on the third Sunday of every month. Paseo Arias, or Callejon del Amor (Lover's Alley), is a charming pedestrian passage between two 1920s bank buildings, Banco Popular and Banco Santander, on Plaza Las Delicias, where outdoor cafe tables invite lingering. Two monumental bronze lions by Spanish sculptor Victor Ochoa guard the entrance to the old section of the city.

In addition to the attractions listed below, the **weekday market-place,** open Monday through Friday from 8am to 5pm, at calles Atocha and Castillo is colorful. Perhaps you'll want to simply sit in the plaza, watching the Ponceños at one of their favorite pastimes—strolling about town.

Cathedral of Our Lady of Guadalupe In 1660 a rustic chapel was built on this spot on the western edge of the Plaza Las Delicias, and since then fires and earthquakes have razed the church repeatedly. In 1919 a team of priests collected funds from local parishioners to construct the Doric- and Gothic-inspired building that stands here today. Designed by architects Francisco Porrato Doría and Francisco Trublard in 1931, and featuring a pipe organ installed in 1934, it remains an important place for prayer for many. The cathedral, named after a famous holy shrine in Mexico, is the best-known church in southern Puerto Rico.

Calle Concordia/Calle Union. ℂ **787/842-0134.** Free admission. Mon–Fri 6am–2pm; Sat–Sun 6am–noon and 3–8pm.

El Museo Castillo Serralles 𝒜 Two miles (3km) north of the center of town is the largest and most imposing building in Ponce, constructed high on El Vigía Hill (see below) during the 1930s by the Serralles family, owners of a local rum distillery. One of the architectural gems of Puerto Rico, it is the best evidence of the wealth produced by the turn-of-the-20th-century sugar boom. Guides will escort you through the Spanish Revival house with Moorish and Andalusian details. Highlights include panoramic courtyards, a baronial dining room, a small cafe and souvenir shop, and a series of photographs showing the tons of earth that were brought in for the construction of the terraced gardens.

El Vigía 17. ℂ **787/259-1774.** Admission $3 adults, $2 seniors over 62, $1.50 children under 16. Tues–Thurs 9:30am–5pm; Fri–Sun 9:30am–5:30pm. Free trolley leaving from Plaza Las Delicias de Ponce.

El Vigía Hill The city's tallest geologic feature, El Vigía Hill (about 300 ft.) dominates Ponce's northern skyline. Its base and steep slopes are covered with a maze of 19th- and early-20th-century development. When you reach the summit, you'll see the soaring Cruz del Vigía (Virgin's Cross). Built in 1984 of reinforced concrete to replace a 19th-century wooden cross in poor repair, this modern 100-foot structure bears lateral arms measuring 70 feet long and an observation tower (accessible by elevator), from which you can see all of the natural beauty surrounding Ponce.

The cross commemorates Vigía Hill's colonial role as a deterrent to contraband smuggling. In 1801, on orders from Spain, a garrison was established atop the hill to detect any ships that might try to unload their cargoes tax-free along Puerto Rico's southern coastline.

At the north end of Ponce. Take a taxi from the Plaza Las Delicias; the ride will cost about $4.

Museo de Arte de Ponce 👁👁👁 Donated to the people of Puerto Rico by Luís A. Ferré, a former governor, this museum has the finest collection of European and Latin American art in the Caribbean. The building itself was designed by Edward Durell Stone (who also designed the John F. Kennedy Center for the Performing Arts in Washington, D.C.) and has been called the "Parthenon of the Caribbean." Its collection represents the principal schools of American and European art of the past 5 centuries. Among the nearly 400 works on display are exceptional pre-Raphaelite and Italian baroque paintings. Visitors will also see artworks by other European masters, as well as Puerto Rican and Latin American paintings, graphics, and sculptures. On display are some of the best works of the two "old masters" of Puerto Rico, Francisco Oller and José Campéche. The museum also contains a representative collection of the works of the old masters of Europe, including Gainsborough, Velázquez, Rubens, and Van Dyck. The museum is best known for its pre-Raphaelite and baroque paintings and sculpture—not only from Spain, but from Italy and France as well. Both the Whitney Museum in New York and the Louvre in Paris have borrowed from its collection. Temporary exhibitions are also mounted here.

Av. de Las Américas 25. ✆ 787/848-0505. www.museoarteponce.org. Admission $4 adults, $1 children under 12. Daily 10am–5pm. Follow Calle Concordia from Plaza Las Delicias 1½ miles (2.5km) south to Av. de Las Américas.

Museum of the History of Ponce (Casa Salazar) Opened in the Casa Salazar in 1992, this museum traces the history of the city from the time of the Taíno peoples to the present. Interactive displays help visitors orient themselves and locate other attractions. The museum has a conservation laboratory, library, souvenir-and-gift shop, cafeteria, and conference facilities.

Casa Salazar ranks close to the top of Ponce's architectural treasures. Built in 1911, it combines neoclassical and Moorish details, while displaying much that is typical of the Ponce decorative style: stained-glass windows, mosaics, pressed-tin ceilings, fixed jalousies, wood or iron columns, porch balconies, interior patios, and the use of doors as windows.

Calle Reina Isabel 51–53 (at Calle Mayor). *①* **787/844-7071**. Admission $3 adults, $1.50 seniors, $1 children. Mon and Wed–Fri 9am–5pm; Sat–Sun 10am–6pm.

Parque de Bombas   Constructed in 1882 as the centerpiece of a 12-day agricultural fair intended to promote the civic charms of Ponce, this building was designated a year later as the island's first permanent headquarters for a volunteer firefighting brigade. It has an unusual appearance—it's painted black, red, green, and yellow. A tourist-information kiosk is situated inside the building (see "Visitor Information," above).

Plaza Las Delicias. *①* **787/284-4141**. Free admission. Wed–Mon 9:30am–6pm.

Teatro la Perla   This theater, built in the neoclassical style in 1864, remains one of the most visible symbols of the economic prosperity of Ponce during the mid–19th century. Designed by Juan Bertoli, an Italian-born resident of Puerto Rico who studied in Europe, it was destroyed by an earthquake in 1918, and rebuilt in 1940 according to the original plans; it reopened to the public in 1941. It is noted for acoustics so clear that microphones are unnecessary. After an extensive restoration completed in 1990, the theater is now the largest and most historic in the Spanish-speaking Caribbean. Everything from plays to concerts to beauty pageants takes place here.

At Calle Mayor and Calle Christina. *①* **787/843-4080**.

NEARBY ATTRACTIONS

Hacienda Buena Vista   Built in 1833, this hacienda preserves an old way of life, with its whirring waterwheels and artifacts of 19th-century farm production. Once it was one of the most successful plantations on Puerto Rico, producing coffee, corn, and citrus. It was a working coffee plantation until the 1950s, and 86 of the original 500 acres are still part of the estate. The rooms of the hacienda have been furnished with authentic pieces from the 1850s.

Rte. 10, Barrio Magüeyes, km 16.8 (a 30-min. drive north of Ponce, in the small town of Barrio Magüeyes, between Ponce and Adjuntas). *①* **787/848-7020** or 787/284-7020. Tours $5 adults, $2 children. Reservations required. 2-hr. tours Sat and Sun at 8:30am, 10:30am, 1:30pm, and 3:30pm (in English only at 1:30pm).

Tibes Indian Ceremonial Center   Bordered by the Río Portuguéz and excavated in 1975, this is the oldest cemetery in the Antilles. It contains some 186 skeletons, dating from A.D. 300, as well as pre-Taíno plazas from A.D. 700. The site also includes a re-created Taíno village, seven rectangular ball courts, and two dance grounds. The arrangement of stone points on the dance grounds, in line with the solstices and equinoxes, suggests a pre-Columbian Stonehenge. Here you'll also find a museum, an exhibition hall that presents a documentary about Tibes, a cafeteria, and a souvenir shop.

Rte. 503, Tibes, at km 2.2 (2 miles/3km north of Ponce). © 787/840-2255. Admission $2 adults, $1 children. Guided tours in English and Spanish are conducted through the grounds. Tues–Sun 9am–4:30pm.

HIKING & BIRD-WATCHING IN GUANICA STATE FOREST

Heading directly west from Ponce, along Route 2, you reach **Guánica State Forest** (© 787/724-3724), a setting that evokes Arizona or New Mexico. Here you will find the best-preserved subtropical ecosystem on the planet. UNESCO has named Guánica a World Biosphere Reserve. Some 750 plants and tree species grow in the area.

The Cordillera Central cuts off the rain coming in from the heavily showered northeast, making this a dry region of cacti and bedrock, a perfect film location for old-fashioned western movies. It's also ideal country for birders. Some 50% of all of the island's terrestrial bird species can be seen in this dry and dusty forest. You might even spot the Puerto Rican emerald-breasted hummingbird. A number of migratory birds often stop here. The most serious ornithologists seek out the Puerto Rican nightjar, a local bird that was believed to be extinct. Now it's estimated that there are nearly a thousand of them.

To reach the forest, take Route 334 northeast of Guánica, to the heart of the forest. There's a ranger station here that will give you information about hiking trails. The booklet provided by the ranger station outlines 36 miles (58km) of trails through the four forest types. The most interesting is the mile-long (1.5km) **Cueva Trail,** which gives you the most scenic look at the various types of vegetation. You might even encounter the endangered bufo lemur toad, once declared extinct but found to still be jumping in this area.

Within the forest, El Portal Tropical Forest Center offers 10,000 square feet of exhibition space and provides information.

BEACHES & OUTDOOR ACTIVITIES

Ponce is a city—not a beach resort—and should be visited mainly for its sights. There is little here in the way of organized sports, but a 10-minute drive west of Ponce will take you to **Playa de Ponce** , a long strip of white sand opening onto the tranquil waters of the Caribbean. This beach is usually better for swimming than the Condado in San Juan.

Because the northern shore of Puerto Rico fronts the often-turbulent Atlantic, many snorkelers prefer the more tranquil southern coast, particularly near Ponce. Water lovers can go snorkeling right off the beach, and it isn't necessary to take a boat trip. Waters here are not polluted, and visibility is usually good, unless there are heavy winds and choppy seas.

La Guancha is a sprawling compound of publicly funded beachfront, located 3 miles (5km) south of Ponce's cathedral. It has a large parking lot, a labyrinth of boardwalks, and a saltwater estuary with moorings for hundreds of yachts and pleasure craft. A tower, which anyone can climb free of charge, affords high-altitude vistas of the active beach scene. La Guancha is a relatively wholesome version of Coney Island, with a strong Hispanic accent and vague hints of New England. On hot weekends, the place is mobbed with thousands of families who listen to recorded merengue and salsa. Lining the boardwalk are at least a dozen emporiums purveying beer, party-colored drinks, high-calorie snacks, and souvenirs. Weather permitting, this free beach is good for a few hours' diversion at any time of the year.

Although snorkeling is good off the beaches, the best snorkeling is reached by boat trip to the offshore island of **Caja de Muertos,** or **Coffin Island,** an uninhabited key that's covered with mangrove swamps and ringed with worthwhile beaches. A government ferry used to take beach buffs to the wild beaches here, but it was needed for passenger service between Fajardo and Vieques. Today, a private outfitter, **Island Adventures,** c/o Rafi Vega, La Guancha (✆ 787/842-8546), will haul day-trippers there for a full-day beachgoers' outing ($20 per person without snorkeling equipment; $35 per person with snorkeling equipment). Advance reservations (which you can make yourself, or leave to the desk staff of whatever hotel you opt for in Ponce) are necessary, as most of this outfit's excursions don't leave unless there are a predetermined number of participants.

The city owns two **tennis complexes,** one at Poly Deportivos, with nine hard courts, and another at Rambla, with six courts. Both are open from 9am to 10pm daily and are lighted for night play. You can play for free, but you must call to make a reservation. For information, including directions on how to get there, call the **Secretary of Sports** at ✆ 787/840-4400.

To play golf, you can go to **Aguirre Golf Club,** Route 705, Aguirre (✆ 787/853-4052), 30 miles (48km) east of Ponce (take Hwy. 52). This nine-hole course, open from 7:30am to sunset daily, charges $15 greens fees Monday through Friday, and $18 on weekends and holidays. Another course, **Club Deportivo,** Carretera

102, km 15.4, Barrio Jogudas, Cabo Rojo (℃ 787/254-3748), lies 30 miles (48km) west of Ponce. This course is a nine-holer, open daily from 7am to 5pm. Greens fees are $30 daily.

SHOPPING

If you feel a yen for shopping in Ponce, head for the Fox-Delicias Mall, at the intersection of Calle Reina Isabel and Calle Union, the city's most innovative shopping center. Among the many interesting stores is **Regalitos y Algo Mas** (no phone), located on the upper level. It specializes in unusual gift items from all over Puerto Rico. Look especially for the Christmas tree ornaments, crafted from wood, metal, colored porcelain, or bread dough, and for the exotic dolls displayed by the owners. Purchases can be shipped anywhere in the world.

At the mall, the best outlet for souvenirs and artisans' work is **El Palacio del Coquí Inc.** (℃ 787/841-0216), whose name means "palace of the tree frog." This is the place to buy the grotesque masks (viewed as collectors' items) that are used at Carnival time. Ask the owner to explain the significance of these masks.

Utopía, Calle Isabel 78 (℃ 787/845-8742), conveniently located in Plaza Las Delicias, has the most imaginative and interesting selection of gift items and handcrafts in Ponce. Prominently displayed are *vegigantes,* brightly painted carnival masks inspired by carnival rituals and crafted from papier-mâché. In Ponce, where many of these masks are made, they sell at bargain prices of between $5 and $500, depending on their size. Other items include cigars, pottery, clothing, and jewelry; gifts imported from Indonesia, the Philippines, and Mexico; and rums from throughout the Caribbean. Julio and Carmen Aguilar are the helpful and enthusiastic owners, who hail from Ecuador and Puerto Rico, respectively.

WHERE TO STAY
EXPENSIVE

Ponce Hilton & Casino 🐸🐸   On an 80-acre tract of land right on the beach at the western end of Avenida Santiago de los Caballeros, about a 10-minute drive from the center of Ponce, this is the most glamorous hotel in southern Puerto Rico. Designed like a miniature village, with turquoise-blue roofs, white walls, and lots of tropical plants, ornamental waterfalls, and gardens, it welcomes conventioneers and individual travelers alike. Each unit has tropically inspired furnishings, ceiling fans, and a terrace or balcony. All the rooms are medium-sized to spacious, with adequate desk and storage space, tasteful fabrics, good upholstery, and fine linens. Each is equipped with a generous tiled bathroom with a tub-and-shower combo. The ground-floor rooms are the most expensive.

The food at one of the hotel's restaurants, La Cava, is the most sophisticated and refined on the south coast of Puerto Rico. All the waiters seem to have an extensive knowledge of the menu and will guide you through some exotic dishes—of course, you'll find familiar fare, too. For less expensive buffet dining, you can also patronize La Terrazza, which serves the best lunch buffet in Ponce (see "Where to Dine," below).

Av. Caribe 1150 (P.O. Box 7419), Ponce, PR 00732. (C) **800/HILTONS** or 787/259-7676. Fax 787/259-7674. www.hilton.com. 153 units. Year-round $185–$280 double, $475 suite. AE, DC, DISC, MC, V. Self-parking $5; valet parking $10. **Amenities:** 2 restaurants; 3 bars; casino; lagoon-shaped pool ringed with gardens; 4 tennis courts; fitness center; watersports; bike rentals; playground; children's program; business center; room service (7am–midnight); babysitting; laundry/dry cleaning. In room: A/C, TV, minibar, coffeemaker, hair dryer, safe.

MODERATE

Meliá (Value) This city hotel with southern hospitality, which has no connection with the international hotel chain, attracts business-people. It is located a few steps from the Cathedral of Our Lady of Guadalupe and from the Parque de Bombas (the red-and-black fire-house). Although this old and somewhat tattered hotel was long ago outclassed by the more expensive Hilton, many people who can afford more upscale accommodations still prefer to stay here for the old-time atmosphere. The lobby floor and all stairs are covered with Spanish tiles of Moorish design. The desk clerks speak English. The small rooms are comfortably furnished and pleasant enough, and most have balconies facing either busy Calle Cristina or the old plaza. The shower-only bathrooms are tiny. Breakfast is served on a rooftop terrace with a good view of Ponce, and Mark's at the Meliá thrives under separate management (see "Where to Dine," below). **Note:** There's no pool here.

Calle Cristina 2, Ponce, PR 00731. (C) **800/742-4276** or 787/842-0260. Fax 787/841-3602. 75 units (shower only). Year-round $82–$131 double, $120 suite. Rates include continental breakfast. AE, DC, MC, V. Parking $3. **Amenities:** Restaurant; bar; room service; babysitting; laundry/dry cleaning. In room: A/C, TV, hair dryer, iron, safe.

Ponce Inn (Kids) This hotel, a 15-minute drive east of Ponce, opened in 1989. Its modest bedrooms are conservative and comfortable, equipped with contemporary furnishings. Each unit has a small tiled bathroom with tub-and-shower combination. The prices appeal to families with children.

Turpo Industrial Park 103, Mercedita, Ponce, PR 00715. (East of Ponce on Hwy. 52, opposite the Interamerican University.) © **866/668-4577.** Fax 787/841-2560. www.hidpr.com. 120 units. $100–$109 double; $129 suite. AE, DC, MC, V. Free parking. **Amenities:** Restaurant; bar/disco; pool; children's wading pool; gym; whirlpool; room service; babysitting; laundry/dry cleaning. *In room:* A/C, TV, coffeemaker, hair dryer, safe.

INEXPENSIVE

Hotel Bélgica   In the hands of a skilled decorator with a large bankroll, this Spanish colonial mansion from around 1911 could be transformed into a very chic bed-and-breakfast. Until then, however, you'll be faced with a combination of historic charm and modern junkiness, overseen by a brusque staff. You might find this cost-conscious spot wonderful or horrible, depending on your point of view and room assignment. The most appealing accommodations are nos. 8, 9, and 10; these rooms are spacious and have balconies that hang over Calle Villa, a few steps from Plaza Las Delicias. Each unit has a small tiled shower-only bathroom. This venue is for roughing it, backpacker style. The hotel is devoid of the standard amenities, and no meals are served, but there are several cafes in the area.

Calle Villa 122 (at Calle Union/Concordia), Ponce, PR 00731. © **787/844-3255.** Fax 787/844-6149. http://hotelbelgica.somewhere.net. 21 units (shower only). $60–$75 double. MC, V. *In room:* A/C, TV.

WHERE TO DINE
EXPENSIVE

La Cava 𝓡𝓡 INTERNATIONAL   Designed like a hive of venerable rooms within a 19th-century coffee plantation, this is the most appealing and elaborate restaurant in Ponce. It has a well-trained staff, a sense of antique charm, well-prepared cuisine, and a champagne-and-cigar bar where the bubbly sells for around $6 a glass. Menu items change every 6 weeks but might include duck foie gras with toasted brioche, Parma ham with mango, cold poached scallops with mustard sauce, fricassee of lobster and mushrooms in a pastry shell, and grilled lamb sausage with mustard sauce on a bed of couscous. Dessert could be a black-and-white soufflé or a trio of tropical sorbets.

In the Ponce Hilton, Av. Caribe 1150. © **787/259-7676.** Reservations recommended. Main courses $24–$30. AE, DC, DISC, MC, V. Mon–Sat 6:30–10:30pm.

Mark's at the Meliá 𝓡𝓡𝓡 INTERNATIONAL   Mark French (isn't that a great name for a chef?) elevates Puerto Rican dishes into haute cuisine at this eatery. You'd think he'd been entertaining the celebs in San Juan instead of cooking at what is somewhat of a Caribbean backwater. French was hailed as "Chef of the Caribbean 2000" in Fort Lauderdale. With his constantly changing menus and his insistence that everything be fresh, he's still a winner. You'll fall in love with this guy when you taste his tamarind barbecued lamb with yucca mojo. Go on to sample the lobster pionono with tomato-and-chive salad or the freshly made sausage with pumpkin, cilantro, and chicken. All over Puerto Rico you get fried green plantains, but here they come topped with sour cream and a dollop of caviar. The corn-crusted red snapper with yucca purée and tempura jumbo shrimp with Asian salad are incredible. The desserts are spectacular, notably the vanilla flan layered with rum sponge cake and topped with a caramelized banana, as well as the award-winning bread pudding soufflé with coconut vanilla sauce.

In the Meliá Hotel, Calle Cristina. © **787/284-6275.** Reservations recommended. Main courses $14–$30. AE, MC, V. Wed–Sat noon–3pm and 6–10:30pm; Sun noon–5pm.

MODERATE

El Ancla 𝕱𝕱 PUERTO RICAN/SEAFOOD   This is one of Ponce's best restaurants, with a lovely location 2 miles (3km) south of the city center, on soaring piers that extend from the rocky coastline out over the surf. As you dine, the sound of the sea rises literally from beneath your feet.

Menu items are prepared with real Puerto Rican zest and flavor. A favorite here is red snapper stuffed with lobster and shrimp, served either with fried plantain or mashed potatoes. Other specialties are filet of salmon in caper sauce and a seafood medley of lobster, shrimp, octopus, and conch. Most of the dishes are reasonably priced, especially the chicken and conch. Lobster tops the price scale. The side orders, including crabmeat rice and yucca in garlic, are delectable.

Av. Hostos 805, Playa Ponce. © **787/840-2450.** Main courses $13–$36. AE, DC, MC, V. Sun–Thurs 11am–9:30pm; Fri–Sat 11am–11pm.

La Montserrate PUERTO RICAN/SEAFOOD   Beside the seafront, in a residential area about 4 miles (6.5km) west of the town center, this restaurant draws a loyal following from the surrounding neighborhood. A culinary institution in Ponce since it was established 20 years ago, it occupies a large, airy, modern building divided into two different dining areas. The first of these is slightly more formal than the other. Most visitors head for the less formal, large room in back, where windows on three sides encompass a view of some offshore islands. Specialties, concocted from the catch of the day, might include octopus salad, several different kinds of asopao, a whole red snapper in Creole sauce, or a selection of steaks and grills. Nothing is innovative, but the cuisine is typical of the south of Puerto Rico, and it's a family favorite. The fish dishes are better than the meat selections.

Sector Las Cucharas, Rte. 2. ℂ **787/841-2740.** Main courses $15–$25. AE, DC, DISC, MC, V. Daily 11am–10pm.

INEXPENSIVE

Café Tomas/Café Tompy *Value* PUERTO RICAN   The more visible and busier section of this establishment functions as a simple cafe for neighbors and local merchants. At plastic tables often flooded with sunlight from the big windows, you can order coffee, sandwiches, or cold beer, perhaps while relaxing after a walking tour of the city.

The family-run restaurant part of this establishment is more formal. The discreet entrance is adjacent to the cafe on Calle Isabel. Here, amid a decor reminiscent of a Spanish *tasca* (tapas bar), you can enjoy such simply prepared dishes as salted filet of beef, beefsteak with onions, four kinds of asopao, buttered eggs, octopus salads, and yucca croquettes.

Calle Isabel at Calle Mayor. ℂ **787/840-1965.** Breakfast $2.25–$4; main courses lunch and dinner $4.50–$10. AE, MC, V. Restaurant daily 11:30am–midnight; cafe daily 7am–midnight.

Lupita's Mexican Restaurante MEXICAN   Lending a note of lighthearted fun to the city, this is the only Mexican restaurant in Ponce. Set in a 19th-century building and its adjoining courtyard, a short walk from Ponce's main square, it's the creative statement of Hector de Castro, who traveled throughout Mexico to find the elaborate fountains and the dozens of chairs and decorative accessories. The trompe l'oeil murals on the inside (featuring desert scenes in an amusing surrealism) were painted by the owner's sister, Flor de Maria de Castro.

A well-trained staff serves blue and green margaritas (frozen or unfrozen) and a wide array of other tropical drinks. These can be followed by Mexican dishes such as tortilla soup, taco salads, grilled lobster tail with tostones, seafood fajitas, and burritos, tacos, or enchiladas with a wide choice of fillings. A mariachi band plays on Friday. Lupita is an affectionate nickname for Guadalupe, the patron saint of both Mexico and the city of Ponce.

Calle Reina Isabel 60. ℭ **787/848-8808.** Reservations recommended. Main courses $8–$15; platters for 2 $12–$30. AE, DC, MC, V. Sun–Thurs 11am–11pm; Fri–Sat 11am–2am.

PONCE AFTER DARK

La Terrazza, above the Puerto Santiago Restaurant, Paseo Tablado, La Guancha (ℭ **787/840-7313**), is the most whimsical bar at La Guancha, the board-laced beachfront of Ponce. Part of the appeal is its location at the top of an open-sided watchtower. The owners define it as "a music pub," and as such, its collection of CDs rivals that of a sophisticated dance club in New York. Come here for an insight into what's hip with the young and restless of Puerto Rico's "second city." The venue is friendly, the drinks stiff, and if you're hungry, you can select from a short list of food items, including fried calamari and lobster empanadas. Hours are Wednesday, Thursday, and Sunday from noon to 10pm, Friday and Saturday from noon to 2am. There is no cover charge.

2 Mayagüez ⟨★

98 miles (158km) W of San Juan, 15 miles (24km) S of Aguadilla

The largest city on the island's west coast, Mayagüez is a port whose elegance and charm reached its zenith during the mercantile and agricultural prosperity of the 19th century. Most of the town's stately buildings were destroyed in an earthquake in 1918, and today the town is noted more for its industry than its aesthetic appeal.

Although it's a commercial city, Mayagüez is a convenient stopover for those exploring the west coast. If you want a windsurfing beach, you can head north of Rincón, and if you want a more tranquil beach, you can drive south from Mayagüez along Route 102 to Boquerón.

Although the town itself dates from the mid–18th century, the area around it has figured in European history since the time of Christopher Columbus, who landed nearby in 1493. Today, in the gracious plaza at the town's center, a bronze statue of Columbus stands atop a metallic globe of the world.

Famed for the size and depth of its **harbor** (the second-largest on the island, after San Juan's harbor), Mayagüez was built to control the **Mona Passage,** a route essential to the Spanish Empire when Puerto Rico and the nearby Dominican Republic were vital trade and defensive jewels in the Spanish crown. Today this waterway is notorious for the destructiveness of its currents, the ferocity of its sharks, and the thousands of boat people who arrive illegally from either Haiti or the Dominican Republic, both on the island of Hispaniola.

Queen Isabel II of Spain recognized Mayagüez's status as a town in 1836. Her son, Alfonso XII, granted it a city charter in 1877. Permanently isolated from the major commercial developments of San Juan, Mayagüez, like Ponce, has always retained its own distinct identity.

Today the town's major industry is tuna packing. In fact, 60% of the tuna consumed in the United States is packed here. This is also an important departure point for deep-sea fishing and is the bustling port for exporting agricultural produce from the surrounding hillsides.

ESSENTIALS

GETTING THERE **American Eagle** (✆ **800/433-7300**) flies from San Juan to Mayagüez twice daily Monday through Friday, three times a day on weekends (flying time: 40 min.). Depending on restrictions, round-trip passage ranges from $99 to $242 per person.

If you're driving from San Juan, head either west on Route 2 (trip time: 2½ hr.) or south from San Juan on the scenic Route 52 (trip time: 3 hr.). Route 52 offers easier travel.

GETTING AROUND **Taxis** meet arriving planes. If you take one, negotiate the fare with the driver first because cabs are unmetered here.

There are branches of **Avis** (✆ **787/833-7070**), **Budget** (✆ **787/832-4570**), and **Hertz** (✆ **787/832-3314**) at the Mayagüez airport.

VISITOR INFORMATION Mayagüez doesn't have a tourist-information office. If you're starting out in San Juan, inquire there before you set out (see "Visitor Information" under "Orientation" in chapter 3).

EXPLORING THE AREA: SURFING BEACHES & TROPICAL GARDENS

Along the western coastal bends of Route 2, north of Mayagüez, lie the best **surfing beaches** in the Caribbean. Surfers from as far away as New Zealand come to ride the waves. You can also check out panoramic **Punta Higüero** beach, nearby on Route 413, near Rincón. For more information, see "Rincón," in chapter 9.

South of Mayagüez is **Boquerón Beach** ★★, one of the island's best, with a wide strip of white sand and good snorkeling conditions.

Mayagüez

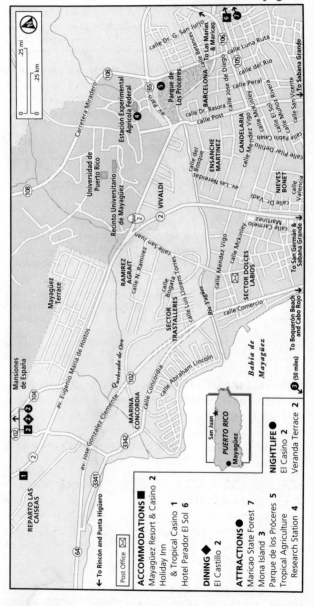

ACCOMMODATIONS ■
Mayagüez Resort & Casino **2**
Holiday Inn
& Tropical Casino **1**
Hotel Parador El Sol **6**

DINING ◆
El Castillo **2**

ATTRACTIONS ●
Maricao State Forest **7**
Mona Island **3**
Parque de los Próceres **5**
Tropical Agriculture
Research Station **4**

NIGHTLIFE ●
El Casino **2**
Veranda Terrace **2**

PUERTO RICO
San Juan ★
Mayagüez ●

Post Office ⊠

163

Mona Island: The Galápagos of Puerto Rico

Off Mayagüez, the unique island of **Mona** ⟨★★★⟩ teems with giant iguanas, three species of endangered sea turtles, red-footed boobies, and countless other sea birds. It features a tabletop plateau with mangrove forests and cacti, giving way to dramatic 200-foot-high limestone cliffs that rise above the water and encircle much of Mona.

A bean-shaped pristine island with no hotels, Mona is a destination for the hardy pilgrim who seeks the road less traveled. A pup tent, backpack, and hiking boots will do fine if you plan to forego the comforts of civilization and immerse yourself in nature. Snorkelers, spelunkers, biologists, and eco-tourists find much to fascinate them in Mona's wildlife, mangrove forests, coral reefs, and complex honeycomb, which is the largest marine-originated cave in the world. There are also miles of secluded white-sand beaches and palm trees.

Uninhabited today, Mona was for centuries the scene of considerable human activity. The pre-Columbian Taíno Indians were the first to establish themselves here. Later, pirates used it as a base for their raids, followed by guano miners,

---

The chief attraction in Mayagüez is the **Tropical Agriculture Research Station (Estación Experimental Agrícola Federal)** ⟨★⟩ (© 787/831-3435). It's located on Route 65, between Post Street and Route 108, adjacent to the University of Puerto Rico at Mayagüez campus and across the street from the **Parque de los Próceres (Patriots' Park).** At the administration office, ask for a free map of the tropical gardens, which have one of the largest collections of tropical plant species intended for practical use, including cacao, fruit trees, spices, timbers, and ornamentals. The grounds are open Monday through Friday from 7am to 5pm, and there is no admission fee.

Mayagüez is the jumping-off point for visits to unique **Mona Island** ⟨★★★⟩, the "Galápagos of the Caribbean." See the box above for details.

Not far from Mayagüez is **Maricao.** You can reach Maricao from Mayagüez by heading directly east along Route 105, which will take

who removed the rich crop fertilizer from Mona's caves. Columbus landed in Mona during his 1494 voyage, and Ponce de León spent several days here en route to becoming governor of Puerto Rico in 1508. The notorious pirate Captain Kidd used Mona as a temporary hideout.

Mona can be reached by organized tour from Mayagüez. Camping is available at $4 per night. Everything needed, including water, must be brought in, and everything, including garbage, must be taken out. For more information, call the **Puerto Rico Department of Natural Resources** at ℂ 787/ 721-5495.

Encantos Ecotours (ℂ 787/272-0005 or 787/808-0005) offers bare-bones but ecologically sensitive tours to Mona Island at sporadic intervals that vary according to the interest of clients. The experience includes ground transport to and from San Juan, sea transport departing from Cabo Rojo (a few miles south of Mayagüez), plus a half-day tour of the island. The tour costs $50 per person (including travel expenses) and takes approximately 4 hours (not including travel time).

you across mountain scenery and along fertile fields until you reach the village.

From Maricao, you can take Route 120 south to km 13.8, or from Mayagüez you can take Route 105 east to the **Maricao State Forest** ℱ picnic area, located 2,900 feet above sea level. The observation tower here provides a panoramic view across the green mountains up to the coastal plains. Trails are signposted here, and your goal might be the highest peak in the forest, Las Tetas de Cerro Gordo, at 2,625 feet. A panoramic view unfolds from here, including a spotting of the offshore island of Mona. Nearly 50 species of birds live in this forest, including the Lesser Antillean pewee and the scaly naped pigeon. Nature watchers will delight to know that there are some 280 tree species in this reserve, 38 of which are found only here.

WHERE TO STAY

Holiday Inn & Tropical Casino   This six-story hotel competes with the Mayagüez Resort & Casino, which we like better. However, the Holiday Inn is well maintained, contemporary, and comfortable. It has a marble-floored, high-ceilinged lobby, an outdoor pool with a waterside bar, and a big casino, but its lawn simply isn't as dramatically landscaped as the Mayagüez Resort's surrounding acreage. Bedrooms here are comfortably but functionally outfitted in motel style; they've recently been refurbished. Each unit is equipped with a tiled bathroom with a tub-and-shower combo.

2701 Rte. 2, km 149.9, Mayagüez, PR 00680-6328. ℂ **800/HOLIDAY** or 787/833-1100. Fax 787/833-1300. www.holiday-inn.com. 142 units. Year-round $100–$131 double, $210–$260 suite. AE, DC, MC, V. **Amenities:** Restaurant; 2 bars; casino; pool; gym; room service; laundry. *In room:* A/C, TV, coffeemaker, hair dryer, safe.

Hotel Parador El Sol   This parador from around 1970 provides some of the most reasonable and hospitable accommodations in this part of Puerto Rico, although it's far more geared to the business traveler than to the tourist, with no-frills furnishings. Each unit has a small bathroom with tub and shower. This six-floor restored hotel is central to the shopping district and to all highways, 2 blocks from the landmark Plaza del Mercado in the heart of the city. (For the location of this parador, see the map "Paradores & Country Inns of Puerto Rico" on p. 45.)

Calle Santiago Riera Palmer, 9 Este, Mayagüez, PR 00680. ℂ **787/834-0303.** Fax 787/265-7567. www.plazapop.com. 52 units. $60–$70 double; $70–$80 triple. Rates include continental breakfast. AE, DC, MC, V. Free parking. **Amenities:** Restaurant; pool; babysitting. *In room:* A/C, TV, hair dryer.

Mayagüez Resort & Casino ℱ   This is one of the largest and best general hotel resorts in western Puerto Rico, appealing equally to business travelers and vacationers. In 1995 local investors took over what was then a sagging Hilton and radically renovated it, to the tune of $5 million. The hotel benefits from its redesigned casino, country-club format, and 20 acres of tropical gardens. The landscaped grounds have been designated an adjunct to the nearby Tropical Agriculture Research Station. Five species of palm trees, eight kinds of bougainvillea, and numerous species of rare flora flourish here, adjacent to the institute's collection of tropical plants, including a pink torch ginger and a Sri Lankan cinnamon tree.

The hotel's well-designed bedrooms open onto views of the pool, and many units have private balconies. Units tend to be small, but they have good beds. Some units are designated as nonsmoking rooms, and others are accessible for people with disabilities. The restored bathrooms are well equipped with makeup mirrors, scales, and tub-and-shower combos.

For details about El Castillo, the hotel's restaurant, see "Where to Dine," below. The hotel is the major entertainment center of Mayagüez. Its casino is open daily from noon to 4am. You can also drink and dance at the Victoria Lounge.

Rte. 104 (P.O. Box 3781), Mayagüez, PR 00709. ✆ **888/689-3030** or 787/832-3030. Fax 787/834-3475. www.mayaguezresort.com. 140 units. Year-round $169–$189 double, $260 suite. AE, DC, DISC, MC, V. Parking $5. **Amenities:** Restaurant; 3 bars; nightclub; casino; Olympic-size pool, children's pool; 3 tennis courts; small fitness room; Jacuzzi; deep-sea fishing; skin-diving; surfing; scuba diving; playground; room service (6:30am–10:30pm); babysitting; laundry. *In room:* A/C, TV, minibar, coffeemaker.

WHERE TO DINE

El Castillo ✻ INTERNATIONAL/PUERTO RICAN   This is the best-managed large-scale dining room in western Puerto Rico, as well as the main restaurant for the largest hotel and casino in the area. Known for its generous lunch buffets, El Castillo serves only a la carte items at dinner, including seafood stew served on a bed of linguine with marinara sauce, grilled salmon with mango-flavored Grand Marnier sauce, and filets of sea bass with cilantro, white-wine, and butter sauce. Steak and lobster can be served on the same platter. The food has real flavor and flair, and it isn't the typical bland hotel fare so often dished up.

In the Mayagüez Resort & Casino, Rte. 104. ✆ **787/832-3030.** Breakfast buffet $11; Mon–Fri lunch buffet $14; Sat–Sun brunch buffet $25; main courses $14–$32. AE, MC, V. Daily 6:30am–11pm.

MAYAGÜEZ AFTER DARK

El Casino   At the completely remodeled casino at the Mayagüez Resort & Casino, with the adjoining Player's Bar you can try your luck at blackjack, dice, slot machines, roulette, and minibaccarat. Open daily from noon to 4am. At the Mayagüez Resort & Casino, Rte. 104. ✆ **787/832-3030.**

Veranda Terrace   On a large and airy covered terrace that opens to a view of a manicured tropical garden, this is a relaxing and soothing place for a cocktail. The bartenders specialize in rum-based concoctions that go well with the hibiscus-scented air. Open daily from 10:30am to 1am. In the Mayagüez Resort & Casino, Rte. 104. ✆ **787/831-7575.**

9

Western Puerto Rico

The scenery of western Puerto Rico varies from a terrain evoking the Arizona desert to a dense blanket of green typical of Germany's Black Forest. The interior has such attractions as the Río Camuy Cave Park and Arecibo Observatory. Along the west and south coasts, you'll find white sandy beaches, world-class surfing conditions, and numerous towns and attractions. There are modest hotels from which to choose, as well as a few noteworthy paradores, a chain of government-sponsored, privately operated country inns.

The waters of the Atlantic northwest coast tend to be rough—ideal for surfers but not always good for swimming.

Some 8 centuries ago, the Taíno Indians inhabited this western part of Puerto Rico, using it as a site for recreation and worship. Stone monoliths, some decorated with petroglyphs, remain as evidence of that long-ago occupation.

There is a tremendous difference between a vacation on the east coast of Puerto Rico and one on the west coast. Nearly all visitors from San Juan head east to explore the El Yunque rain forest (see chapter 7). After that, and perhaps a lazy afternoon on Luquillo Beach, they head back to San Juan and its many resorts and attractions. Others who remain for a holiday in the east are likely to do so because they want to stay at one of the grand resorts such as Doral Palmas del Mar or Wyndham El Conquistador (see chapter 10).

Western Puerto Rico, particularly its southwestern sector, is where the Puerto Ricans themselves go for holidays by the sea. The only pocket of posh here is the Horned Dorset Primavera Hotel at Rincón (see "Rincón" below). Rincón is also the beach area most preferred by windsurfers.

Other than that, most locals and a few adventurous visitors seeking the offbeat and charming head for the southwestern sector of the island. This is the real Puerto Rico; it hasn't been taken over by high-rise resorts and posh restaurants.

Puerto Rico's west coast has been compared to the old U.S. Wild West. There is a certain truth to that. The cattle ranches on the rolling upland pastures south of the town of Lajas will evoke home for those who come from northwest Texas. Others have compared the peninsula of Cabo Rojo in Puerto Rico to Baja, California.

This western part of Puerto Rico also contains the greatest concentration of paradores, attracting those who'd like to venture into the cool mountainous interior of the west, a wonderful escape from pollution and traffic on a hot day.

1 Rincón

100 miles (161km) W of San Juan, 6 miles (9.5km) N of Mayagüez

North of Mayagüez, on the westernmost point of the island, lies the small fishing village of Rincón, in the foothills of La Cadena mountains. It's not a sightseeing destination unto itself, but surfers from as far away as New Zealand say the area's reef-lined beaches, off Route 2 between Mayagüez and Rincón, are the best in the Caribbean. Surfers are particularly attracted to **Playa Higüero** ★★★, the beach at Punta Higüero, on Route 413, which ranks among the finest surfing spots in the world. During winter, uninterrupted swells from the North Atlantic form perfect waves, averaging 5 to 6 feet in height, with ridable rollers sometimes reaching 15 to 25 feet.

The best snorkeling is at a beach gringos have labeled **"Steps."** The waters here are more tranquil than at the beaches attracting surfers. Steps lies right off Route 413, just north of the center of Rincón.

Endangered humpback whales winter here, attracting a growing number of whale-watchers from December to March. The lighthouse at El Faro Park is a great place to spot these mammoth mammals.

Many nonsurfers visit Rincón for only one reason: the Horned Dorset Primavera Hotel, not only one of the finest hotels in Puerto Rico, but one of the best in the entire Caribbean.

ESSENTIALS

GETTING THERE & GETTING AROUND **American Eagle** (✆ **800/352-0714** or 787/749-1747) flies from San Juan to Mayagüez, the nearest airport, four times daily (flying time: 40 min.).

Taxis meet planes arriving from San Juan. Because the taxis are unmetered, you should negotiate the fare with your driver at the outset.

There are branches of **Avis** (✆ **787/833-7070**), **Budget** (✆ **787/832-4570**), and **Hertz** (✆ **787/832-3314**) at the Mayagüez airport.

If you're driving from San Juan, either travel west on Route 2 (trip time: 2 hr.) or travel south on scenic Route 52 (trip time: 3½ hr.).

VISITOR INFORMATION   There is no tourist-information office in Rincón. Inquire in San Juan before heading here (see "Visitor Information" under "Orientation" in chapter 3).

SURFING & OTHER OUTDOOR PURSUITS

Despite its claim as the windsurfing capital of the Caribbean, there are very definite dangers in the waters off Rincón. In November 1998 three surfers (two from San Juan, one from the U.S. mainland) drowned in unrelated incidents offshore at Maria's Beach. These deaths are often cited as evidence of the dangerous surf that has misled some very experienced surfers. Local watersports experts urge anyone who's considering surfing at Rincón to ask a well-informed local for advice. When the surf is up and undertows and riptides are particularly strong, losing a surfboard while far offshore seems to be one of the first steps to eventually losing your life.

Windsurfing is best from November to April. The best beaches for surfing lie from Borinquén Point south to Rincón. There are many surfing outfitters along this strip, the best of which is **West Coast Surf Shop,** 2 E. Muñoz Rivera at Rincón (© **787/823-3935**), open Monday through Saturday from 9am to 6pm.

The windsurfers who hang out here like **Sandy Beach** because it does not have the stone and rocks found on some of the other beaches in the area. Also, from December to February it gets almost constant winds every day. Windsurfers wait on the terrace of Tamboo Tavern for the right wind conditions before hitting the beach.

West Coast Charters, located in the Marina at Rincón (© **787/823-4114**), offers a number of options for fun in the water, ranging from whale-watching (Dec–Mar) and other fun cruises to renting diving or fishing equipment. Expeditions are arranged to Desecho Island Reef, one of the best reefs in the Caribbean for snorkeling and diving. Desecho Island is an uninhabited island 14 miles (22km) offshore. A Federal Wildlife Preserve, it consists of 360 acres. The highest point rises 715 feet. West Coast Charters also attracts sports fishermen in search of tuna, grouper, marlin, wahoo, and dolphin (the fish, not the mammal). Fishermen are taken out for a half day aboard a fully equipped boat, with a licensed and experienced charter captain. A snorkeling trip costs $35, a one-tank scuba dive $85. A half-day fishing charter is $450 per boat, including the guide.

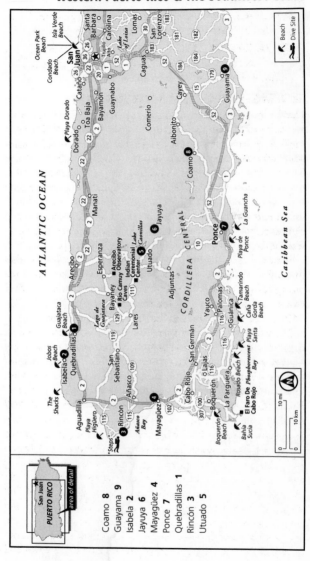

Coamo 8
Guayama 9
Isabela 2
Jayuya 6
Mayagüez 4
Ponce 7
Quebradillas 1
Rincón 3
Utuado 5

Another good scuba outfitter is **Taíno Divers,** Black Eagle Marina at Rincón (© **787/823-6429**), which offers local boat charters along with scuba and snorkeling trips. Other activities include whale-watching expeditions and sunset cruises. Fees are $95 for a one-tank dive, $475 for a half-day fishing-boat rental, and $45 for snorkeling.

The most visible and sought-after whale-watching panorama in Rincón is **Parque El Faro de Rincón (Rincón's Lighthouse Park),** which lies on El Faro Point peninsula at the extreme western tip of town. Within its fenced-in perimeter are pavilions that sell souvenirs and snack items, rows of binoculars offering 25¢ views, and a stately looking lighthouse built in 1921. The park is at its most popular from December to March for whale-watching and in January and February for surfer gazing. The park is locked every evening between midnight and 7am. Otherwise, you're free to promenade with the locals any time you like.

The park's snack bar is called **Restaurant El Faro,** Barrio Puntas, Carretera 413, km 3.3 (no phone). Platters of American and Puerto Rican food, including mofongos, steaks, and burgers, cost from $13 to $19. When is it open? The owner told us, "I open whenever I want to. If I don't want to, I stay home."

Punta Borinquén Golf Club, Route 107 (© **787/890-2987**), 2 miles (3km) north of Aquadilla's center, across the highway from the city's airport, was originally built by the U.S. government as part of Ramey Air Force Base. Today, it is a public 18-hole golf course, open daily from 7am to 6:30pm. Greens fees are $20 for an all-day pass; a golf cart that can carry two passengers rents for $26 for 18 holes. A set of clubs can be rented for $10. The clubhouse has a bar and a simple restaurant.

WHERE TO STAY
VERY EXPENSIVE

Horned Dorset Primavera Hotel ✿✿✿   This is the most sophisticated hotel on Puerto Rico, and it's one of the most exclusive and elegant small properties anywhere in the Caribbean. It was built on the massive breakwaters and seawalls erected by a local railroad many years ago. Guests here enjoy a secluded, semiprivate beach; this narrow strip of golden sand is choice, if small.

The hacienda evokes an aristocratic Spanish villa, with wicker armchairs, hand-painted tiles, ceiling fans, seaside terraces, and cascades of flowers. This is really a restful place. Accommodations are in a series of suites that ramble uphill amid lush gardens. The decor is tasteful, with four-poster beds and brass-footed tubs in marble-sheathed bathrooms. Rooms are spacious and luxurious, with Persian rugs over tile floors, queen sofa beds in sitting areas, and fine linen. Bathrooms are equally roomy and luxurious, with tub-and-shower combinations. Eight suites are located in the separate Casa Escondida villa, set at the edge of the property. Some of these units have private pools; others offer private verandas or sun decks.

The hotel's restaurant, Horned Dorset Primavera, is one of the finest on Puerto Rico (see "Where to Dine" below).

Hotel Rte. 429 (P.O. Box 1132), Rincón, PR 00677. © **800/633-1857** or 787/823-4030. Fax 787/823-5580. www.horneddorset.com. 31 units. Winter $380–$440 double, $540–$800 suite for 2; off-season $280–$340 double, $420–$650 suite for 2. MAP (breakfast and dinner) $82 per person extra. AE, MC, V. Children under age 12 not accepted. **Amenities:** 2 restaurants; bar; 2 pools; tennis court; fitness center; deep-sea fishing; room service (breakfast and lunch); massage; laundry; library. *In room:* A/C, minibar, hair dryer, iron, safe, no phone.

MODERATE

Casa Isleña Inn *Finds*   "Island House" is created from a simple oceanfront former home right on the beach. Behind its gates, away from the water, is a private and tranquil world that offers a series of medium-sized and comfortably furnished bedrooms decorated in bright Caribbean colors and designs. Each room has a neatly maintained shower-only bathroom. A natural tidal pool formed by a reef is an 8-minute stroll from the inn. At the tidal pool and from the inn's terraces guests can enjoy views of Aguadilla Bay and Mona Passage. In winter, while standing on the terraces, you can often watch the migration of humpback whales.

Barrio Puntas Carretera Int. 413 km 4, Rincón, PR 00677. © **888/289-7750** or 787/823-1525. Fax 787/823-1530. www.casa-islena.com. 9 units (shower only). Year-round $125–$135 double. AE, MC, V. **Amenities:** Restaurant for breakfast and lunch; bar. *In room:* A/C, TV, no phone.

Lemontree Waterfront Cottages *Finds*   Right on a good, sandy beach, these spacious apartments with kitchenettes are for those who don't want to limit themselves to hotel rooms and meals. With the sound of the surf just outside your private back porch, these well-furnished seaside units can provide a home away from home, with everything from ceiling fans to air-conditioning, from paperback libraries to custom woodworking details. The property is well maintained. Families enjoy the three-bedroom, two-bathroom oceanfront suite called "Papaya." "Mango" and "Pineapple" are ideal for two persons. Each unit contains a midsize shower-only bathroom. The least expensive units, "Banana" and "Coconut," are studio units for those who want a kitchen but don't require a living room. The cottages lie a 10-minute drive west of Rincón.

Rte. 4290 (P.O. Box 3200), Rincón, PR 00677. ✆ 787/823-6452. Fax 787/823-5821. www.lemontreepr.com. 6 units (shower only). Winter $110–$140 double, $165 quad, $185 for 6; off-season $95–$125 double, $145 quad, $165 for 6. AE, MC, V. **Amenities:** Laundry. *In room:* A/C, TV, kitchenette, coffeemaker.

INEXPENSIVE

Lazy Parrot   Set within an unlikely inland neighborhood, far from any particular view of the sea, this place has a better-than-average restaurant and clean, well-organized bedrooms. Each unit is comfortable, even if not overly large, with light-grained and durable furnishings that might seem appropriate for the bedroom of a high-school senior in a suburb on the U.S. mainland. Bathrooms are simple, functional, and workable, each with a shower, but not at all plush. Lazy Parrot was built as a private home in the 1970s, and then transformed into the inn you see today. The place is just as well known for its restaurant as it is for its rooms. Meals are served in an open-sided aerie on the building's uppermost floor.

Rte. 413, km 4.1. Barrio Puntas, Rincón, PR 00677. ✆ 800/294-1752 or 787/823-5654. Fax 787/823-0224. www.lazyparrot.com. 11 units. Winter $95–$125 double; off-season $75–$95 double. AE, MC, V. **Amenities:** Restaurant; bar; pool; room service; babysitting. *In room:* A/C, TV.

Villa Cofresi   Set about a mile (1.5km) south of Rincón's center, this is a clean, family-run hotel with a view of the beach. Thanks to the three adult children of the Caro family, the place is better managed than many of its competitors. Bedrooms are comfortable and airy, with well-chosen furniture that might remind you of something in southern Florida. Each unit has a white tile floor and a small bathroom with a tub and shower. Most rooms have two double beds; some have two twin beds. The two units that tend to be reserved out long in advance are nos. 47 and 55, which have windows opening directly onto the sea.

The in-house restaurant, La Ana de Cofresi, is named after the ship that was captained by the region's most famous 18th-century pirate, Roberto Cofresi. Hand-painted murals highlight some of his adventures. Open Monday through Friday from 5 to 10pm, Saturday and Sunday from noon to 10pm; it charges $8 to $30 for well-prepared main courses that are likely to include fish consommé, four kinds of mofongo, breaded scampi served either with Creole sauce or garlic, and very good steaks, including a 12-ounce New York sirloin.

Rte. 115, km 12.3, Rincón, PR. 00677. ✆ 787/823-2450. Fax 787/823-1770. www.villacofresi.com. 70 units. Winter $105 double, $135 suite; off-season $95 double, $115 suite. AE, DC, MC, V. **Amenities:** Restaurant; bar; pool; room service; babysitting; laundry/dry cleaning. *In room:* A/C, TV, fridge, hair dryer, iron.

WHERE TO DINE
VERY EXPENSIVE

Horned Dorset Primavera FRENCH/CARIBBEAN This is the finest restaurant in western Puerto Rico—so romantic that people sometimes come from San Juan just for an intimate dinner. A masonry staircase sweeps from the garden to the second floor, where soaring ceilings and an atmosphere similar to that in a private villa awaits you.

The menu, which changes virtually every night, based on the inspiration of the chef, might include chilled parsnip soup, a fricassee of wahoo with wild mushrooms, grilled loin of beef with peppercorns, and medallions of lobster in an orange-flavored beurre-blanc sauce. The grilled breast of duckling with bay leaves and raspberry sauce is also delectable. Mahimahi is grilled and served with ginger-cream sauce on a bed of braised Chinese cabbage. It's delicious.

In the Horned Dorset Primavera Hotel, Rte. 429. ℂ **787/823-4030.** Reservations recommended. Lunch $8–$20; fixed-price dinner $68–$72 for 5 dishes, $92 for 8 dishes. AE, MC, V. Daily noon–2pm and 7–9pm.

MODERATE

The Landing INTERNATIONAL This is the most substantial of the many bars in Rincón, with a popularity so widespread that it's likely to attract as many as 800 customers on a Friday or Saturday night. The restaurant, which looks like a stylish private house, is adjacent to a beach favored by a cadre of devoted surfers. Its focal point is a sprawling bar where popular drinks include an M&M ($5.50 each)—loosely defined as a piña colada capped with layers of both light and dark rum. Edwin Nault, a former dental technician from Boston, is the competent entrepreneur who runs this place. Menu items include fried calamari, scampi, T-bone steaks, jerk chicken, churrasco, barbecued ribs, stuffed chicken breast, and lobster kebabs. The view of Rincón's legendary surf, complete with dozens of surfers trying their luck on the deep blue, is panoramic.

Carretera 413 (Interior), Barrios Puntas/Playa Antonio. ℂ **787/823-3112.** Reservations recommended for dinner Fri–Sat. Burgers and sandwiches $6.75–$9.75; platters $16–$33. AE, MC, V. Fri–Sat and Mon 11am–2am.

INEXPENSIVE

Calypso Café AMERICAN Set on a bend in the road between the Black Eagle Marina and the lighthouse (El Faro de Rincón), this sometimes-charming bar attracts many of Rincón's young singles. One of the simplest drinking emporiums in the region, it consists of a roof, a fiesta-colored balustrade, and a collection of surfers, many from New York, New Jersey, and Florida. Maria's Beach, a well-known surfer's hangout, is a few steps away. A deejay or live band performs every Friday and Saturday night. The ambience might remind you of a latter-day remake of *The Endless Summer.*

Maria's Beach. No phone. Reservations not accepted. Burgers and simple platters $6–$8. No credit cards. Daily noon–2am.

2 Paradores of Western Puerto Rico

One program that has helped the Puerto Rico Tourism Company successfully promote the commonwealth as "The Complete Island"—the paradores puertorriqueños—will help make your travels even more enjoyable.

The *paradores puertorriqueños* (see chapter 2 for more details about these government-sponsored inns and a map pinpointing their locations) are a chain of privately owned and operated country inns under the auspices and supervision of the Commonwealth Development Company. These hostelries are easily identified by the Taíno grass hut that appears in the signs and logos of each one. The Puerto Rico Tourism Company started the program in 1973, modeling it after Spain's parador system, although many of the paradores here are mere shanties compared to some of the deluxe Spanish hostelries. Each parador is situated in a historic or particularly beautiful spot. They vary in size, but most share the virtues of affordability, hospitable staffs, and high standards of cleanliness. Most but not all of their rooms are air-conditioned, and each room has a bathroom.

For reservations or further information, contact the **Paradores Puertorriqueños Reservation Office,** P.O. Box 9023960, San Juan, PR 00902 (© **800/443-0266**).

JAYUYA

The village of Jayuya, southwest of San Juan and north of Ponce, lies in the middle of the Cordillera Central, a mountain massif. From San Juan, travel west along Highway 22, going past the town of Barceloneta until you come to the junction of Route 140; head south to the town of Florida, passing through some of the most dramatic scenery in Puerto Rico. Continue along Route 140 until you come to the junction of Route 141, signposted southwest into Jayuya.

> ### (Tips) Mesónes Gastronómicos
>
> Except for those in major hotels, you'll find few well-known restaurants as you tour the western part of the island. However, there are plenty of roadside places and simple taverns. For authentic island cuisine, you can rely on the *mesónes gastronómicos* (gastronomic inns). This established dining network, sanctioned by the Puerto Rico Tourism Company, highlights restaurants recognized for excellence in preparing and serving Puerto Rican specialties at modest prices.
>
> Mesón gastronómico status is limited to restaurants outside the San Juan area that are close to major island attractions. Membership in the program requires that restaurants have attractive surroundings and comply with strict standards of service. Members must specialize in native foods, but if you order fresh fish, chances are you'll be pleased. Regrettably, there are no maps listing these myriad restaurants, but their signs are easy to spot as you drive around the island.

Jayuya is a small town that still retains strong Taíno cultural influences, particularly in the language. At the Jayuya Indian Festival in mid-November, you'll see craft markets, parades, and displays of Taíno dances. The festival honors the patron saint of the town, Nuestra Señora la Monserrate.

Here you'll also find the Parador Hacienda Gripiñas (see below), a former coffee plantation, where you can glimpse the good old days on Puerto Rico. In 1950 Jayuya received worldwide attention when *independentistas* proclaimed the "Republic of Puerto Rico" and held the town under siege until the National Guard was called in.

WHERE TO STAY & DINE

Parador Hacienda Gripiñas 𝒢   A former coffee plantation about 2½ hours from San Juan, Parador Hacienda Gripiñas is reached via a long, narrow, and curvy road. This home-turned-inn is a delightful blend of old-world hacienda and modern conveniences. The plantation ambience is created by ceiling fans, splendid gardens, porch hammocks, and more than 20 acres of coffee bushes. You'll taste the homegrown product when you order the inn's aromatic brew.

The modest rooms vary in size and all are kept very tidy. Each unit has a small, tiled shower-only bathroom. For meals, we suggest the restaurant's Puerto Rican dishes rather than the international cuisine. You can swim in the two chilly mountain pools, soak up the sun, or enjoy the nearby sights, such as the Taíno Indian Ceremonial Park at Utuado. Boating and plenty of fishing are just 30 minutes away, at Lake Caonillas. The parador is also near the Río Camuy Caves.

Rte. 527, km 2.5 (P.O. Box 387), Jayuya, PR 00664. ℂ **787/828-1717.** 20 units (shower only). Year-round $125 double. Rate includes 2 meals a day. AE, MC, V. From Jayuya, head east via Rte. 144; at the junction with Rte. 527, go south 1½ miles/2.5km. **Amenities:** Restaurant; pool. *In room:* A/C, TV.

UTUADO

Another good base in the Cordillera Central massif is the little mountain town of Utuado, which lies northwest of Jayuya (see above). This is the heartland of karst, an irregular limestone terrain with sinkholes, underground streams, and caverns. This unique landscape was created over several millennia by heavy rainfall. Utuado is a stronghold of *jíbaro* ("hillbilly") culture, reflecting the mountain life of the island as few other settlements do.

Petroglyphs left over from the Taíno civilization have been found in the area. One depicted an Indian woman with frog legs and an elaborate headdress. From Utuado, you can continue west for 20 miles (32km) on Route 111 to km 12.3, to reach the Taíno Indian Ceremonial Park (see "Life After Death" below).

WHERE TO STAY & DINE

Casa Grande Mountain Retreat ✦ This parador, situated on 107 lush and steeply inclined acres of what used to be a coffee plantation in the Caonillas Barrios district, about 1½ hours drive from San Juan, originated in the late 19th century as a hacienda. Thanks to renovations by Steve Weingarten, a retired lawyer from New York City, the isolated compound functions today as a simple, eco-sensitive hotel. It's oldest part is the much-restored cement-sided core of the original hacienda, site of the lobby and a likeable eatery, Jungle Jane's restaurant, which serves an array of well-prepared international and Puerto Rican Creole–style dishes. Even if you're not registered as a guest, you can eat here daily from 7:30am to 9:30pm. It's a good spot for lunch if you're touring in the area.

Accommodations lie within five wood-sided cottages (four units to a cottage, some of them duplex) scattered throughout the surrounding acreage. Each is kept as rustic and simple as possible, thanks to lots of exposed wood, airy verandahs, and sparse decor. Each unit has a balcony, a hammock, a view of the mountains, and a small bathroom with shower. Without TVs, phones, or air conditioning, the accommodations are favored by those with an interest in getting back to nature. Some guests come to brush up on yoga and meditation skills. A nature trail is carved out of the surrounding forest. Under separate management, a riding stable offers the option of horseback riding a short distance away.

P.O. Box 1499, Utuado, PR 00641. ✆ 888/343-2272 or 787/894-3939. Fax 787/894-3900. www.hotelcasagrande.com. 20 units. Year-round $80–$90 double. AE, DISC, MC, V. From Arecibo, take Rte. 10 south to Utuado; then head east on Rte. 111 to Rte. 140; head north on Rte. 140 to Rte. 612 for ¼ mile/.5km. **Amenities:** Restaurant; bar; pool. *In room:* No phone.

QUEBRADILLAS

Quebradillas is one of the sleepy municipalities of northwest Puerto Rico. With its flamboyantly painted houses, narrow streets, and spiritualist herb shops, it is like a town of long ago. Quebradillas lies 70 miles (113km) west of San Juan, only about a 15-mile (24km) trip from the city of Arecibo along Route 2.

The Atlantic waters along the northwest coast of Puerto Rico tend to be rough, with the rugged coastline seemingly plunging right into the ocean. Both snorkelers and scuba divers are drawn to a protected beach area known as **"The Shacks,"** close to the town of Isabela, northwest of Quebradillas. The reefs and coral caverns here are some of the most dramatic in Puerto Rico. Surfers also flock to Isabela's Jobos Beach. Neither beach, however, is ideal for swimming.

Also northwest of Quebradillas lies beautiful **Guajataca Beach,** with its white sands, raging surf, and turbulent, deep waters. This is a fine beach for sunning and collecting shells, but it's a *playa peligrosa* (dangerous beach) unless you're a skilled swimmer. You can also visit **Lago de Guajataca,** another beautiful spot, by heading south for 7 miles (11km) on Route 113. This man-made lake is a lovely place for hiking, and it's the site of two paradores (see below). The staff at these government-sponsored inns will give you advice about jaunts in the **Guajataca Forest Reserve** to the immediate west.

WHERE TO STAY & DINE

Parador El Guajataca   You'll find this place on a rolling hillside reaching down to a surf-beaten beach along the north coast. Stay here for the stunning natural setting and don't expect too much,

Life After Death

The Taíno Indians who lived in Puerto Rico before Europeans came here were ruled by *caciques,* or chiefs, who controlled their own villages and several others nearby. The Taínos believed in life after death, which led them to take extreme care in burying their dead. Personal belongings of the deceased were placed in the tomb with the newly dead, and bodies were carefully arranged in a squatting position. Near Ponce, visitors can see the oldest Indian burial ground uncovered in the Antilles, Tibes Indian Ceremonial Center (p. 153).

Even at the time of the arrival of Columbus and the conquistadores who followed, the Taínos were threatened by the warlike and cannibalistic Carib Indians coming up from the south. But though they feared the Caribs, they learned to fear the conquistadores even more. Within 50 years of the Spanish colonization, the Taíno culture had virtually disappeared, the Indians annihilated through either massacres or due to European diseases.

But Taíno blood and remnants of their culture live on. The Indians married with Spaniards and Africans, and their physical characteristics—straight hair, copper-colored skin, and prominent cheekbones—can still be seen in some Puerto Ricans today. Many Taíno words became part of the Spanish language that's spoken on the island even today. Hammocks, the weaving of baskets, and the use of gourds as eating receptacles are part of the heritage left by these ill-fated tribes.

because the hotel itself is somewhat seedy. Each room is rather standard and has its own entrance and private balcony opening onto the turbulent Atlantic. Bathrooms are slightly battered but functional, each with a tub.

Served in a glassed-in dining room where all the windows face the sea, the cuisine isn't much more memorable than the accommodations, with little care going into the preparation of the often-canned ingredients. A local musical group plays for dining and dancing on Friday and Saturday evenings. There are two swimming pools (one for adults, another for children), plus a playground for children.

Still standing near Utuado, a small mountain town, **Parque Ceremonial Indígena-Caguaña (Indian Ceremonial Park at Caguaña),** Route 111, km 12.3 (✆ **787/894-7325**), was built by the Taínos for recreation and worship some 800 years ago. Stone monoliths, some etched with petroglyphs, rim several of the 10 *bateyes* (playing fields) used for a ceremonial game that some historians believe was a forerunner to soccer. The monoliths and petroglyphs, as well as the *dujos* (ceremonial chairs), are existing examples of the Taínos' skill in carving wood and stone.

Archaeologists have dated this site to approximately 2 centuries before Europe's discovery of the New World. It is believed that the Taíno chief Guarionex gathered his subjects on this site to celebrate rituals and practice sports. Set on a 13-acre field surrounded by trees, some 14 vertical monoliths with colorful petroglyphs are arranged around a central sacrificial stone monument. The ball complex also includes a museum, which is open daily from 8:30am to 4pm; admission is free.

There is also a gallery called Herencia Indígena, where you can purchase Taíno relics at reasonable prices, including the sought-after *Cemis* (Taíno idols) and figures of the famous little frog, the coquí. The Taínos are long gone, and much that was here is gone, too. This site is of special interest to those with academic pursuits, but of only passing interest to the lay visitor.

Rte. 2, km 103.8 (P.O. Box 1558), Quebradillas, PR 00678. ✆ **800/964-3065** or 787/895-3070. Fax 787/895-3589. www.elguajataca.com. 38 units. $89–$96 double. AE, DISC, MC, V. From Quebradillas, continue northwest on Rte. 2 for 1 mile/1.5km; the *parador* is signposted. **Amenities:** Restaurant; bar; 2 pools; room service; babysitting; laundry/dry cleaning. *In room:* A/C, TV, coffeemaker, iron.

Parador Vistamar   In the Guajataca area, this parador, one of the largest in Puerto Rico, sits like a sentinel surveying the scene from high atop a mountain overlooking greenery and a seascape. There are gardens and intricate paths carved into the side of the mountain, where you can stroll while enjoying the fragrance of the tropical flowers. Or you might choose to search for the calcified fossils that abound on the carved mountainside. For a unique experience, visitors can try their hand at freshwater fishing just down the hill from the hotel (bring your own gear). Flocks of rare tropical birds are frequently seen in the nearby mangroves.

Bedrooms are comfortably furnished in a rather bland motel style. Bathrooms with either shower or tub are functional, but without much decorative zest. There's a dining room with an ocean view where you can have a typical Puerto Rican dinner or choose from the international menu.

A short drive from the hotel will bring you to the Punta Borinquén Golf Course. Tennis courts are just down the hill from the inn itself. Sightseeing trips to the nearby Arecibo Observatory (see chapter 7)—the largest radar/radio-telescope in the world—and to Monte Calvario (a replica of Mount Calvary) are available. Another popular visit is to the plaza in the town of Quebradillas.

6205 Rte. 113N (P.O. Box T-38), Quebradillas, PR 00678. ✆ 787/895-2065. Fax 787/895-2294. www.paradorvistamar.com. 55 units (each with either shower or tub). Year-round $71–$95 double. Up to 2 children under 12 stay free in parent's room. AE, DC, MC, V. At Quebradillas, head northwest on Rte. 2, then go left at the junction with Rte. 113 and continue for a half mile/1km. **Amenities:** Restaurant; bar; pool; room service; laundry/dry cleaning. *In room:* A/C, TV, coffeemaker (in some), hair dryer (in some), iron.

ISABELA

On the northwestern coast, a 1½-hour drive west of San Juan, the town of Isabela captures the flavor of the west, although it's far less known by visitors than Rincón and Mayagüez. Its pastel-colored, whitewashed houses border the sea, known for its surfing and swimming beaches.

The locals don't survive on tourism, but on such industries as shoemaking and textiles. In spite of manufacturing, many small farms still dot the area.

Tragedy has struck repeatedly in the area because of the geographical location of Isabela, which has made it the victim of both tidal waves and earthquakes since it was first settled.

Isabela enjoys a reputation for horse breeding. This activity is centered around Arenales, south of the town, where a number of horse stables are located.

The area abounds in good beaches, including Jobos Beach, directly west of Isabela on Route 466. The beach is set against a backdrop of cliffs, the most dramatic of which is El Pozo de Jacinto. Nearby at a beach called "The Shacks," both snorkelers and scuba divers enjoy swimming among the reefs, teeming with rainbow-hued fish and the coral caverns.

WHERE TO STAY & DINE

Villas del Mar Hau *(Kids)*   Opening onto a long private beach, this family-friendly parador complex is peppered with West Indian–style cottages in vivid Caribbean pastels with Victorian wood trim. The location is midway between the west coast cities of Arecibo in the east and Aguadilla in the west, right outside the smaller town of Isabela. Under the shelter of Causuarina pine trees, most guests spend their days lying on Playa Montones. The huge tidal "wading" pool is ideal for children. The place is unpretentious but not completely back to nature, as the beachfront cottages are well furnished and equipped, each with a balcony and with capacities for two to six guests. Some have ceiling fans, others have air-conditioning, and all units are equipped with small, tiled, shower-only bathrooms. Since 1960 the Hau family has run this little beach inn. The on-site restaurant is well-known in the area for its creative menu featuring fresh fish, shellfish, and meats.

Carretera 466, km 8.3, Playa Montones, Isabela, PR 00662. © **787/872-2045.** Fax 787/830-2490. www.villahau.com. 38 units (shower only). Year-round $95 for 2, $138 for 4, $155 for 6. From the center of Isabella, take Rte. 466 toward Aguadilla. **Amenities:** Restaurant; bar; pool with snack bar; barbecue area; tennis; beach toy rental; photocopy and fax; convenience store; babysitting; laundry; horseback riding; volleyball court. *In room:* A/C, TV (in most rooms), kitchenette, coffeemaker.

COAMO

Legend has it that the hot springs in this town, located inland on the south coast about a 2-hour drive from San Juan, were the Fountain of Youth sought by Ponce de León. It is believed that the Taíno peoples, during pre-Columbian times, held rituals and pilgrimages here as they sought health and well-being. Between 1847 and 1958, the site was a center for rest and relaxation for Puerto Ricans and others, some on their honeymoons, others in search of the curative powers of the geothermal springs, which lie about a 5-minute walk from **Parador Baños de Coamo.** Nonguests can come here to use the baths, but the experience is hardly special today. The baths are in poor condition.

South of Coamo you can get on the expressway (no. 52) and head east for a 40-minute drive to **Guayama,** a green and beautiful small town with steepled churches, and the Casa Cautiño Museum on the main plaza of town (© **787/864-0600**). It is open Tuesday through Sunday from 10am to 4pm. Admission is $1 for adults and 50¢ for seniors, students, and children 7 to 12 (free for children 6 and under). This museum is in a turn-of-the-20th-century mansion that once was occupied by the Cañuelo family. It contains all of the family's original belongings and is a showplace for fine turn-of-the-century furnishings and pictures of the prize horses for which Guayama is famous. Just minutes from town is Arroyo Beach, a tranquil place to spend an afternoon, but lacking facilities.

WHERE TO STAY & DINE

Parador Baños de Coamo   The spa at Baños de Coamo features this parador, offering hospitality in traditional Puerto Rican style. The Baños has welcomed many notable visitors over the years, including Franklin D. Roosevelt, Frank Lloyd Wright, Alexander Graham Bell, and Thomas Edison, who came here to swim in the on-site hot springs, said to be the most radioactive in the world. Since those days and since those long-departed visitors, the spa world is now state-of-the-art in many places, including San Juan and some nearby resorts. Such is not the case here; maintenance is poor, and the baths show signs of aging. (Locals sometimes purchase a day pass and use the pool, which leads to noise, confusion, and overcrowding on weekends.)

The buildings range from a lattice-adorned two-story motel unit with wooden verandas to a Spanish colonial pink stucco building, which houses the restaurant. The bedrooms draw a mixed reaction from visitors, so ask to see your prospective room before deciding to stay here. Many of the often-dark rooms are not well maintained, and the bathrooms seem more appropriate for a campsite. Mildew is also evident. The cuisine here is both Creole and international, and the coffee Baños-style is a special treat.

P.O. Box 540, Coamo, PR 00769. ✆ **787/825-2186.** Fax 787/825-4739. www. banosdecoamo.com. 48 units. Year-round $81 double. AE, DC, DISC, MC, V. From Rte. 1, turn onto Rte. 153 at Santa Isabel; then turn left onto Rte. 546 and drive west 1 mile/1.5km. **Amenities:** Restaurant; bar; pool; laundry/dry cleaning. *In room:* A/C, TV.

10

Eastern Puerto Rico

The northeast corner of the island, only about 45 minutes from San Juan, contains the island's major attractions, El Yunque rain forest and Luquillo Beach (see chapter 7), as well as a variety of landscapes, ranging from miles of forest to palm groves and beachside settlements. Here you will also find two of the best resorts on the island, Wyndham El Conquistador Resort and Doral Palmas del Mar Resort, and Fajardo, a preeminent sailor's haven, where you can catch ferries to the islands of Vieques and Culebra.

1 Las Croabas

35 miles (56km) E of San Juan

Las Croabas, near Fajardo, is the site of the Wyndham El Conquistador Resort. El Conquistador was the leader in luxury resorts in the Caribbean from the 1960s to the late 1970s. Celebrities Elaine May, Jack Gilford, Celeste Holm (with her husband and two poodles), Elaine Stritch (and her dog), Amy Vanderbilt, Jack Palance, Burt Bacharach, Angie Dickinson, Omar Shariff, Marc Connelly, Maureen O'Sullivan, and Xavier Cugat attended its grand inaugural festivities in 1968. Later, its circular casino, in black and stainless steel, appeared in the James Bond movie *Goldfinger.* The original hotel closed in 1980, but it was reborn in 1993 as the distinctive $250 million El Conquistador we have today.

GETTING THERE

Wyndham El Conquistador staff members greet all guests at the San Juan airport and transport them to the resort. Guests at the resort can take a taxi or a hotel courtesy car, or they can drive a rental car to Luquillo Beach.

The cost of a taxi from the San Juan airport averages around $60.

If you're driving from San Juan, head east on Route 3 toward Fajardo. At the intersection, cut northeast on Route 195 and continue to the intersection with Route 987, at which point you turn north.

To the Lighthouse: Exploring Las Cabezas de San Juan Nature Reserve

Las Cabezas de San Juan Nature Reserve is better known as El Faro, or "The Lighthouse." In the northeastern corner of the island, it is one of the most beautiful and important areas in Puerto Rico. Here you'll find seven ecological systems and a restored 19th-century Spanish colonial lighthouse. From the lighthouse observation deck, majestic views extend to islands as far off as St. Thomas in the U.S. Virgin Islands.

Surrounded on three sides by the Atlantic Ocean, the 316-acre site encompasses forestland, mangroves, lagoons, beaches, cliffs, offshore cays, and coral reefs. Boardwalk trails wind through the fascinating topography. Ospreys, sea turtles, and an occasional manatee are seen from the windswept promontories and rocky beach.

The nature reserve is open Wednesday through Sunday. Reservations are required; for reservations during the week, call © **787/722-5882,** and for reservations on weekends, © **787/860-2560** (weekend reservations must be made on the day of your visit). Admission is $5 for adults, $2 for children under 13, and $2.50 for seniors. Guided 2½-hour tours are conducted at 9:30am, 10am, 10:30am, and 2pm (in English at 2pm).

OUTDOOR ACTIVITIES

In addition to the lovely beach and the many recreational facilities that are part of the Wyndham El Conquistador (p. 188), there are other notable places to play in the vicinity. Don't forget that not far from Las Croabas is **Luquillo Beach,** one of the island's best stretches of sand (see chapter 7).

WATERSPORTS   For a cruise, your best bet in Las Croabas is **Erin Go Bragh Charters** (© **787/860-4410**). The 50-foot ketch is operated by Capt. Bill Henry, who is licensed to carry six passengers. The boat is available for day charters and sunset and evening cruises, and it has equipment for watersports, including Windsurfers and masks and fins. A full-day tour costs $75 per person, including a barbeque lunch.

For scuba divers, the best deal is offered by the PADI outfit **La Casa del Mar,** at the Puerto del Rey marina, the lowest level of the

Map labels:
ATLANTIC OCEAN
Condado Beach | Ocean Park Beach | Isla Verde Beach
San Juan
Loiza
Luquillo Beach
Cabezas de San Juan Nature Reserve
165 | 26
Cataño
22 | 36 | 26
Santa Barbara
Las Croabas **8**
7
Bayamón | 20
Carolina
Río Grande
6
Guaynabo
1 | 18
Trujillo Alto
3
194
Fajardo **5**
Fajardo Beach
Lake of Loiza
186 | 191
El Yunque **1**
Ceiba
To Culebra
191
Comerio
Lomas
Río Blanco
Daguao
Caguas
30
Juncos
Naguabo
Cayey
San Lorenzo
La Permina
31 | 192
Naguabo Beach
52
183
183
30
Punta Santiago
Naguabo **4**
184
181
Humacao
Cayo Santiago
Playa de Humacao
15 | 184
179
182
Humacao **2**
Palmas del Mar **3**
To Vieques
179
3
Yabucoa
Guayama
Pasaje de Vieques
3
3
Caribbean Sea
0   10 mi
0   10 km
To Vieques

El Yunque	1
Fajardo	5
Humacao	2
Las Cabezas de San Juan Nature Reserve	7
Las Croabas	6
Luquillo Beach	8
Naguabo	4
Palmas del Mar	3

Wyndham El Conquistador (℡ **787/863-1000,** ext. 7917). You can go for ocean dives on the outfitter's boats, a one-tank dive costing $69 or a two-tank dive for $99, including tanks and weight belt. A PADI snorkel program, at $50 per person, is also available.

In Fajardo, the Caribbean's largest and most modern marina, **Puerto del Rey** (℡ **787/860-1000**), has facilities for 70 boats, including docking and fueling for yachts up to 200 feet and haul-out and repair for yachts up to 90 feet. The marina has boat rentals, yacht charters, and watersports, plus shops and a restaurant.

Some of the best snorkeling in Puerto Rico is in and around Fajardo. Its beach, **Playa Seven Seas,** is not as hotsy-totsy as Luquillo Beach, but is an attractive and sheltered strip of sand. The beach lies on the southwestern shoreline of Las Cabezas peninsula and is crowded on weekends. For even better snorkeling, walk along this beach for about half a mile (1km) to another beach, called **Playa Escondido ("Hidden Beach").** Coral reefs in clear waters lie right off this beach. We'll let you in on a secret: East from Las Cabezas is a marine wildlife refuge known as **La Cordillera,** or "The

Spine." Off the mainland of the island, these are the most gin-clear and tranquil waters we have found to date in Puerto Rico. They are teeming with wildlife, including several species of fish such as grouper, but also lobster, moray eels, and sea turtles. On these islets you might even see a rare crested iguana. **Aqua Sports** in Fajardo (© 787/888-8841) will take you there.

TENNIS   The seven Har-Tru courts at the **Wyndham El Conquistador** are among the best tennis courts in Puerto Rico, rivaling those at Palmas del Mar. The staff at the pro shop is extremely helpful to beginning players. Courts are the least crowded during the hottest part of the day, around the lunch hour. If you're a single traveler to the resort and in search of a player, the pro shop will try to match you up with a player of equal skill.

WHERE TO STAY

Wyndham El Conquistador Resort & Country Club

One of the most impressive resorts in the Caribbean, with a flash and glitter that remains supremely tasteful, El Conquistador has an incredible array of facilities. Rebuilt in 1993 at a cost of $250 million, it encompasses 500 acres of forested hills sloping to the sea. Accommodations are divided into five separate sections that share the common themes of Mediterranean architecture and lush landscaping. A replica of an Andalusian hamlet, Las Casitas Village seems straight out of the south of Spain; each of the plush, pricey units here has a full kitchen. A short walk downhill takes you to Las Olas Village, a cluster of tastefully modern accommodations. At sea level, adjacent to an armada of pleasure craft bobbing at anchor, is La Marina Village, whose balconies seem to hang directly over the water. All the far-flung elements of the resort are connected by serpentine, landscaped walkways and by a railroad-style funicular that makes frequent trips up and down the hillside. The accommodations are outfitted with comfortable and stylish furniture, soft tropical colors, and robes.

The resort has an array of restaurants and lounges; you could live here for a month and always sample something new and different. One of the most comprehensive spas in the world, The Golden Door, maintains a branch in this resort. The hotel is sole owner of a "fantasy island" (Palomino Island), with caverns, nature trails, horseback riding, and watersports such as scuba diving, windsurfing, and snorkeling. About half a mile (1km) offshore, the island is connected by free ferries to the main hotel at frequent intervals. Camp Coquí on Palomino Island is for children 3 to 12 years old.

Av. Conquistador 1000, Las Croabas, Fajardo, PR 00738. (C) **800/468-5228** or
787/863-1000. Fax 787/863-6500. www.wyndham.com. 915 units. Winter
$455–$765 double, from $1,375 suite for 1–4, from $1,195 casita with kitchen for
1–6; off-season $295–$525 double, from $1,125 suite for 1–4, $325–$1,025 casita
with kitchen for 1–6. MAP (breakfast and dinner) $92 extra per adult per day, $46
extra per child age 12 and under. Children age 15 and under stay free in parent's
room. AE, DC, DISC, MC, V. Parking $10 per day. **Amenities:** 6 restaurants; 7 bars;
nightclub; casino; 6 pools; golf course; 7 Har-Tru tennis courts; health club and spa;
watersports; 25-slip marina; fishing; sailing; dive shop; children's programs; room
service; massage; laundry/dry cleaning. *In room:* A/C, TV, minibar, coffeemaker, hair
dryer, iron, safe.

WHERE TO DINE
VERY EXPENSIVE

Isabela's Grill *&* AMERICAN/STEAK   If Dwight Eisenhower
were to miraculously return, he'd feel comfortable with this 1950s
American menu. The massive gates are among the most spectacular
pieces of wrought iron in Puerto Rico. The service is impeccable, the
steaks are tender, and the seafood is fresh. You can begin with the
lobster bisque or French soup, then move on to the thick cut of veal
chop or the perfectly prepared rack of lamb. Prime rib of beef is a
feature, as are the succulent steaks, especially the New York strip and
porterhouse.

In the Wyndham El Conquistador Resort. (C) **787/863-1000.** Reservations recommended. Main courses $24–$35. AE, DISC, MC, V. Mon–Sat 6–10pm; Sun 6pm–midnight. Parking $2.50–$15.

EXPENSIVE

Blossoms *&&* CHINESE/JAPANESE   Blossoms boasts some of
the freshest seafood in eastern Puerto Rico. Sizzling delights are prepared on teppanyaki tables, and there's a zesty selection of Hunan
and Szechuan specialties. On the teppanyaki menu, you can choose
dishes ranging from chicken to shrimp, from filet mignon to lobster.
Sushi bar selections range from eel and squid to salmon roe and
giant clams.

In the Wyndham El Conquistador Resort. (C) **787/863-1000.** Reservations recommended. Main courses $19–$40. AE, DC, MC, V. Daily 6–11:30pm.

Otello's *&* NORTHERN ITALIAN   Here you can dine by candlelight in the old-world tradition, with a choice of indoor or outdoor
seating. You might begin with one of the soups, perhaps pasta fagioli,
or select one of the zesty Italian appetizers, such as excellently prepared clams Posillipo. Pastas can be ordered as a half-portion appetizer
or as a main dish, and they include the likes of homemade gnocchi
and fettuccine with shrimp. The chef is known for his superb veal

dishes. A selection of poultry and vegetarian food is offered, as are shrimp and fish dishes.

In the Wyndham El Conquistador Resort. ✆ 787/863-1000. Reservations required in winter, recommended off-season. Main courses $20–$37. AE, DISC, MC, V. Daily 6–11pm.

2 Palmas del Mar

46 miles (74km) SE of San Juan

An hour east of San Juan, the residential resort community of Palmas del Mar lies near Humacao. Here you'll find one of the most action-packed sports programs in the Caribbean, offering golf, tennis, scuba diving, sailing, deep-sea fishing, and horseback riding. Palmas del Mar's location is one of its greatest assets. The pleasing Caribbean trade winds steadily blow across this section of the island, stabilizing the weather and making Palmas del Mar ideal for outdoor sports.

The resort is no longer what it was in its heyday in the early 1990s. Today it is a real estate conglomerate that promotes vacation properties to investors, although outsiders can stay here as well. Many of the occupants are residents of San Juan who come here on weekends. Tourists are welcome, but most first-time visitors will find better accommodations up the coast, at the Westin Rio Mar (p. 145) or the Wyndham El Conquistador (p. 188).

GETTING THERE

Humacao Regional Airport is 3 miles (5km) from the northern boundary of Palmas del Mar. It accommodates private planes; no regularly scheduled airline currently serves the Humacao airport. Doral Palmas del Mar Resort will arrange minivan or bus transport from Humacao to the San Juan airport for $36 per person for two passengers or $24 per person for four passengers. For reservations, call ✆ 787/285-4323. Call the resort if you want to be met at the airport.

If you're driving from San Juan, take Highway 52 south to Caguas, then take Highway 30 east to Humacao. Follow the signs from there to Palmas del Mar.

BEACHES & OUTDOOR ACTIVITIES

Doral Palmas del Mar Resort offers a variety of choices to keep active vacationers in shape (many are also open to the public, with prior reservation). Following are details on some of the most popular, along with a few other offerings in the area that are not connected with the resort complex.

BEACHES   Doral Palmas del Mar Resort has 3 exceptional miles (5km) of white-sand beaches (all open to the public). Nonguests pay a $1 charge for parking and 25¢ for a changing room and a locker. The waters here are calm year-round, and there's a watersports center and marina (see "Scuba Diving & Snorkeling," below).

GOLF   Few other real-estate developments in the Caribbean devote as much attention and publicity to their golf facilities as the **Palmas del Mar Golf Club** ☆☆ (© 787/285-2256). Today, both the older course, the Gary Player–designed Palm course, and the newer course, the Reese Jones–designed Flamboyant course, have pars of 72 and layouts of around 6,800 feet each. Crack golfers consider holes 11 to 15 of the Palm course among the toughest five successive holes in the Caribbean. The pro shop that services both courses is open daily from 7am to 5:30pm. The Flamboyant course costs $176 for 18 holes; the Palm Course costs $160 for 18 holes.

HIKING   Palmas del Mar's land is an attraction in its own right. Here you'll find more than 6 miles (9.5km) of Caribbean ocean frontage—3½ (5.5km) miles of sandy beach amid rocky cliffs and promontories. Large tracts of the 2,700-acre property have harbored sugar and coconut plantations over the years, and a wet tropical forest preserve with giant ferns, orchids, and hanging vines covers about 70 acres near the resort's geographic center.

SCUBA DIVING & SNORKELING   Some of the best dives in Puerto Rico are right off the eastern coast. Two dozen dive sites south of Fajardo are within a 5-mile (8km) radius offshore. Refer to "The Best Beaches" in chapter 1 for more on the best snorkeling sites.

Set adjacent to a collection of boutiques, bars, and restaurants at the edge of Palmas del Mar's harbor, **Palmas Dive Center** ☆, Anchors Village, 110 Harbor Drive (© 787/633-7314 or cellphone 787/504-7333), owns a 44-foot-long diveboat with a 16-foot beam to make it stable in rough seas. Pennsylvania-born Bill Winnie, a 5-year veteran of other dive operations in and around Palmas del Mar, offers $120 full-day "Discover Scuba" resort courses that are geared to beginners. They include classroom testing, presentation of a video on water safety, a practice session in a swimming pool, and a one-tank afternoon dive in the open sea. Also available are both morning and afternoon sessions of two-tank dives that are available only to experienced and certified divers, priced at $95 each. Half-day snorkeling trips, priced at $55 per participant and departing for both morning and afternoon sessions, go whenever there's demand to the fauna-rich reefs that encircle Monkey Island, an offshore cay.

TENNIS   The **Tennis Center at Palmas del Mar** 🏾🏾 (⍤ 787/852-6000,** ext. 51), the largest in Puerto Rico, features 15 hard courts and 5 clay courts, open to hotel guests and nonguests. Fees for hotel guests are $20 per hour during the day and $25 per hour at night. Fees for nonguests are $24 per hour during the day and $29 per hour at night. Tennis packages, including accommodations, are available. Within the resort's tennis compound is a **fitness center,** which has the best-equipped gym in the region; open daily from 7am to 9pm. The center is free for guests of the resort; nonguests can use the center for $7 per day.

WHERE TO STAY

Doral Palmas del Mar Resort 🏾🏾 *Kids*   Although the acreage within the Palmas del Mar development contains thousands of privately owned villas, many of which can be rented or purchased outright, this is the only conventional, full-service hotel in Palmas del Mar. At least some of its business derives from newcomers who want to experience firsthand what Palmas del Mar is like before buying a villa. It was radically renovated in 1997, and again in 1999. None of the well-furnished bedrooms overlook the sea, but many have private patios or verandas, and most are roomier than you might expect. Each room has tile floors, tropical furnishings, large closets, fine linens, and either a king- or two queen-size beds, plus a tiled bathroom with a tub-and-shower combo.

The resort has an Adventure Club for children ages 3 to 13. Supervised activities include crafts and sports, plus horseback riding for older children. For nonguests, the cost is $30 per half day or $35 per day, including lunch; it's free for guests. The beach, tennis center, and golf courses are close at hand. Palma's Café (see "Where to Dine," below) is one of the panoply of dining options here.

170 Candalero Dr., Palmas del Mar, Humacao, PR 00791. ⍤ **800/725-6273** or 787/852-6000. Fax 787/852-6320. www.palmasdelmar.com. 102 units. Winter $225–$260 double; off-season $160–$195 double. MAP (breakfast and dinner) $45 per person extra. AE, DC, MC, V. **Amenities:** Restaurant; 2 bars; casino; pool; 2 18-hole golf courses; 20 tennis courts (7 lit); health club; dive shop; fishing; bikes; children's program; car rental; room service (6am–10pm); babysitting; laundry/dry cleaning; horseback riding. *In room:* A/C, TV, hair dryer.

The Villas at Palmas 🏾 *Kids*   Set almost adjacent to Doral Palmas del Mar Resort, this complex of red-roofed, white-walled town houses is a good choice for a family vacation. Divided into five separate clusters and carefully landscaped with tropical plants, the units are furnished and decorated according to the tastes of their individual owners. Each contains a working kitchen, a sense of privacy, views of either the ocean or the gardens, and a midsize and comfortable private bathroom with tub-and-shower combo. Rental fees depend on the unit's proximity to the beachfront or golf course. A handful of villas built against a steep hillside overlook the Palmas del Mar tennis courts.

170 Candelero Dr., Palmas del Mar, Humacao, PR 00792. © 800/725-6273 or 787/852-6000. Fax 787/852-6320. 135 town house–style suites. Winter $400–$560 1-bedroom suite, $600–$760 2-bedroom suite, $800–$960 3-bedroom suite; off-season $280–$380 1-bedroom suite, $380–$480 2-bedroom suite, $480–$580 3-bedroom suite. Minimum bookings ranging from 3–7 nights required during some peak seasons, depending on the accommodation. AE, DC, MC, V. **Amenities:** Bar; pool; gym; babysitting. *In room:* A/C, TV, kitchen, coffeemaker, hair dryer, iron, safe, washing machine/dryer.

WHERE TO DINE

Thanks to the kitchens that are built into virtually every unit in Palmas del Mar, many guests prepare at least some of their meals "at home." This is made relatively feasible thanks to the on-site general store at the Palmanova Plaza, which sells everything from fresh lettuce and sundries to liquor and cigarettes. In addition, there are several other dining options in the Doral Palmas del Mar complex.

Barracuda Bistro ✦ PUERTO RICAN/INTERNATIONAL The most active bar scene in the early evening takes place here, as yachters gather to talk about the adventures of the day. The sautéed mahimahi in tequila butter and lime sauce alone is worth the trip. Fresh red snapper is sautéed in butter and lemon zest, and you can also count on the chef throwing a T-bone steak on the grill. You can also order both Mexican and Creole specialties, including roast pork and fajitas with either chicken or beef. If you're visiting at lunch or during the afternoon, you can also order fast food, including hot dogs, sandwiches, and burgers.

La Marina. © 787/850-4441. Reservations recommended. Main courses $5–$30. DC, MC, V. Daily noon–10pm.

Blue Hawaiian CHINESE   This is the best Chinese restaurant in the region. It combines Polynesian themes (similarly to a toned-down Trader Vic's) with an Americanized version of Chinese food that's flavorful and well suited to Puerto Rico's hot, steamy climate. Menu items include lobster with garlic-flavored cheese sauce; blackened salmon or steaks reminiscent of styles in New Orleans; and a superb house version of honey chicken. You'll find the place within the dignified courtyard of the resort's shopping center, with tables for alfresco dining. Your host is Tommy Lo, former chef aboard the now-defunct ocean liner SS *United States.*

In the Palmanova Shopping Center. ℭ 787/852-0897. Reservations recommended. Main courses $11–$25. AE, MC, V. Daily noon–10:30pm.

Chez Daniel/Le Grill ℛ FRENCH　It's French and it's the favorite of the folks who tie up their yachts at the adjacent pier. Normandy-born Daniel Vasse, the owner, along with his French Catalonian wife, Lucette, maintain twin dining rooms that in their way are the most appealing in Palmas del Mar. Le Grill is a steakhouse with a Gallic twist and lots of savory flavor in the form of béarnaise, garlic, peppercorn sauce, or whatever else you specify. Chez Daniel shows a more faithful allegiance to the tenets of classical French cuisine, placing emphasis on such dishes as bouillabaisse, onion soup, and snails, as well as lobster and chicken dishes. For dessert, consider a soufflé au Cointreau.

Marina de Palmas del Mar. ℭ 787/852-6000. Reservations required. Main courses $8–$12 at lunch, $22–$35 at dinner. AE, MC, V. Wed–Sun noon–3pm; Wed–Mon 6:30–10pm. Chez Daniel open only Dec–Apr; Le Grill closed June.

Palma's Café INTERNATIONAL　Cooled by trade winds, this restaurant overlooking a courtyard and pool is an ideal choice for a casual meal. Lunch includes sandwiches and burgers; if you want heartier fare, ask for the Puerto Rican specialty of the day, perhaps red snapper in garlic butter, preceded by black-bean soup. Dinner is more elaborate. Begin with stuffed jalapeños or chicken tacos, followed by lobster, New York sirloin, paella, or the catch of the day. The hearty cooking, although of a high standard, is never quite gourmet.

In Doral Palmas del Mar Resort. ℭ 787/852-6000, ext. 50. Reservations required only for groups of 6 or more. Main courses $5–$11 breakfast, $12–$17 lunch and dinner. AE, DC, DISC, MC, V. Daily 6:30–11am, noon–5pm, and 6–10:30pm.

PALMAS DEL MAR AFTER DARK

The **casino** in the Palmas del Mar complex (ℭ 787/852-6000, ext. 10142), has 12 blackjack tables, 2 roulette wheels, a craps table, and dozens of slot machines. The casino is open daily year-round, Sunday through Thursday from 4pm to 2am and Friday and Saturday from 6pm to 3am. Under Puerto Rican law, alcoholic beverages cannot be served in a casino.

Index

See also Accommodations and Resorts and Restaurant indexes below.

ACCOMMODATIONS & RESORTS

FROMMER'S® MEMORABLE WALKS

Chicago
London

New York
Paris

San Francisco
Washington, D.C.

FROMMER'S® GREAT OUTDOOR GUIDES

Arizona & New Mexico
New England

Northern California
Southern New England

Vermont & New Hampshire

SUZY GERSHMAN'S BORN TO SHOP GUIDES

Born to Shop: France
Born to Shop: Hong Kong,
 Shanghai & Beijing

Born to Shop: Italy
Born to Shop: London

Born to Shop: New York
Born to Shop: Paris

FROMMER'S® IRREVERENT GUIDES

Amsterdam
Boston
Chicago
Las Vegas
London

Los Angeles
Manhattan
New Orleans
Paris
Rome

San Francisco
Seattle & Portland
Vancouver
Walt Disney World®
Washington, D.C.

FROMMER'S® BEST-LOVED DRIVING TOURS

Britain
California
Florida
France

Germany
Ireland
Italy
New England

Northern Italy
Scotland
Spain
Tuscany & Umbria

HANGING OUT™ GUIDES

Hanging Out in England
Hanging Out in Europe

Hanging Out in France
Hanging Out in Ireland

Hanging Out in Italy
Hanging Out in Spain

THE UNOFFICIAL GUIDES®

Bed & Breakfasts and Country
 Inns in:
 California
 Great Lakes States
 Mid-Atlantic
 New England
 Northwest
 Rockies
 Southeast
 Southwest
Best RV & Tent Campgrounds in:
 California & the West
 Florida & the Southeast
 Great Lakes States
 Mid-Atlantic
 Northeast
 Northwest & Central Plains

Southwest & South Central
 Plains
 U.S.A.
Beyond Disney
Branson, Missouri
California with Kids
Chicago
Cruises
Disneyland®
Florida with Kids
Golf Vacations in the Eastern U.S.
Great Smoky & Blue Ridge Region
Inside Disney
Hawaii
Las Vegas
London

Mid-Atlantic with Kids
Mini Las Vegas
Mini-Mickey
New England and New York with
 Kids
New Orleans
New York City
Paris
San Francisco
Skiing in the West
Southeast with Kids
Walt Disney World®
Walt Disney World® for Grown-up
Walt Disney World® with Kids
Washington, D.C.
World's Best Diving Vacations

SPECIAL-INTEREST TITLES

Frommer's Adventure Guide to Australia &
 New Zealand
Frommer's Adventure Guide to Central America
Frommer's Adventure Guide to India & Pakistan
Frommer's Adventure Guide to South America
Frommer's Adventure Guide to Southeast Asia
Frommer's Adventure Guide to Southern Africa
Frommer's Britain's Best Bed & Breakfasts and
 Country Inns
Frommer's Caribbean Hideaways
Frommer's Exploring America by RV
Frommer's Fly Safe, Fly Smart
Frommer's France's Best Bed & Breakfasts and
 Country Inns
Frommer's Gay & Lesbian Europe

Frommer's Italy's Best Bed & Breakfasts and
 Country Inns
Frommer's New York City with Kids
Frommer's Ottawa with Kids
Frommer's Road Atlas Britain
Frommer's Road Atlas Europe
Frommer's Road Atlas France
Frommer's Toronto with Kids
Frommer's Vancouver with Kids
Frommer's Washington, D.C., with Kids
Israel Past & Present
The New York Times' Guide to Unforgettable
 Weekends
Places Rated Almanac
Retirement Places Rated